# FAMILIAR VIOLENCE

# FAMILIAR VIOLENCE

Gender and Social Upheaval
in the Novels
of Frances Burney

## Barbara Zonitch

DELAWARE

Newark: University of Delaware Press
London: Associated University Presses

Associated University Presses
440 Forsgate Drive
Cranbury, N.J. 08512

Associated University Presses
16 Barter Street
London WC1A 2AH, England

Associated University Presses
P.O. Box 338, Port Credit
Mississauga, Ontario
Canada L5G 4L8


The paper used in this publication meets the requirements
of the American National Standard for Permanence of Paper
for Printed Library Materials Z39.48–1984.

**Library of Congress Cataloging-in-Publication Data**

Zonitch, Barbara.
    Familiar violence : gender and social upheaval in the novels of
Frances Burney / Barbara Zonitch.
        p.    cm.
    Includes bibliographical references (p.    ) and index.
    ISBN 0-87413-618-0  (alk. paper)
    1. Burney, Fanny, 1752–1840—Political and social views.
Feminism and literature—England—History—18th Century.
3. Women and literature—England—History—18th century.
4. Aristocracy (Social class) in literature.  5. Women—England-
Social conditions.  6. Social problems in literature.  7. Sex role
in literature.  8. Violence in literature.  I. Title.
PR3316.A4Z96    1997
823'.6—dc20                                                      96-42178
                                                                    CIP

PRINTED IN THE UNITED STATES OF AMERICA

To the memory of my dearest friend,
Felice Ronca

# Contents

# Acknowledgments

It gives me great pleasure to thank the many teachers who have provided me with encouragement, patience, and wisdom. At the University of Rochester, Paula Backscheider's classes gave me a safe forum in which to find my voice, and I am much indebted to her for nurturing my early interest in the eighteenth-century novel.

Special thanks are due to Michael McKeon for his endless patience and support as I struggled to work out my ideas. I will always be grateful to him for holding me to the highest standards; it is hard to imagine this work coming to fruition without him. I owe a great debt as well to Carol Barash and Kate Ellis for pushing me beyond my usual safe limits to read Burney in new ways; their help was invaluable.

For their support before, during, and after I wrote this work, I would like to thank my family, and my dear friends, Susan Morris and Marie Sawaya.

Finally, this book is dedicated in memory of a friend who taught me, in too short a time, the best things about friendship, and they were many.

# FAMILIAR VIOLENCE

# Social Transformations:
# The Crisis in the Aristocracy
# and the Status of Women

In her preface to an 1810 edition of *Evelina*, Anna Letitia Barbauld complains of Frances Burney's "propensity . . . to involve all her heroines not only in difficult but in degrading adventures. . . ."[1] Barbauld refers to those scenes in Burney's novels that have perpetually troubled the novelist's readers; and more often than not, literary critics have dismissed these disturbing episodes as signs of Burney's moral or aesthetic failure. Two twentieth-century critics—Walter Allen and J. M. S. Tompkins—have attributed them to Burney's aberrant "love of humour" and roundly criticized her for unnecessarily embarrassing or even distressing her readers.[2] Camilla's experiences with abusive and unscrupulous shopkeepers, the old women's race in *Evelina*, and those troubling moments when lecherous men chase or attempt to abduct frightened heroines are episodes typical of the kinds of "degrading adventures" that discomfited Barbauld and others. Yet these rather patronizing charges turn out to be astute observations as well, for these critics have focused on a narrative dilemma that is one of the most distinguishing features of Burney's work. Why, we must ask, is the otherwise calm and polished surface of Burney's novels suddenly and frequently disturbed by scenes of disorder and violence?

Recently, a few feminist critics have begun to reexamine these "degrading adventures," and they have read them as symptomatic of the harsh social conditions faced by eighteenth-century women and as signs of Burney's angry recognition of the limits imposed on her as a woman writer in a patriarchal culture. In her important literary biography, *Frances Burney: The Life in the Works*,[3] Margaret Anne Doody both recognizes and stresses the thematic centrality of the many acts of physical and emotional violation that disrupt Burney's narratives.

13

Doody's literary biography is a major development in Burney studies not only
for the emphasis it places on the novels that follow *Evelina* but also for bringing
into high relief the vast range of complex themes and problems that recur in
Burney's work.

Whereas Doody considers a wide range of literary and biographical issues,
in *The Iron Pen: Frances Burney and the Politics of Women's Writing,* Julia Epstein
attends particularly to this problem of violence in Burney's novels and private
journals. Epstein argues that these moments of violence and harassment are
often symptomatic of Burney's "disguised anger" towards the "constrained
cultural situation" of women writers in the eighteenth century. Epstein poses
and investigates the following question: "Why has the gulf between the social
self/proper lady and private self/angry writer been dismissed or glossed over
for two centuries?"[4] Epstein concludes that Burney's rage, as manifested in
these episodes of violence, is precipitated by the struggle to "synthesize propriety with public achievement."[5] I am indebted to both Doody and Epstein, as
well as to other Burney scholars, for paving the way for my own work. Without
their groundbreaking studies, which legitimized Burney's novels as worthy of
serious book-length treatment, this work would not have been possible.

In the study that follows I will build upon the work done by these and
other recent feminist critics,[6] but I intend to contextualize Burney's novels more
fully in their historical moment in order to show how she engages the ideological conflicts of the late-eighteenth century in more complicated ways than some
of her previous readers have suggested. And for this reason, her novels, like her
social context, often seem ambiguous and contradictory. I will argue that
Burney's preoccupation with violence originates in the fear that the death of
aristocratic social domination subjects women to the escalating violence of the
modern world. And the central question is: What will replace the traditional
means of protection and paternalistic care? On the evidence of Burney's novels, the choice for women is an untenable one: a choice between the harsh and
even violent restraints of aristocratic rule and the alternative forms of violence
created by newer versions of social control.

What kinds of behavior do I include within the wide range of violence in
Burney's novels? Here I will lay out briefly what I will develop further in subsequent chapters. Many times Burney figures violence as a sexual harassment
that is often associated with aristocratic rule and the gradual decline in its authority. At the opposite end of this spectrum of sexual and physical abuse is an
activity I will describe as a cruel social shaming; this form of emotional violation is most often affiliated with bourgeois authority and with those women
who are implicated in the maintenance of aristocratic patriarchal rule. Throughout her career, Burney will explore the ways in which the deliberate inflicting

of embarrassment is a means of violence that effectively controls the powerless. In many ways, the violation of emotional boundaries, in effect a lack of sympathetic restraint, is one instrument of violence in a middle-class culture. Burney's heroines are particularly susceptible to these kinds of violations because they lack one or all of the social signs that putatively promise respect and protection, most centrally family origin, name, social status, and wealth. Indeed, the scenes of violation in Burney's novels are marked by an anxiety over lost, inadequate, or absent social protection.

Burney does not only explore externally inflicted violence; she also investigates the ways in which this violence is internalized. This self-imposed violence includes a range of emotional and physical maladies, including strokes, episodes of madness and hallucinatory illnesses, and suicide. The strict internalization of a code of manners, I will argue shortly, can give rise to this type of self-mutilating behavior. I will contend that the changing ways in which patriarchy orders itself during the eighteenth century account in part for some of the new patterns of violence that Burney exposes and investigates. That is, we must see Burney's violence not simply within the framework of an unchanging patriarchal rule[7] but as a historically specific and contradictory phenomenon that intimates the altered form that dominance will take in the modern world.

## I

During the period that Frances Burney wrote her four novels (*Evelina*, 1778; *Cecilia*, 1782; *Camilla*, 1796; *The Wanderer*, 1814), England was experiencing a volatile economic and political transformation that would profoundly and permanently affect its social institutions. As Burney recognized, the daunting scope of these changes would have a momentous but as yet still uncertain effect on women, and thus she uses her novels to explore and to enter into the early modern debates surrounding these social transformations. To this end, in each of her novels Burney takes up the following questions in increasingly complex and innovative ways: What are the social ramifications of the demise of aristocratic domination? More specifically: What happens to women faced with a shifting patriarchal rule, who thus are confronted with the need not only for security but also for a new social identity? Do these changes offer an opportunity for women's greater empowerment or do they simply extend and aggravate their subjugation in a male-dominated culture? Burney addresses these questions in part through the representation of varying motifs of violence, and also by imagining alternative social forms to replace the ones that were steadily disappearing, most of all the aristocratic patriarchal family and community.

Thus Burney is most immediately concerned with the status group of gentility (though certainly not exclusively), and for this reason, the present chapter will concentrate on the social institutions that are most relevant to this order.

The patriarchal family looms large in all of Burney's narratives, and the rule of the father is deeply implicated in her novels' episodes of violence. Any discussion of Burney's representation of the patriarchal family, then, must begin with an examination of this structure in late-eighteenth-century England. Social historians have shown us that the patriarchal family has always been a repressive and coercive structure for both women and children. The legal status of an eighteenth-century wife has by now been well documented, but a brief summary of marital law seems in order here. Her husband assumed almost total control of her property upon marriage, and even if she were protected by a "separate estate," he could, because of his considerable power and influence, arrogate her property. Having no legal identity separate from her husband's, moreover, she could not obtain credit, sign a contract, sue or be sued. His rights to her property and person even extended over her children; he was the sole legal parent and could remove them from her at his will. If she ever tried to leave him, he could force her to return, making her a virtual prisoner in her own home; and divorce was nearly impossible without a parliamentary act.[8] Sarah Chapone, a contemporary of Burney's, angrily articulates this legal disempowerment as a virtual loss of self: "[A]ccording to established rule, a wife is dead in law," and therefore "it would be ridiculous for the law to consider the interests of a non-entity"; but this same "non-entity may nevertheless be called into being occasionally at the pleasure and direction of the husband. . . ."[9]

Chapone's view of a married woman's status was most notably (and notoriously) codified by Sir William Blackstone in *Commentaries on the Laws of England,* in which he championed this legal nonexistence: "By marriage, the husband and wife are one person in law . . . the very being or legal existence of the woman is suspended during the marriage, or at least is incorporated and consolidated into that of the husband; under whose wing, protection, and *cover,* she performs everything."[10] For the purposes of my argument, this legal account is important on two fronts: it signals the almost total obliteration of the wife's identity upon marriage, in part to ensure that she relinquished all her property rights to her husband and his family;[11] but it also, following Blackstone's logic, secures her absolute protection. Since her husband was considered more adept in dealing with the responsibilities of a legal existence, she would naturally be subsumed under his legal identity. And thus, Blackstone argues, the law exists to safeguard the vulnerable wife.

In this way, for many of Burney's contemporaries the patriarchal family could be ideally imagined to sustain a sense of permanence, stability, and safety

in an era of uncertainty and change. And while the patriarchal family had
historically been a rigid system of male dominance, the social instability of this
period paradoxically helped strengthen its ideological power. In other words, it
is when this system seemed most vulnerable that its harsh methods of protection
were particularly susceptible, in the absence of known alternatives, to nostalgic
idealization. Susan Staves has noted that the patriarchal model of marriage
entailed "a reciprocal exchange of the husband's support and protection for
the wife's services and chastity."[12] In this fashion, the patriarchal family seemed
to have the virtues of its defects. In its very coerciveness—its "familiar" violence—it protected women from legal responsibility and gave them a social
and familial identity, what Staves calls a "status security."[13] Until the rise of the
modern state, with its welfare and disciplinary services, the patriarchal family
was the main source of public order and private morality. To be sure, by securing
public order, the gentry was merely protecting its own property and authority.[14] Nevertheless, it was this cultural centrality that led men like Edmund Burke
to see the love of family as "the first link in the series by which we proceed
towards a love to our country and to mankind."[15]

The patriarch who was also an aristocratic landowner had significant communal power, for he played a major role in the political and judicial government of the surrounding county, and his protective duties were presumably
extended to those outside of his immediate family.[16] This aristocratic, familial
arrangement is an integral part of the social system that Harold Perkin has
called "vertical friendship," a deferential relationship between patrons and cli-
ents, landlords and tenants—in short, symbolic fathers and children—that justified inequalities by protecting the most vulnerable: women, children, and the
impoverished.[17] The aristocratic model of social relations was therefore predicated in part on communal and familial values like paternalistic care, status
values that served to legitimize and uphold aristocratic dominance.

E. P. Thompson has argued that "[p]aternalism as myth or as ideology is
nearly always backward-looking. It offers itself in English history less as actual-
ity than as a model of an antique, recently passed, golden age from which
present modes and manners are a degeneration."[18] Burney's social vision often
seems to participate in this myth, a myth of social relations as seen from the
comfortable perspective of well-to-do gentility.[19] Burney's representation of
aristocratic patriarchy—most especially in *Evelina*'s Lord Orville—is often suf-
fused with the utopian air of a "new aristocracy" composed of traditionally
paternalistic but also modernized and feminized men. Yet at the same time, it
is in this nostalgically framed attempt to modernize the aristocracy that Burney
registers her severe and scathing critique of traditional aristocratic values. Despite her increasing skepticism of any merit in this "old-style" aristocratic
order, however (indeed, there is no completely positive example of traditional

aristocratic values in her novels), Burney's social vision is often colored by the elegiac tone that characterizes John Langhorne's contemporary poem, *Country Justice* (1774). Langhorne, suspicious of the innovations of modernity, laments that the "rural patron is beheld no more":

> When thy good father held this wide domain,
> The voice of sorrow never mourn'd in vain.
> Sooth'd by his pity, by his bounty fed,
> The sick found medicine, and the aged bread.
>
> He left their interest to no parish care,
> No bailiff urged his little empire there;
> No village tyrant starved them, or oppress'd;
> He learn'd their wants, and he those wants
>                                    redress'd.[20]

The benevolent gentleman landowner, surrounded by his contented tenants, was the moral locus of this ideal community. Indeed, paternalistic responsibility promised a host of protections: no member of the community would ever be hungry, destitute, physically exposed, or isolated. "Feudal hospitality" idealizes a past where all exchange between people was figured as voluntary and spontaneous. As Raymond Williams has argued in *The Country and the City*, the figure of the house in the country-house poems of the eighteenth century (like Pope's *Epistle to Bathurst*) becomes subsidiary to the theme of usefulness. In order to preserve community cohesiveness, the aristocrat was obligated to spend his money wisely and for the benefit of all.[21]

In the following pages, I will argue that Burney's view of the aristocratic patriarchal model is often a paternalistic one, tied to a "feudal" vision of the aristocratic landowner's magnanimous protections. It is within this conservative and nostalgic climate that her novels partly took shape. But her novels are deeply colored as well by the knowledge that "familiar" aristocratic rule is irreparably flawed. Indeed, a major feature of early modern social crisis is a critique of aristocratic institutions and ideology; and, if Burney's social vision can at times seem to idealize the aristocracy, it just as forcefully reflects a general disenchantment with a "traditional" aristocratic order. How can the contradictory nature or status of this system best be understood? Aristocratic marriage and inheritance practices—especially patrilineage and primogeniture—and the modifications they underwent during this period provide the best context to illustrate how the early modern alterations in aristocratic rule and ideology seem at once to humanize it, to mark its demise, and yet paradoxically to fortify its power.

Patrilineal ideology was founded on property laws that recognized descent through the father; patrilineage itself was a system of inheritance that assured male landowners that women or outsiders would never be allowed to gain control of the land and the family seat. The family name, house, estate, honor, and ancestral heirlooms were the components of this patrilineal line. Thus this ideology assumed a genealogical permanence and, to some, promised social stability. It is this belief that shapes Edmund Burke's celebration of patrilineage: "The power of perpetuating our property in our families is one of the most valuable and interesting circumstances belonging to it, and that which tends the most to the perpetuation of society itself."[22] When a demographic crisis toward the end of the seventeenth century caused a severe attrition in the male line, greater reliance was placed on strategies of "patriline repair"—name hyphenation, surrogate heirship, name changing—means by which the alarming image of female ownership and succession might be resisted and evaded.[23]

The doctrine of primogeniture was the cornerstone of eighteenth-century patrilineage. The institution of primogeniture insured that the firstborn son would inherit the family estate and title in order to preserve family integrity and continuity. Quite obviously, younger sons and daughters could suffer under this system, since they were totally dependent on their father's or their eldest brother's wishes; younger sons, especially, might slide down through the social order.[24] A later seventeenth-century invention required fathers to provide for younger sons and daughters in a "strict settlement" drawn up before their birth. Such a revision in settlement practices must certainly have afforded them more reassurance, as they now were legally provided for by their father. Yet at the same time, the strict settlement preserved patrimony for the eldest son while making him a tenant for life, thus reinforcing primogenitural and patrilineal assumptions. Michael McKeon, for one, reads these amendments in inheritance customs as testimony to the perception that the family was splintering into a series of differing interests that had formerly been tacitly subsumed under a unified patriarchal "family" interest.[25] Important questions remain, of course, as to whether these settlements were actually honored and if provisions for daughters were sufficient for subsistence.[26] Nonetheless, these contracts at the very least suggest a significant ideological crisis in traditional patriarchal authority. As Amy Louise Erickson has argued, the prevalence of these settlements qualifies, at the very least, the notion of women's complete "legal 'annihilation' in marriage."[27]

What were the effects of the inheritance practices of patrilineage and primogeniture on young, marriageable women like Burney's heroines? Marriage-settlement laws served to promote the conveyance of property from male to male, in part to obviate the possibility of women accumulating property and the considerable power annexed to it.[28] Women were crucial in the transmission of property, but expendable when they no longer served this purpose. As heiresses or dowagers, they were vastly instrumental in preserving the patrilineal line, but once they outlived their utility they were deemed irrelevant; they could be viewed as a drain on familial resources or even as men's competitors. Women who were single or past childbearing age were completely dependent, a situation that Mary Wollstonecraft deplored as utterly "humiliating."[29] Indeed, one contemporary commentator observed that many avaricious brothers resented providing subsistence for their unmarried sisters; a typical brother, he observes, "considers such payment as a heavy incumbrance on his paternal estate. Such is the condition in which the unmarried daughters of English gentlemen are too frequently found."[30]

That single women had great difficulty finding legitimate and satisfying work to support their basic economic needs is an attendant issue, for they, like their married counterparts, often found themselves powerless to achieve financial autonomy. The painful stories of governesses and paid companions (their job to entertain and serve wealthy gentlewomen) attest to this problem. Wollstonecraft, a paid companion for a number of years, resented the fact that she was forced to spend "many hours of anguish" at her job; she complained that she was treated no better than a dependent servant.[31] Because women were primarily educated in the polite arts, such as drawing, needlework, and music, they were hardly prepared to become self-supporting. As Leonore Davidoff and Catherine Hall have shown, women had few employment opportunities, since the idea of a working woman contradicted the prevailing cultural image of women as passive, retiring, and genteel.[32] And with the advent of capitalism and the gradual disappearance of the household as the main site of production, the kinds of work open to women sharply declined, so that only those "traditional" female occupations—milliner, mantua-maker, and seamstress— were open to women, and even then they would need significant capital if they hoped to set up their own businesses in these trades. Because the needle trades were considered the only labor proper for the daughters of the respectable, moreover, they tended to be overcrowded, thus driving down wages.[33] Hence, not only were single women barred from finding adequate work but they were denied a positive social identity as well, since, being unmarried, they were deemed to be almost completely useless to a patriarchal regime that stressed the transmission of property between men.[34] For this reason, as Bridget Hill has argued, single women could be viewed as a threat, since they were not under the visible control of a husband.[35] Juliet Granville, the heroine of *The Wanderer*, will face repeated scorn and abuse as she attempts to survive as an unmarried working woman in late-eighteenth-century England.

Circumstances proved no better for heiresses; they, too, might have problems attaining economic and social independence. Lord Hardwicke's Marriage Act (1753), for example, required that all women under the age of twenty-one receive their parents' consent before marrying, in part to prevent rich heiresses from absconding with family property and possibly depleting both aristocratic power and wealth.[36] Erica Harth has shown that Hardwicke's Marriage Act was a victory for patriarchy, since it attempted to keep money out of women's hands; it simply reinforced women's social and economic dependency on men.[37] If an heiress were to succeed to an estate because of the absence of a male heir, moreover, she might be forced to forfeit it unless her future husband took her family's name, thus preserving the patrilineal line. Burney's Cecilia will suffer the loss of her estate by this means of patriline repair. And yet the very explicitness of these methods used to shore up aristocratic patriarchy points to a systemic weakness that Burney recognizes as having a profound effect on women's social possibilities. By investigating the consequences of a legal device like patriline repair, Burney exposes not only the vulnerability of the old system but also the contradictory effects its weakening had on women's lives. Burney often figures this crisis in authority in moments of aristocratic violence, frequently manifested as a kind of sexual harassment, that suggests the anxiety of a perceived loss of control.

In her study of the changes in the laws regulating married women's separate property during the early modern period, Susan Staves has argued that older views of marriage as a status institution began to be challenged by contract ideology, resulting in attempts to give women the right to own and alienate property. But efforts to apply these new ideas to marriage were found to be "socially intolerable" by the courts, who, by the end of the eighteenth century, retreated from bringing these tenets to bear on marital law.[38] For our purposes, Staves's findings—that these modern alterations were ultimately found to be subversive of patriarchy and thus, in the end, paradoxically relegitimized male domination—speak to the general systemic weakness of aristocratic rule that Burney sees as central to women's contradictory experience in the eighteenth century.[39] Generally speaking, during the early-modern period, men appeared publicly as the owners of property, while women largely functioned as the transmitters of property and inheritances. In material terms, a woman's role largely entailed the maintenance of property within the domestic household. (I will discuss shortly how the spiritual and moral authority that women wielded in the domestic household exacerbated the ideological weakening of the aristocratic order). During this era, however, we do see some modifications in aristocratic rule with the development and growth of married women's pin money and separate maintenance contracts.[40] But as Staves's argument makes clear, the question of whether this separate property gave women added power and independence is the subject of a heated, expanding controversy. While some historians, for instance, read the advent of pin money as evidence of a married woman's growing financial independence, Staves shows how the courts created "idiosyncratic" laws in response to these new contracts in order to ensure the use of pin money exclusively for family maintenance.[41] We can say, though, that while women certainly did experience some important gains in the eighteenth century because of legal doctrines like separate maintenance contracts, individual husbands could flagrantly break these agreements. Instances of husbands coercing, even threatening, their wives out of their independent holdings find documentation in both fact and fiction. In *Cecilia*, one desperate husband forces his wife to relinquish her separate fortune, the kind of behavior that Mary Astell complained of some eighty years earlier: "There have been but too many instances of husbands that by wheedling or threatening their wives, by seeming kindness or cruel usage, have persuaded or forced them out of what has been settled on them . . . covenants between husband and wife, like laws in an arbitrary government are of little force; the will of the sovereign is all in all."[42]

What Lawrence Stone has called the "companionate marriage" is an important component to the social organization of Burney's fictional communities, and it was as much a contentious subject for Burney as it is for present-day historians. Briefly, Stone, among others, argues that the rise of affective individualism helped create a new conception of marriage: companionship and affection were now viewed as essential for a successful and satisfying marriage, thus precipitating some significant modifications in family relationships and the status of women. He argues that women gained a certain degree of independence from this new arrangement, since if affection partially supplanted dynastic and economic concerns as the primary motive for marriage, husbands and fathers presumably would more likely want to provide for their loved ones.[43] But many social historians and feminist critics have vehemently questioned this hypothesis. This mating arrangement, according to Staves, sentimentalized women, making them seem even less able to manage money and property capably and independently. Once married, women could be severely limited by this new cult of affection; the rhetoric of "free choice," for instance, might place "an added sense of responsibility" on them for the ultimate success of the marriage.[44] Nevertheless, as Staves argues, there can never be a clear separation between the private and public spheres; economic and state forces began to bear down hard in the eighteenth century on the supposedly private haven of the family. The ideology of the market would necessarily intrude on the individual's decisions, including marital choices. Thus affection and personal preferences could never be completely divorced from economic concerns and public interests.[45]

If companionship and romantic love became the overriding motives (or expected motives) for marriage,[46] then it follows that there would be increased agitation for the children's right to select their own marriage partners. This development challenged one of the basic tenets of patriarchal control. Eldest sons had always been particularly vulnerable to paternal pressure, since under the doctrine of primogeniture they were responsible for securing the future of the family and the family estate. Any perceived defiance of the father's authority in the marriage choice could threaten existing social and familial alignments. The impassioned debate ignited in Parliament over Lord Hardwicke's Marriage Act, whose eventual passage further tightened paternal control over a child's marital choice, testifies to the anxiety rampant in a society struggling with the competing ideologies of individualism and aristocratic patriarchy.[47] Some historians have indeed pointed to the rise of affective individualism as a factor contributing to just this sort of defiance. According to this argument, the individual's emotional needs came to seem at least competitive with the family's monetary interests.[48]

And yet the new ties of affection between parents and children could be as coercive as the older paternal control: children could be manipulated in their life choices by this new bond. They would feel psychologically compelled to comply with paternal and kindred aspirations; this would especially hold true for daughters who might fear disinheritance at a time of economic uncertainty. Close bonding between parent and child, moreover, might ensure that the children would have internalized their parents' social values. While individual cases may have varied, the children of the gentry would rarely come in contact with those outside of their own social group; there was little danger, therefore, of exogamous unions. Thus the issue of free choice at once questioned the unlimited authority of the father and potentially reinforced the tenets of patriarchy on more sentimental grounds.[49] In this way, we see yet again how important alterations in aristocratic rule paradoxically only seemed to exacerbate women's oppressed status, and, in this case, the bourgeois patriarchy that replaced this rule proved to be just as coercive and perhaps even more inclined to violence; indeed, the ideology and practice of feeling spawned new methods of psychological violation.

What are the implications of this deeply contradictory narrative of aristocratic marriage and inheritance practices for our reading of Burney's novels? The breadth of modern historical controversy obviously does not yield one indisputable reading of the past; but the partial credibility of each opposing position suggests the full contradictory range of late-eighteenth-century social life. Similarly, I will argue, Burney's novels reflect this complex and ambiguous social context in that they do not provide a single "correct" reading of women's experience, but offer instead a deeply ambivalent and inevitably contradictory story of the social institutions and ideologies that govern the possibilities for women's lives.

## II

A central theme of this chapter has been the uncertain status of aristocratic institutions and ideology. A major feature of the aristocratic crisis was the beginning of a slow transformation from a status to a class society. Social historians and literary critics have long debated the question of whether eighteenth-century society was a class society. Harold Perkin, for example, argues that classes—groups of people self-consciously banded together because of shared economic and political interests—were not part of eighteenth-century society; he argues for a nineteenth-century rise of class.[50] But others have suggested that the eighteenth century was in fact characterized by protoclasses with significant economic, political, and cultural differences. R. S. Neale, for example, delineates the early-modern period as a time when the activities and attitudes that define a class society were infiltrating eighteenth-century status culture, and he argues that a well-developed preclass conflict was slowly crystallizing by the time Burney began writing. The early part of the century saw the rise of credit and financial institutions like the Bank of England, and as the century progressed, manufacturing, commercial, and other capitalist interests gained force and credibility. The articulation of an opposition between a "landed interest" and a "monied interest" suggests this early formation of class and class conflict.[51]

Michael McKeon has argued that the novel emerged when it did to engage some of the social and ethical problems that existing fictions could no longer accommodate. He identifies one such problem as the emergent opposition between status and class criteria of social organization. He posits that class criteria—financial income and occupational identity—increasingly replace status criteria, which become subsumed under the new class categorization. Yet, he argues, the appearance and even the aura of aristocratic social relations persist during this period even as the social groups and practices to which they refer are transformed and modernized from within.[52] Similarly, Keith Wrightson has argued that what is germane here is not whether the eighteenth century was a status or a class society but rather that it presented a contradictory landscape: these two social alignments coexisted uneasily for a period of time, varying in their measure of importance, until a class society was to emerge as the dominant social arrangement in early-modern England.[53]

At the nucleus of emergent class conflict in the eighteenth century was this transition from status to class, which entailed the gradual replacement of the ideology of paternalism and the primacy of the landed estate by the values of a class society based on the laws of the market. We have already seen that there was a growing sense in the eighteenth century that paternalistic institutions were failing. Many contemporary writers linked their failure to the rise of an antagonistic class society, as a wide range of capitalist values were seen as re-shaping the social landscape and subverting older values. Perkin has conceptu-alized the developing capitalist system as a nexus of "horizontal solidarities" that challenged the "vertical" relationships of a more traditional hierarchical model.[54] In short, the forces of the market, rooted in the profit motive, created new and unfamiliar social relationships. In her novels, Burney is particularly concerned with the burgeoning ascendancy of consumerism and credit, and she at times criticizes these seemingly alien and potentially precarious develop-ments by invoking what E. P. Thompson has called the "ghostly image of pa-ternal responsibilities,"[55] well aware that this older order was available to her only as a corrective myth. That is, the conventions of paternalism could be exploited and manipulated by the gentry and its sympathizers as a way to handle the constant threat of new conflict in what was historically a highly stratified society.[56] Yet at the same time, Burney will draw unmistakable connections between these two social orders, exposing how bourgeois society only seems to extend the abuses of the system it seeks to replace.

Credit was a highly volatile creation of this new market economy. J. G. A. Pocock has argued that to some Augustan social critics, credit was a fantasy based solely on human appetite. In brief, Pocock argues that the function of property (i.e., land) during the early-modern period was to maintain the reality of personal autonomy (at least for those of the uppermost ranks), a reality that would span the generations through the vehicle of primogeniture. But once property came to possess a symbolic value—figured in credit or coin—the foun-dations of personality could appear to be imaginary. The "individual could exist, even in his own sight, only at the fluctuating value imposed upon him by his fellows. . . ."[57] In addition, as Pocock and others have noted, "credit" was often depicted as a goddess, illustrating the instability of human appetite.[58] Because there was no formal procedure in place to regulate credit (creditors, for instance, largely determined when a debt became one for which the debtor had legal responsibility), and because of the ready availability of money, the eighteenth-century economy was especially volatile, leading men to be bold and often reckless in their financial dealings.[59] With the nostalgia of hindsight, then, the rise of a credit economy could seem to threaten the very structure of a society within which everyone supposedly knew his or her own place and relationships were secure and deferential.

Burney extends and alters this earlier Augustan criticism by centering the debate on the particular financial problems faced by women;[60] that is, she will explore the violating consequences of credit and the economic difficulties caused in part by the new capitalism in the lives of vulnerable, unmarried women. She will show in particular how economic vulnerability invites sexual vulnerability, as both rapacious aristocrats and rising parvenus can easily manipulate women because of their debts, fiscal naïveté, and economic disempowerment. These characters commodify Burney's heroines by imposing a market value on them. Once again the parliamentary debates concerning the Marriage Act of 1753 serve as a useful cultural and social marker, as they bring into high relief the ideological differences between aristocratic patriarchs and the new capitalists. During these debates, it became increasingly clear that the meaning of love, courtship, and marriage was inseparable from contemporary perceptions of money. As Erica Harth has astutely observed, both love and money have an "anarchic" potential that can threaten the status quo, and both the backers and the opponents of Lord Hardwicke's bill recognized that the flow of wealth was either to be controlled by regulating love and marriage or wealth and love were to be left alone to "circulate 'freely.'" As Burney would show, the future that women faced was largely shaped by the consequences of a burgeoning class conflict whose battleground was a highly explosive and precarious economy.[61]

For the gentry, one of the dangers of the transition to a capitalist society lay in the mixing of status groups. They feared the total collapse of the traditional social order and the principles upon which it was constructed if gentlemen were indistinguishable from wealthy upstarts. The role that consumerism played in this social dynamic is integral to the world that Burney delineates in her fiction. Perkin coins the expressions "emulative spending" and "competitive spending" to denote the cultural values and behavior of the rising parvenus. Many of these fiscal ventures involved the commercialization of leisure activities, such as dancing, music, theater, and sporting events, that brought the different classes together in public, often making them indistinguishable.[62] To imitate their superiors required extravagant spending, and by becoming consumers these rising parvenus began to alter the social landscape.[63] In 1770, the *London Magazine* warned that consumerism created "such an emulation in fashionable follies, such an emulation for power, and pre-eminence, as renders the lowest orders impatient of controul [*sic*]." [64] This writer feared the prospect of an unsubmissive and potentially dangerous lower class. As the personification of credit as a goddess would suggest, moreover, women especially came under fire for being capricious consumers. To be sure, this criticism was part of the sexism of eighteenth-century censure, which focused on contemporary changes that seemed to offer women more financial independence,[65] but it also speaks to the concern that one's preoccupation with the demands of the self necessarily diminished one's sense of duty to the larger community. If a woman focused solely on her desire for expensive dresses, for example, then, it was feared, she could easily neglect the needs of others.[66] Like credit, the principles of consumerism threatened to undermine the communitarian values—nostalgically idealized by the very fact of their apparent endangerment—that existed under an older cultural model. Both Burney's men and women will be the victims of this unleashing of human appetite.

## III

Current historical research has noted the importance of the rise of "domestic ideology" to eighteenth-century culture. This development played a central role in late-century social and cultural changes, including the transformation and modernization of the aristocracy, new configurations of gender, and a renewed emphasis on the efficacy of women's behavior. One important result of the rise of domestic ideology, as Mitzi Myers has argued, is that women writers were to adopt and alter the progressive critique of aristocratic society in order to develop arguments advancing the domestic empowerment of women.[67] And yet the implications and consequences of domestic ideology are deeply complicated. A contemporary wife's lament suggests the general contradiction of this development: she has visited homes "where they tell of ladies that manage their domestic affairs in such a manner as argues they have much power: Then I come home a humble mouse gnawing on the thought that in forty years I have not gained the privilege to change a cook maid on any account whatsoever . . . [a wife's power] is but subordinate if the husband who is supreme suspend her power."[68] In the privacy of her diary, Sarah Cowper both acknowledges here the genuine authority that women began to wield during the eighteenth century and their continued subjection to oppressive husbands. Burney's novelistic engagement with domestic ideology captures the contradictory nature of the social context that Cowper's complaint vividly evokes.

Some of the most significant precepts of the new domestic ideology included emotional self-regulation and economic frugality. These new values, associated with the middle class in general and the middle-class woman in particular, helped change cultural attitudes toward the country house and its system of aristocratic values. The country estate no longer paraded the signs of aristocratic patrimony; instead, it modestly displayed the qualities associated with the new "domestic" female: regulation and charity.[69] In this fashion, the persistence of the aristocracy, as Christopher Lasch has noted, depended in large part on its acceptance of progressive values and behavior.[70] At the same time, however, this new ideology was rooted in the more traditional aristocratic ethos and signaled the felt need to correct the abuses generated by the spread of capitalist activity and by the perceived loss of an older, paternalistic charity. In what ways did women specifically combine the ethos of paternalistic care with their new domestic identity? Tending to the poor, arranging for smallpox inoculations, and significant involvement in educational reform were just some of the volunteer projects that women performed at the turn of the century that were reminiscent of paternalistic virtues.[71] Nancy Armstrong argues that it was through the vehicle of charity that women were able to enter the public sphere in new, more empowering ways. If, in a precapitalist view of the world, the patriarchal household took in all ranks of people, then in the new economic order, charity becomes more a mark of sensibility than an obligation or prescribed duty. We could argue that women were assuming the mantle of responsibility that the corrupt aristocrat had abdicated. Moreover, as the private and public spheres became increasingly separate, the demarcations of gender became that much more significant.[72] The essential qualities of the new aristocrat—practicing politeness to equals and social inferiors (this latter code connected closely to acts of charity)—were based on these new delineations of the feminine. In their behavior, women were to remind men of the best virtues of their paternalistic history.

Armstrong and Mary Poovey have both argued that the proliferation of conduct books during the eighteenth century testified to a growing middle-class readership concerned with replacing corrupt aristocratic values with a new middle-class creed, which included self-regulation and less-violent approaches to socialization.[73] Even as the aristocracy as a group was tenacious in its staying power, its "traditional" values and behavior came to be seen as corrupt and degenerate. Progressive thinkers attacked those vices they saw as specifically linked to a dissolute aristocracy. Gambling and dueling, two such vices, suggest the recklessness of the battlefield, the impulsiveness, perhaps, of aristocrats who hold a highly self-conscious yet often insouciant attitude towards their slowly eroding social dominance.[74] Dueling and the attendant codes of male violence were a frequent subject of dispute during the eighteenth century. Such violence came under attack by progressive thinkers because it symbolically recalled an aristocratic version of society in which privilege and inherited status were the dominant principles.[75] The rise of a discourse of "manners" (to which I will return) was consistent with the reformation in the codes of honor and morality in which domestic ideology participated.

Domestic ideology has customarily been seen as confining the activity and efficacy of women to the private sphere of the household. The decline of domestic industry and its relocation in the public sphere played an important role in the formation of specifically gendered realms. During the Restoration and early-eighteenth century, women were conspicuous participants in public life. The theater, public gardens, and social centers like Bath and Tunbridge Wells were just some of the sites where women took part in public activities. But with the gradual separation of the spheres, women found themselves increasingly restricted to the private realm. Self-regulation and a growing interest in manners and proper behavior became the focus of late-century thinking, and how women were to fulfill their domestic obligations was a central preoccupation of this new cultural ethos. The self-control needed to rehabilitate the rash and degenerate aristocrat was to find its model in both middle-class and gentle women. These women were expected to practice self-regulation—emotionally, physically, and monetarily—and by their example to reform men, to socialize both lecherous and corrupt aristocrats and climbing, untutored parvenus. In other words, women were to regulate the most morally dangerous desires. They were expected to disappear from public arenas, for being seen outside the home devalued them as wives, mothers, and domestic supervisors. As objects of display, they not only brought a potentially hazardous attention to themselves; they might also learn to crave the seductive public gaze, thus sacrificing their supposedly natural proclivity for domestic life. In addition, frequent public appearances suggested an "unnatural" disorder and unlicensed sexuality, behaviors that patriarchal thinking has historically deemed as women's equally "natural" inclination.[76]

Thus, as Staves observes, the responsibility for order and happiness in the new domestic family was relocated in the wife.[77] But the new ethical responsibilities that might empower women also paved the way for condemning them for instances of domestic—even public—disorder. In fact, some moralists counseled women that they had the power and the duty to reform licentious or adulterous husbands into proper and chaste men; according to this argument, women might only have themselves to blame for wandering husbands.[78] In an era of sexual and economic tumult, women were charged as well with maintaining social order because of their special relationship to virtue; as the traditional holders of chastity, they were expected to save marriage from the dangerous and unruly innovations of capitalism.[79] James Fordyce, speaking in the voice of a "brother," lays the blame for both domestic turmoil and public licentiousness at the feet of women: "To see that time which should be laid out in examining

the accounts, regulating the operations, and watching over the interests of perhaps a numerous family—to see it lost, worse than lost, in visiting and gaming,
'in chambering and wantonness,' is shocking." [80] This contradiction—the means
of women's potential empowerment only being used to reauthorize patriarchal
control—is by now familiar. And this domestic responsibility also exposed
women to new, more innovative forms of violence. Women were schooled in
their new domestic obligations by learning to internalize a patriarchal surveillance that had historically, under "old-style" authority, controlled their behavior from without. Now this external regulation would become self-control,
self-censorship, self-abnegation—ultimately, self-violation.

    It can be argued that the novels of Burney and Austen are some of our
most solid evidence of the importance that "manners" had for eighteenth-century social life. Because of the unstable social climate of the last decades of the
century, gentlewomen found themselves particularly vulnerable to violence.
Laetitia Hawkins, a contemporary writer, offers an angry account of her increased defenselessness: "I feel it impossible . . . with any degree of comfort, or
even security, to walk in London, unprotected by a gentleman. The levelling
principle has rendered all persons, making an appearance at all above the common rank, obnoxious to the most galling abuse, and often to personal insult." [81]
Obviously, Hawkins gravely doubts her ability to interpret social practices and
behavior at a time that saw the "increasing licentiousness of the plebeian classes."
Traditional social signifiers such as dress no longer distinguished rank and character. Learning manners and a vertiginous array of social codes, therefore,
might be a woman's only possible means of protection. In the eighteenth century, especially, one's manners referred to those forms of behavior that were
estimated as proper or improper according to the degree to which they con-
formed to received standards of propriety. At the same time, manners embodied a
moral code: one's external behavior was an index to one's moral character. [82]
Thus the discourse of manners retained in part the regard for reputation and
honor that had traditionally been associated with elevated birth. Once this key
principle of aristocratic ideology—that virtue was inherited—came under attack, it was slowly replaced by the progressive notion that if one mastered a
complex set of social practices (manners), one was recognized as a member of
a "new aristocracy" of manners, an "aristocracy" shorn of more traditional
aristocratic values and ideas.

    Yet for women, "learning manners" was fraught with contradictions. It
was only in the public world that a young woman could acquire manners, yet it
was also in this realm that she was most susceptible to criticism and assault.
Burney's Evelina suffers the consequences of this social dilemma. And this social crisis was part of a larger, more dangerous problem: to be seen on the street
was to invite abuse, yet in the context of the social transformation I have been

discussing, it was "on the street" that women increasingly found themselves. All of Burney's heroines at one time or another find themselves separated from the family and familial community, only to be lost in the maze of a chaotic social sphere and confronted with bold and dangerous men and women.

The concern with manners and standards of behavior at this historical juncture bespeaks a contemporary anxiety about the possibility of turbulent and unruly desires erupting at the social surface. In other words, a preoccupation with manners suggests not social stability but a volatile instability. In his voluminous work on the history of manners, Norbert Elias notes that only in a culture where a high degree of self-restraint is assured and the rules of etiquette are deeply ingrained do public activities that involve both sexes become prevalent and acceptable.[83] Elias's observation is helpful here, for it suggests that late-eighteenth-century society was wary of the steadfastness of individual restraint. Laetitia Hawkins's harsh criticism of the "levelling principle" attests to a common fear that a breakdown in social hierarchy could unleash a dark instinctual life that would especially endanger those formerly protected by traditional marks of social distinction.

One theme of this chapter has been that the transition from an aristocratic status society to an antagonistic class society based on a capitalist model led contemporaries to question how this development would affect social relationships. Manners, as contemporary critics of dueling saw them, partially replaced the more violent manifestations of aristocratic codes of honor and promised a more tranquil environment among social unequals. A writer in the *Edinburgh Review* felicitously makes this observation:

> Whenever and wherever duelling has most prevailed, then and there manners and morals have been most rude and lax. . . . As dissoluteness and absence of all that comely self-control and consideration for the feelings of others, of all classes, which is the essence of good manners, rose or fell, so precisely did duelling flourish or decay.[84]

Capitalist relations leveled the social landscape to some degree, thus giving new weight to the moral virtues of sympathy and self-control. Adam Smith believed that these virtues were the key to socialization. Ideally, he argued, people would police their conduct by internalizing the judgments and regard of real and imagined spectators.[85] Dueling, for example, had been an instrument of civility in a bygone age, for it in essence obviated "bad manners" by regulating social life and preventing accusations of dishonor from going unheeded. But by the late-eighteenth century, self-control and sympathy took the place of this more violent alternative.[86]

A central aim of this study is to reexamine this cultural preoccupation with

manners and behavior, because some of Burney's most recent readers have
considered the classification of her works as "novels of manners" to be pejora-
tive and limiting.[87] But as James R. Kincaid has argued, the "novel of manners"
is no less political than any other novelistic category. In particular, manners are
affiliated with forms of power; they are part of an elaborate code that upholds
prevailing ideologies.[88] If we historicize this definition within an eighteenth-
century context, we can begin to understand how the innovative discourse of
manners participates in the complex reordering of patriarchal domination that
results from the weakening of aristocratic ideology. I will show that in Burney's
hands, the "novel of manners" is in many ways a cultural articulation of this
new bourgeois patriarchy. From this working definition, we can more effectively trace Burney's growing skepticism about the possibilities for women's
protection in a changing world. That is, we can better see and understand how
the more optimistic Burney of *Evelina* (1778) comes to write a more pessimistic
"anti" novel of manners, *Camilla* (1796). As I will show, Burney works both with
and against this complex genre.

## IV

In the preceding pages, I have tried to intimate the interrelated sociocul-
tural factors at work in Burney's historical context that are most salient to her
insistent and profound concern with violence in her novels. In the chapters
that follow, I will turn my attention to her narrative representations of these
factors. As enduring agents of cultural history, Burney's novels provide us with
an arresting and frequently trenchant perspective on one of the most turbulent
and uncertain periods in English history. As I have suggested, Burney tells the
stories of these struggles through the medium of the novel of manners and its
paradigmatic gesture towards closure, the companionate marriage. But she
often disrupts the seemingly polite and civilized surface of this genre in order
to highlight the chaotic and violent world that surrounded and at times in-
vaded the polished homes of the gentry. Thus Burney urges her readers to see
that the placid surface of these novels can barely conceal the disorder and
violence that constantly threatens the seemingly stable and decorous world of
eighteenth-century culture.

In the following chapters, I argue that Burney's novels, each one in dialogue with the others, compose a series whose comprehensive aim is to investigate the alternative social "replacements" for aristocratic protection in the
modern world. Burney explores different social forms designed to help women
adopt a new identity, or mode of being, in order to survive in a radically transformed society. These replacements include a reformed and feminized aristoc-

racy; familial experiments of various sorts (most centrally, affective fatherhood); bourgeois patriarchy; a self-supporting community of women; and an internalized form of protection—a code of manners. The metaphor of "replacement" proves especially useful because it suggests how innovative social forms undertake those functions traditionally performed by older aristocratic forms, extending and preserving their essential social tasks under new conditions that require a change in the means of its achievement. But the metaphor also implicitly questions the extent and degree of "replacement": Can the social and ethical efficacy of the new forms improve upon that of the old? Do they instead perpetuate the injustices and inequities of tradition, or even, under the claim of "progress," devise new and more effective means of social violation? More specifically: What becomes of the inveterate violations of aristocratic rule, inseparable as they are from codes of paternalistic protection, once new models of social responsibility attempt to replace that rule?[89]

In *Evelina* (1778), the promise of a reformed aristocracy still seems plausible to Burney, but she begins there to intimate the vast social and economic problems that shape and govern the lives of contemporary women, and she begins there as well to explore the connections between cultural change and violence. Some of the socioeconomic problems that are adumbrated and yet not fully explored in *Evelina* find a more volatile and troubling representation in *Cecilia* (1782) and *Camilla* (1796). In these two novels, the latter profoundly influenced by her disturbing experiences at the royal court of George III, Burney's experiments in women's self-protection and their search for a new social identity lead to and seem inseparable from moments of madness, self-destruction, and even death. Episodes that explore the causes and consequences of women's suicidal behavior are the astonishing climaxes of both novels.

My reading of *The Wanderer; Or, Female Difficulties* (1814), Burney's final novel, stresses its status as a revision, or rewriting, of *Evelina*. The role of the "wanderer" proves to be a felicitous expression for what is most crucial in Burney's social vision. It suggests the frightening dangers of a woman cut off from her familiar social being, but it also points to the exhilarating possibility of freedom from all inhibiting constraints. In *The Wanderer*, Burney enters a feminist and revolutionary discourse galvanized by the debate of radically different thinkers like Wollstonecraft and Burke over the social and political implications and possibilities of the French Revolution. Like many others, Burney was both attracted to and repelled by what she saw, and it deeply affected her representation of violence and of the possibilities of social replacement. Claudia Johnson has written that for some late-century novelists, the "unthinkable is living outside sacred and time-honored structures; for others . . . it is living inside of them."[90] I will argue that for Burney, the "unthinkable" can be both, an argument that will help account for the powerfully contradictory ambivalence we associate with her novels. The simple and central question remains the same, however, throughout her thirty-six-year career: How does a woman of her time find physical and psychological safety and economic security? Burney will begin her career in 1778 by turning to a nostalgically framed yet ultimately modernized vision of aristocratic possibility for the answer.

# 1

## *Evelina* and the
## Politics of Nostalgia

FRANCES Burney's description of her first and most celebrated novel proves to be a fitting synopsis of the basic story that she would rethink, retell, and reshape in her three ensuing novels. Attempting to forestall the criticism that a young woman writer of twenty-six, "whose knowledge of the world is very confined," would have been able to write such pointed social criticism, Burney purposely eschews any claims of historical accuracy: "All I can urge is, that I have only presumed to trace the accidents and adventures to which a 'young woman' is liable; I have not pretended to show the world what it actually *is*, but what it *appears* to a girl of seventeen. . . ."[1] Her slightly defensive, even apologetic, tone belies the significance of what even she calls a "bold attempt": her novels will offer a decidedly female perspective on early-modern social crisis. How does the late-eighteenth century "appear" to this typical young woman? It often seems like one in which attack is sudden and unexpected, where protectors are indistinguishable from harassers, and where the lack of social and familial protection particularly exposes her to the endemic violence of the modern world. At some point, each of Burney's heroines is an orphan or wanderer searching for economic security, social acceptance, and, above all, protection from the ubiquitous violence of her world.

Late in *Evelina,* just after the old women's race, Lord Merton repeatedly seizes Evelina's hands, impedes her progress, and molests her with sexual innuendo; her visible anger only serves to entice him further. He exploits her defenselessness, treating her with what she labels a "freedom of gallantry."[2] After facing such unwelcome and violent attentions for much of her life away from the patriarchal home of Berry Hill, Evelina wishes for the putative protections of an older familial order: "'Would to heaven,' cried I, frightened to see how much Lord Merton was in liquor, 'that I too had a brother! — and then I should not be exposed to such treatment'" (*E*, 296). Her wish bespeaks a paternalistic ideology that nostalgically looks to a past where the aristocratic patriarchal community (in particular fathers and brothers) was supposed to have protected her from such assaults.[3] Indeed, Evelina believes she would not even have been "exposed" to this violence. In *Evelina*, Burney often seems to share her heroine's belief in the plausibility of such a system of social control (albeit in altered forms), but as I will show, her representation of this social order also includes a trenchant and insistent critique of its systemic flaws.

In *Evelina* sexual assault, incest, suicide, parricide, and the more figurative death of social identity are constant and serious threats. It is this omnipresent anxiety of potential violation and ruin that registers the impact that the patriarchal family has on the heroine. As a means of protection, it subjects her to its inveterate violence. At the same time, its loss only exposes her to alternative forms of violation. Consequently, one of *Evelina's* most important aims is to experiment in possible replacements for traditional aristocratic rule. These replacements will find varying degrees of emphasis in the later novels, and thus *Evelina* serves as the narrative model with which the others are in continual dialogue. Along with an affective patriarchy these replacements include bourgeois authority, a community of supportive women, and a code of manners. This last replacement, a means of internalized protection—a "new aristocracy" of manners—finds its most hopeful representation in *Evelina*, as the heroine's well-known development of an identity manifests the internalization of the power of the social actor in the heroine. And in *Evelina*, this neoaristocratic means of safety depends not on traditional aristocratic principles but on the progressive tenet that honor rests in behavior rather than in one's birth. Lord Orville, a feminized and modernized aristocrat, knows this code well and hence can restore order, protect Evelina from further violence, and provide her with a stable social identity. Thus even as Burney debunks this myth of aristocratic protection, she attempts to reform and preserve it for the modern world.

I

The opening letters of *Evelina* emphasize the central role that the aristocratic model of the patriarchal family will play in the heroine's quest for legal, social, and familial recognition. Lady Howard's and Rev. Villars's correspondence focuses on the obscurity of Evelina's birth and the "peculiar cruelty" of her situation: her legal father, Sir John Belmont, will not "*properly* own her" (*E*, 8). Because Evelina is not permitted to use her legitimate name, her entrance into the social sphere is marked by the shadow of shame and scandal. In her letters to Villars, she is anxious about this aura of illegitimacy: "I cannot to you sign Anville, and what other name may I claim?" (*E*, 14).[4] That Evelina is prevented from bearing the name of her lawful father places her in a vulnerable position, for names indicate a woman's (non)possession of honor and status. According to this aristocratic assumption, gentlewomen are only able to find protection or a respected social identity in a more traditional status society based on elevated birth. Of immediate concern, of course, is marriage. When Lady Howard suggests taking action to force Belmont to acknowledge, name, and thus legitimize Evelina, she underlines the possible lasting effects of his continued rejection: "The admiration she met with in town, though merely the effect of her external attractions, was such, that Mrs. Mirvan assures me, she would have had the most splendid offers, had there not seemed to be some mystery in regard to her birth" (*E*, 112). The prevailing wisdom is that Evelina cannot marry until a lawful patriarch gives her away, and even the progressive Orville "frankly" admits at the conclusion that he had intended to make detailed inquiries into her "family and connections"(*E*, 371). Given the force of this social reality, when Evelina calls herself an "orphan" (*E*, 368), she points as much to her loss of the privileges (and protections) of social distinction as to her fatherlessness.

But Evelina's familial situation is marked by more than the simple absence of the aristocratic father. Villars, as her adoptive affective father, complicates her predicament. The doubling of the fathers, who often hold conflicting aims, figures the disorder and internal strife Burney sees in eighteenth-century patriarchy. Although she will reaffirm this familial system at the end of the novel, Burney is not afraid to identify and criticize its worst features. Part of this criticism involves an exploration of Villars's dubious motives for purposely hindering attempts to reconcile Evelina with Belmont. While he acknowledges the profoundly perilous situation in which Evelina's namelessness places her—"The supposed obscurity of your birth and situation, makes you liable to a thousand disagreeable adventures" (*E*, 104)—he does little to change it. Lady Howard openly questions his reasons for not pursuing the obvious legal solutions: "[W]ithout knowing, I respect [your motives], from the high opinion that I have of your character and judgment: but I hope they are not insuperable; for I cannot but think, that it was never designed for one who seems so meant to grace the world, to have her life devoted to retirement" (*E*, 112). And yet it is in fact Villars's plan to obviate these "disagreeable adventures" with Evelina's permanent and restricted retirement in the country, rather than helping her achieve a respectable public and social position.

In his letters to Lady Howard, Villars indirectly reveals his selfish purposes for secluding Evelina. On the one hand, he is honoring the memory and final wishes of Evelina's mother, Caroline Evelyn; he promised the dying mother that Evelina *"should know no father but myself, or her acknowledged husband"* (*E*, 113). On the other, that Caroline Evelyn left his "protection" and fell into a "gulph of misery" (at the hands of Belmont) reinforces his belief that he is the only father able to protect Evelina (*E*, 114). Since Evelina's mother rebelled against his patriarchal authority, he is expressly determined not to lose her daughter to the same aristocratic rake: "[T]hen did I flatter myself, that to follow my own inclination, and to secure her welfare, was the same thing. . . . My plan, therefore, was not merely to educate and to cherish her as my own, but to adopt her the heiress of my small fortune . . ." (*E*, 114–15). In Villars we see a father figure who assumes that his desires are coextensive with his adoptive daughter's "welfare." Burney shows us that one of the consequences of such protection is the father's ability to shape his daughter's life to meet his personal ends. Indeed, if Villars accomplishes his design to make Evelina his "heiress," then he has knowingly usurped the legal father's place. That he has given Evelina the surname of "Anville" (*E*, 9)—not only an anagram of "Evelina" but a variant of his appellation as well—throws into high relief how he has effaced both the daughter and the real father.[5]

Burney can displace conflict and anxiety onto either father, and thus she can at once condemn the principles of patriarchy and redeem both men. While Belmont made no overtures to Evelina because he believed Polly Green, the daughter of Evelina's first nurse, to be his legitimate daughter, Villars made no attempt to prevent the inevitable embarrassment and violence Evelina would be subjected to as a bastard. He assumed, for example, that Belmont would destroy her life if a reconciliation were attempted. Dame Green's daughter, though, is not ruined but in fact leads a life similar to Evelina's: "[T]he child was instantly sent to France; where being brought up in as much retirement as myself, nothing but accident could discover the fraud" (*E*, 357). As Evelina marvels, Belmont wished to fulfill his paternal role: "[A]t the very time we concluded I was unnaturally rejected, my deluded father meant to show me most favour and protection" (*E*, 357). No series of passages testify more to Burney's ambiguous treatment of the fundamental principle of patriarchal rule. Both men, for example, imprison their daughters in rural retirement, sustaining the mystery: Evelina is denied her rightful inheritance and the pseudoheiress is thrown into a dangerous web of incest and threatened parricide. But for all this, the true patriarch is still often idealized. Using words such as "accident," "imposition," and "error" to explain Belmont's apparent rejection of her, Evelina excuses him from any responsibility and places the blame on a bold social-climbing woman, Dame Green; like some innocent victim, he was "deluded" by her deliberate "fraud" (*E*, 357). Given a chance, then, the aristocratic father would have provided Evelina with both a social identity and protection. Thus at times *Evelina* is Burney's most conservative and nostalgic depiction of the patriarchal family; in the end, as I will show, Burney's hesitation to reject either father suggests her wish to reaffirm patriarchy on more modern grounds. At the same time, however, this reformed aristocratic patriarchy contains the signs of its own inevitable demise.

How is Evelina affected by the volatile state of the patriarchal family? We can argue that much of the violence Evelina encounters is due to the fact that she is swept up in this early-modern familial crisis. Without the traditional social signs provided by the father (name, wealth, and male guardianship), Evelina is subjected to a series of attempted sexual and physical attacks. She is the first of four Burney heroines to find herself adrift in a world in which she can be suddenly attacked by drunken, aggressive men but also by seemingly respectable aristocrats like Sir Clement Willoughby. Because Evelina is an apparent "bastard," she becomes the object of aristocratic anger, frustration, and corrupted desire. Of course, that Burney even gives her readers a "bastard" heroine suggests a greater tolerance of illegitimate status. However, as Margaret Doody points out, Evelina's apparent illegitimacy restricts the way aristocrats like Sir Clement can perceive her: he tacitly assumes that she will be his kept mistress.[6] Two disturbing scenes specifically highlight the dynamics of this kind of sexual violence. Evelina's first evening at the opera is more like a prolonged nightmare when she becomes separated from her companions; Sir Clement readily exploits her precarious situation. As she frantically tries to find an appropriate way back to her proper guardian Mrs. Mirvan, Sir Clement mocks her dilemma: "'[I]t is impossible for me to go and leave you alone.' The truth of this was indisputable, and totally silenced me" (*E*, 84). At this historical juncture, social customs demanded that a young woman have proper guardians in public. And yet Evelina is in public—a site of increasing violence due in part to class unrest—because she is separated from her aristocratic family. As a virtual "orphan" with no male protection, she must rely on Sir Clement. Thus a crisis in the social efficacy of the aristocracy (Belmont was duped by an upstart woman) has forced Evelina to search for alternative social forms to replace this absent (or lost) protection. In this example, custom, acting with the force of codified law, limits Evelina's actions; her movements, even in the opera house, are circumscribed because she fears the loss of her reputation. She must carefully monitor her own conduct (and stay silent) in order to remain unsullied until the legal father (or husband) accepts her. Her dilemma is complicated, moreover, because of her lack of an education in manners—a code that might help her negotiate such potentially dangerous situations (a theme to which I will return).

Not only does Burney closely explore the physical terrors of such violence but she also exposes the social sanctions that further violate the threatened heroine. During her ride with Sir Clement, Evelina experiences the panic of physical vulnerability. She is simply unable to repel his repeated attempts to grab her: "I would fain have withdrawn my hand, and made almost continual attempts; but in vain, for he actually grasped it between both his, without any regard to my resistance" (E, 86). Her missive teems with like instances— "again seizing my hand," "still holding me" —and Sir Clement forcibly obstructs her attempts to escape the moving carriage (E, 86–87). And all the while he can taunt her with the fact that certain social constraints victimize her further: an eighteenth-century construction of femininity required that she pretend to be ignorant of sex and violence. As Mary Poovey has argued, if a woman indicated any sense that she had a knowledge of the world or of her own sexuality—even just by blushing—then she might lose men's protection and instead be considered their ready prey.[7] To answer Sir Clement's bold and intrusive questions is to show awareness of his sexual intentions: "He began by making many complaints of my unwillingness to trust myself with him, and begged to know what could be the reason?" (E, 85). Following her attempted escape, he again sneers, "What can you fear?" Evelina writes that this question "embarrassed" her (E, 85), and we and Sir Clement know that her mortification stems from the fact that in order to respond, she would have to be explicit about her body. What she "fears" is obviously rape. She finally answers "murder" to his unceasing interrogations, but the threat of sexual assault shapes their language and behavior.

An obvious consequence of the breakdown of aristocratic domination is the violence generated by the rise of competing systems. One of Burney's aims is to explore the connections between the seemingly growing ubiquity of violence in the public sphere and developing class conflict. Because public sites of leisure activities are often frequented by a volatile mix of classes, they are the scene of disorder and possible violence. In a frightening sequence at Vauxhall,[8] men literally jump out from behind bushes to accost Evelina: "By the time we came near the end, a large party of gentlemen, apparently very riotous, and who were hallooing, leaning on one another, and laughing immoderately, seemed to rush suddenly from behind some trees and, meeting us face to face . . . we were presently entirely enclosed" (E, 180–81). That the men are obviously drunk and aimlessly wandering through the dark alleyways suggests such social disorder. Once she escapes from this first group of ominous men, though, she is just as quickly surrounded by another. And the men who menacingly encircle her seem inseparable from each other and from Sir Clement, who soon arrives.

When Sir Clement arrives, he can profit by Evelina's fear and isolation by "rescuing" her, but his form of protection is no different than the other men's mode of abuse. If the breakdown in social hierarchy results in violence, this disorder is caused in part, as Burney implicitly suggests, by the moral decay of the aristocracy. Indeed, one of Evelina's tormentors abusively jokes that if she should run away from him, he would "accompany [her] in a race" (E, 181). Her wildly panicked search for safety is but a mere "race" to these men, prefiguring the old women who will have to race in order to satisfy some idle and dissolute aristocrats' need to gamble and harass.

Thomas Edwards has argued that embarrassment "conscripts its victim into a scene without allowing a choice of role; it is a blocking or barring of the freedom we claim for our selfhood."[9] In this case, Evelina is ashamed that Sir Clement has found her in an improper situation: embarrassment restricts and silences her, permitting him to lead her into a whole new set of "dark alleys." Evelina's surprise at his behavior reveals her belief in a lost idealistic world: "[F]rom you, who know me, I had a claim for protection — not to such treatment as this" (*E*, 182). The allusion is to a time and a place where a Sir Clement was supposed to have defended her. Villars obviously schooled Evelina in this ideology; in fact, in one letter, he praises Lord Orville for waiting at the Mirvans' until Evelina arrived there safely from her frightening carriage ride with Sir Clement. His comments succinctly delineate this trust in the reliability of an older paternal order. But more importantly, they suggest that Evelina has been taught to put faith in a code of moral authority that has no credibility: "*Many men of this age*, from a false and pretended delicacy to a friend, would have quietly pursued their own affairs, and thought it more honorable to leave an unsuspecting young creature to the mercy of a libertine, than to risk his displeasure by taking measures for her security" (*E*, 104; my emphasis). Orville is a good example of an aristocrat who uses rather than abuses his social position, and Burney encourages her readers to see that his behavior is atypical in Evelina's world. As Mrs. Selwyn notes, he is a relic in the present era: "[T]here must have been some mistake in the birth of that young man; he was, undoubtedly, designed for the last age, for he is really polite!" (*E*, 265). His progressive and feminine traits are based on this nostalgic model of the aristocrat. While condemning late-eighteenth-century aristocrats whose brutal treatment of the heroine seems endemic to their social position, Burney is unable to reject completely a hierarchical model of society; she will feminize this model to meet the exigencies presented by new social patterns.

Not only is the old women's race the most notorious moment of violence against women in *Evelina;* it also reveals the ultimate failure of traditional aristocratic rule.[10] The female participants "were to be proved more than eighty years of age, though, in other respects strong and healthy as possible" (*E*, 277). Yet as Evelina notes, "[T]hey looked so weak, so infirm, so feeble . . ." (*E*, 293). They are clearly beyond eighty, literally running for their lives or speeding to their deaths. In their abuse of these elderly women, the drunken Lord Merton and Coverley symbolically enact the anxiety of a perceived loss of status and power. This scene lends itself to an allegorical reading: aristocrats are trying to kill women who are either useless or threatening to them. As Lord Merton had announced earlier, no women should live after thirty, for they only get in men's ways (*E*, 257). In other words, since they are past their prime childbearing years, they no longer fulfill their functional role in the aristocratic order.[11] Consequently, women like Mrs. Selwyn can now direct their energies to defending young Evelinas. And they often prove to be strong and tenacious guardians who are able to frustrate the ominous designs of such gentlemen.

The old women's race is a travesty of an idealized world: here aristocratic institutions have become parodies of themselves. Just as Evelina expected Sir Clement to protect her because of his social position, so, according to the same logic, one might anticipate that Lord Merton and Coverley would take care of these poor old women. Burney satirically exposes the emptiness of this belief; as Kristina Straub suggests, the scene is a parody of chivalry.[12] When the women fall, the men "flew to their assistance" to give them wine in order to speed their recovery (*E*, 293). Authentic notions of chivalry belong now only to Lord Orville, who, as is reiterated frequently, is unique in his times. But even he is more disturbed by his future brother-in-law's intoxication than by the race itself. Thus the promise of traditional aristocratic protection is merely empty rhetoric, a fact that has perilous consequences for those women who still need to depend on it.

What further distinguishes this scene is that no one attempts to stop, much less vigorously complain about, this abusive treatment of older women. Presumably no one wants to challenge the authority of Merton and Coverley. When Evelina first expresses surprise at such an "extraordinary method" for settling a wager, Orville praises her for not as yet being influenced by "custom" (*E*, 277). Violence against women is apparently custom or condoned behavior.[13] So to question "custom" is to question the status quo, something that one as vulnerable as Evelina cannot afford to do. Yet when she instinctively tries to help one of the old women, Lord Merton calls out "no foul play"—no breaking his rules. According to Merton, this elderly female does not "belong" to him; like Evelina, she has been rejected by those who should putatively help her. And when one of the old women dares to tell Coverley that she cannot finish the race, he "swore at her with unmanly rage, and seemed scarce able to refrain even from striking her" (*E*, 294). The old woman's impulse is to defend herself, but this requires her manifest defiance. In this faceless woman, we see the consequences of women attempting to defy one who holds power through his gender and his status. For women to assert themselves alienates the very ruling structure on which they are often forced to depend; they risk "unmanly rage." As Evelina resignedly notes, she needs the markings of family and status to survive: "But I knew not, til now, how requisite are birth and fortune to the attainment of respect and civility" (*E*, 276). We may suppose that the possible effects of losing traditional social forms of protection are as problematic as the price of relying on them indefinitely.

## II

We have seen the violence Evelina faces because of her lack of an aristocratic patriarchal family setting. What then are the implications of a restructuring of the patriarchal family on more sentimental grounds?[14] As I have already suggested, Burney investigates the crisis in the patriarchal family by both disrupting and doubling familial roles; she also experiments with new definitions of these roles. Because Evelina does not have a secure place as either a daughter or a sister, she adopts others to play family roles. But the multiplication of the father figure threatens violence and emotional anguish even as it promises support. Villars especially can exploit the tenuousness of her situation. Just as Evelina is highly self-conscious of her lack of a proper surname, she is as anxious to refer to Villars as her "father": "Adieu, my most honored, most reverenced, most beloved father! for by what other name can I call you?" (*E*, 13). Poovey argues that Belmont is the "tyrant who blocks a woman's social and psychological autonomy."[15] I would argue that Villars also plays this blocking role, for he can take advantage of her psychological need for a father.

One enterprise of *Evelina* is to show that the progressive notion that family bonds should be based on feeling rather than solely on blood only serves to recreate the abuse of power associated with more traditional aristocratic authority. In these instances, the father's power is not attenuated; rather, its persistence depends on rationales foreign to aristocratic ideology. For example, Villars is able to break down Evelina's reluctance and discover her true feelings for Orville by exploiting their affective ties: "At last, with a deep sigh, 'I see,' said he, 'I see but too plainly, that though Evelina is returned, — I have lost my child!'" (*E*, 249). What he does not say, of course, is that his child has been replaced by a woman with sexual desires. Villars's wish to have Evelina remain with him, safely sheltered in his country retirement, eroticizes their relationship; indeed, he often expresses the desire to die in her arms (*E*, 14, 104, 387). The sexualizing of their bond is reinforced in Evelina's association of Orville with Villars; if this paradigm necessarily de-eroticizes the lover, then surely it sexualizes the affective father. Even Villars alludes to this dynamic: she *"should know no father but myself, or her acknowledged husband"* (*E*, 113). In many ways, then, Villars's fantasy is the most extreme version of patriarchal protection: Evelina would presumably be free of a Sir Clement's harassment at Berry Hill, but her sexual, emotional, and social life would be strictly confined to the father's home. A father's "ownership" is tacitly linked to the threat of incest: Villars's ability to manipulate their affective ties necessarily inhibits any hopes of her achieving sexual independence. Anthropological accounts of kinship relations have taught us that patriarchal marriage depends on the willingness of men to exchange daughters and sisters.[16] Consequently, if fathers initiate exchange, they can also prohibit it. In effect, Villars has refused to release Evelina since her birth. Women, Burney shows us, will always be dependent on men to play their proper familial roles so long as the widespread belief in the efficacy of patriarchal rule remains unchanged.

And what of the legal, blood father? This sexual dynamic that partly shapes Evelina's relationship with her affective father is a more visible and powerful force in her meetings with Belmont (*E*, 353). Evelina's response to their first encounter is similar to her reaction to being surrounded by men in the Vauxhall gardens or to being entrapped in Sir Clement's carriage. She uses the language of fear: "I was almost senseless with terror! . . . I believe I was carried into the house . . . an involuntary scream escaped me, and, covering my face with my hands, I sunk on the floor" (*E*, 352, 354). In the tradition of the sentimental heroine, Evelina loses consciousness in a highly charged situation. On the one hand, the language of terror brings the connections between violence and the coercive protection of the patriarch into high relief. To be renounced by the aristocratic (blood) patriarch is almost sure social death, for, as we have seen, a status society particularly demands that a woman be recognized by her father to assure her legitimacy and rectitude. On the other hand, Evelina is sexually threatened here by the same man who destroyed her mother; that Belmont repeatedly calls Evelina by her mother's name bespeaks this sexual confusion (*E*, 354). His ability to name and bestow identity—one of the most powerful functions in the novel—is linked to his power to abuse. By calling Evelina "Caroline," for example, he can recast her as his sexual object.[17] In a meaningful letter that Caroline Evelyn leaves for Belmont, she berates him for abdicating all his proper roles: she cannot name him "husband," "lover," "father," or "friend" (*E*, 320). He has doomed his child to "infamy" and caused his wife unending "misery" because he has ignored not only the duties of rank but also the obligations of family.[18] Yet the novel's unrelenting movement toward Evelina's reconciliation with Belmont seems to endorse (with obvious reservations) the social instrumentality of aristocratic patriarchy.

As the incident with which I introduced this chapter demonstrates, the fantasy of brotherly protection is one feature of paternalistic ideology. By picturing Orville as much a father and brother to Evelina as a lover, Burney is able to reflect on the social implications of this familial relation.[19] When Orville takes on the role of Evelina's brother, he is able to claim increased rights; he immediately questions her relationship with McCartney: "But, do you know that I shall not suffer *my sister* to make a private appointment?" (*E*, 300). Orville is now authorized to demand information that a jealous lover might find awkward to request. Like the affective father, the affective brother can manipulate her because of the disruption in her family. In fact, it is the internal strife in Evelina's various families that causes her to depend on Lord Orville's help.

But it is also important to note that Orville respects Evelina's decision to not reveal McCartney's secrets; he not only trusts her but he also arranges a meeting between Evelina and McCartney that discloses the latter's relationship to her as her brother (*E*, 302–3). Here we see the positive effects of the doubling of roles; the affective brother facilitates reconciliation with the real, albeit illegitimate, brother. And Evelina connects Orville's generosity in this episode with one other man: her affective father at Berry Hill (*E*, 302). At times, the affective family can lessen some of the pain caused by the traditional aristocratic father.

Given the hazards associated with the multiplication of the father figure, however, how does the doubling of the brother role sharpen our sense of the ways in which violation is endemic to the patriarchal family? McCartney is an arresting figure, for he is implicated in many of the novel's motifs of family violence: incest, parricide, and suicide. In McCartney's case, we see how the possibility of parricide and incest bespeak the confusion of familial roles (particularly children's), the internalization of social violence in the family, and the threat to family continuity. The first significant encounter between McCartney and Evelina is marked by the potential for violence. Evelina spies a pistol in his pocket and immediately assumes that he is about to commit suicide. Atypically, Evelina leaps into action as she seizes the pistols from him (*E*, 168). He later explains that robbery, not suicide, was his intention (*E*, 215). It is hard to resist the notion, however, that McCartney is bent on self-destruction. What makes this idea persuasive is that suicide, like incest, is a sign of moral decay. McCartney's "suicide" attempt suggests not so much a troubled individual but the moral turmoil that threatens to undermine the traditional aristocratic family.

We soon learn that McCartney's story is governed by the same factors as Evelina's, and this point tells us a great deal about the relative power of brothers and sisters. Assuming his father is dead, McCartney faces the world, like Evelina, without the privileges and protections of the father; he too is raised in a country retirement, ignorant of his origins (*E*, 211). Sexual difference, though, affects the two orphans' experiences of the world. Unable to claim Belmont's name and status, McCartney has a clandestine affair with the baronet's "daughter." Ironically, his own father berates him as a mere "beggarly Scotchman," an inappropriate spouse for an aristocratic heiress (*E*, 212). He is "beggarly," though, because his father has disowned him. Here class conflict infiltrates the family: the apparently upstart son is at odds with the aristocratic patriarch.

While Evelina is a passive victim and subject to assault because of her lack of a proper identity, McCartney can be openly violent; he can defend his apparently lower-class status (unlike his sister) against the aggression of an old-style aristocrat. In this fashion, we see how McCartney retains the legacy of gender authority while challenging the absolute rule of his father.[20] Nonetheless, McCartney's one overt act of violence—dueling his own father—causes a severe psychological crisis when he discovers the identity of his victim.

It is not surprising, then, that McCartney can also abuse Evelina: he can defeat his father and yet lay claim to Belmont's "daughter." McCartney's sexually suggestive verses about his sister—he describes her body, her "blushing cheek" and "downcast eye"—subject her to the unwanted attentions of aggressive gentlemen. Typically, she is "rescued" by Sir Clement (E, 308–9). Instead of protecting his sister, he unwittingly occasions further violence. The shifting of familial roles and the gradual deterioration of the aristocracy generate this confusion of identity; hence sexual feelings are dangerously misdirected. It can therefore be argued that the temporary legacy of the aristocratic father is not structure and honor but violence, distrust, and moral chaos.

Yet although Burney's critique of the patriarchal model of the family is often incisive and forceful, she clearly redeems its basic structure. In the end, we have a partial reassembling of the Belmont clan, as recognition and reconciliation obviate further violence. Just at the moment that McCartney is told to forget his "sister," Evelina reveals herself as his true sister (E, 345). And although Dame Green's daughter, who passes as the Belmont heiress, is suddenly disinherited, just as quickly Evelina insists on calling her "sister," while Orville promises that she will always be treated as "the daughter of Sir John Belmont" with all the attendant privileges (E, 369). The doubling is now complete.[21] Evelina's concluding vision is of its heroine retreating to the home of her affective father with her aristocratic husband. Doody argues that the central lesson of the novel is the fact that Evelina must leave the patriarchal home of Berry Hill in order to find an identity.[22] I would argue, however, that it is equally important that Evelina returns to patriarchal and "brotherly" protection at the conclusion of her entrance into the world. Such a familial and communal model solidifies her social identity and psychological well-being.

## III

Up to this point I have shown that Evelina's separation from and connection to the aristocratic patriarchal family—and its affective counterpart— exposes her to the threat of incest and sexual assault. Despite being fraught with problems of violence, however, its basic structure prevails. Nevertheless, questions remain. What new class and gender constellations may be able to replace this often violent means of social control? Something like a bourgeois "family" seems logical, since progressive values were slowly replacing older aristocratic beliefs. But this new familial model only sustains, albeit in altered forms, the violations of the order it seeks to supplant. Thus Evelina's bourgeois relations, who are also blood relatives, prove as ineffectual as her aristocratic guardians. The Branghtons, along with her maternal grandmother, Mme. Duval (to whom I will return), represent a disturbing version of a surrogate family. In effect, they expose Evelina to emotional and psychic violence, to social embarrassment. In all of her novels, Burney explores the links between physical abuse and embarrassment: both types of assault render their victims powerless. Humiliating moments might threaten the dissipation of identity, or at least, as Thomas Edwards argues, constrict one's social self.[23] Just as Sir Clement Willoughby and the dissolute aristocrats at Vauxhall can take advantage of Evelina because of her unstable social position, so the Branghtons can manipulate her for the same reasons. In the latter case, violence is associated with new social patterns. Early in her career, Burney fears that the influx of parvenus into genteel social life can only lead to new types of psychic violence. As social distinctions become less concrete, the individual's boundaries become more vulnerable to invasion as well.

The Branghtons "assault" Evelina by constantly mortifying her in public; what is most frightening to her is that they frequently betray her situation to a public audience. Like physical assault, deliberate, almost ritualistic, public shaming violates personal boundaries. If in an aristocratic order, dueling and other forms of physical assault were the usual vehicles of aggression, then the violation of emotional boundaries, in effect a lack of sympathetic restraint, is the instrument of violence in a middle-class culture. In fact, both Villars and Evelina often describe these bourgeois characters as "violent"; it is their "total ignorance of propriety," their inability to restrain their emotions, that makes them violent social actors (*E*, 148, 154). The young Frances Burney complained of the conduct of a family friend who felt the freedom "to ask any question that occurs upon other people's affairs and opinions."[24] The future novelist was determined one day to recommend that his "code" (as she termed his social behavior) be abolished, and I would argue that she tries to do just that with her novels, using them to highlight the violating features of this "code." In this case, the Branghtons' lack of public restraint threatens Evelina's already tenuous social position. When Polly Branghton innocently muses about her cousin's missing father, Evelina flees the scene: "But, is it not extraordinary, that she can put me in situations so shocking, and then wonder to find me sensible of any concern?" (*E*, 59).

That the Branghtons and Mme. Duval feel they have the freedom to violate

Evelina's fragile psychological and social selves, to make her a public subject, is much like an aristocratic rake's assumption that he can violate her body. This similarity calls for a revision of a commonplace in Burney criticism: in Burney's hands, the novel of manners is more than just a textbook for distinguishing proper from rude behavior. Ronald Paulson argues that the novel of manners involves the juxtaposition of the manners of two different classes and a protagonist who is touched by both. Most important for our purposes, this protagonist is usually attempting to solidify her position in relation to these classes.[25] Burney herself claims that the genesis of her first novel lay in a vision of Evelina hung suspended "between the elegant connections of her mother, and the vulgar ones of her grandmother."[26] Suspended between two classes, Evelina faces the violence posed by each; moreover, pressure from both sides creates a volatile environment, one that is ripe for violation and trauma. In the end, Evelina learns a neoaristocratic system of manners, a set of codes that will allow her some degree of self-protection; but before achieving this education we see her desperately trying to negotiate this new terrain of class conflict.

These class tensions are explored in detail during Evelina's first night at the opera. How Evelina ends up in Sir Clement's carriage is a problematic question for many critics, as it appears that Evelina is an apologist for the evils of aristocratic behavior.[27] Evelina is preparing to accompany the Mirvans to the opera, when the Branghtons suddenly intrude and insist that she attend with them; she is "extremely disconcerted at this forward and ignorant behavior" (*E*, 73). Yet in her previous letter, she had expressed a desire for a book explaining the social rules, since she had acted imprudently at her early public appearances: "But, really, I think there ought to be a book of the laws and customs *à la mode*, presented to all young people upon their first introduction into public company" (*E*, 72). Practicing these rules would not only prevent further humiliation but also designate her as a member of a "new aristocracy" of manners. But Burney makes clear that the problem here is that social class shapes and determines public behavior; the Branghtons follow their own code. In short, Evelina blames her cousins for their ignorance of aristocratic forms. Despite her own humiliating experiences, she is unable to sympathize with their social position. Burney's contemporary Adam Smith criticizes a society in which there is a "disposition to admire, and almost to worship, the rich and powerful, and to despise, or, at least, to neglect persons of poor and mean condition." While this serves to uphold the distinction of ranks, it also causes the "corruption of our moral sentiments."[28] Evelina withholds sympathy for fear of being linked to her cousins; sympathy, of course, presupposes an ability to imagine and identify with their feelings.

The great irony of this scene, however, is that Evelina manages to escape humiliation only to be subjected to Sir Clement's physical and verbal abuse.

First, Mme. Duval arrives in a "great rage," forcing Evelina to come with them; Evelina is so frightened that she sits "mute and motionless" (*E,* 74). Next, at the opera Mr. Branghton causes a slight public spectacle by refusing to purchase proper seats; they are simply too expensive. It is Evelina's fear of being associated with her public companions that determines her subsequent actions. When she sees Sir Clement approaching their theater box, her only thought is how to "avoid immediate humiliation" (*E,* 83). She ineluctably falls under his power because of her desperate attempt to maintain an illusion before him and before Lord Orville, who suddenly arrives. She hurriedly climbs into Sir Clement's carriage the moment she hears Mme. Duval descending from the gallery, hoping that she is eluding violation and social ruin (*E,* 85). To be rejected by the Branghtons is socially innocuous; to be rebuffed by Sir Clement, however, is to be renounced by her proper social equals. Once Evelina is safe, she can forgive Sir Clement because he uses the rules of politeness so effortlessly and effectively (*E,* 88). It has been suggested that Evelina "insists on existing against the will of a father . . .who insists she has no being."[29] But if she is existing against his will, she is trying to exist on his terms and in his social milieu. Playing the proper role in public might somehow win back her father. *Evelina* suggests that bourgeois guardians perpetuate, albeit in psychic forms, the worst excesses of aristocratic social control, but, at least for the heroine (if not for her creator) they offer no apparent benefits.

## IV

Claudia Johnson claims that Burney never openly challenges the basic principle of patriarchal authority; hence, she often displaces conflict away from the formidable figure of the father onto an imposing female character.[30] I would counter that Burney's aim is more complicated and sophisticated than this. At a time when women's friendships often became more important because of the gendered separation of the spheres,[31] she intends to show how women's collusion in the aristocratic patriarchal system contributes to the plight of the less fortunate of their sex. With the trio of Mrs. Selwyn, Mrs. Beaumont, and Mme. Duval, Burney explores the possibility of women's communities or friendships serving as replacements for a more traditional male-bound protection; but this society of other women is a problematic alternative. Mrs. Selwyn, for example, is the first in a long line of women characters (which includes *Cecilia's* Mrs. Delvile, *Camilla's* Mrs. Arlbery, and *The Wanderer's* Elinor) who have the ability to protect and empower the vulnerable heroines, yet not only fail to do so but also perpetuate the inveterate violations posed by male domination.

In Mrs. Beaumont we have a character who helps maintain aristocratic fictions. She is introduced through the satiric voice of Mrs. Selwyn, as recorded by Evelina: "She is an absolute *Court Calendar bigot;* for, charming herself to be born of a noble and ancient family, she thinks proper to be of opinion, that birth and virtue are one and the same thing . . .and thinks it incumbent upon her to support the dignity of her ancestry" (*E*, 265–66). As an evident supporter of aristocratic ideology in her equation of "birth" with "virtue," Mrs. Beaumont is implicated in a stratified social order that can ignore or even abuse the most vulnerable: women and the poor. It is fitting, then, that the old women's race should take place on the grounds of her estate (*E*, 293). She upholds the ruling men's interests at the expense of the old women's welfare; instead of guarding them, she protects and enshrines her dead ancestors. (In *Cecilia* aristocratic ideology will be linked with death in bolder and more complicated ways.) By depicting a woman as one of the most conspicuous advocates of aristocratic values, Burney is able to show that women's power is at best tenuous, since they derive it from a male-dominated system that can just as easily efface them. Doody has noted a key difference between the names of Bel*mont* and Du*val:* the former signifies the imposing mountain of the aristocratic father while the latter suggests the lower value of the grandmother's social ties.[32] It is arguable that Mrs. Beau*mont* is implicated in this paradigm. If her position in the social order is symbolized by her affiliation with the formidable aristocratic father who has the power to withhold names and thereby consign women to a life of uncertainty and violation, then we see how fragile her authority actually is.

Evelina, too, as I have suggested, has a collusive relationship with the institutions that repress women. Just as she was lost and abused in Vauxhall's dark alleys, so is her young cousin, Biddy Branghton. Evelina has safely returned and is sharing a disdainful laugh with Sir Clement at the expense of the bourgeois Mr. Smith's ignorance of art, when Miss Biddy dashes out of the gardens. She tells a tale—as logged by Evelina—that sounds uncannily like Evelina's own ordeal: "[S]he proceeded to tell us how ill she had been used, and that two young men had been making her walk up and down the dark walks by absolute force, and as fast as ever they could tear her along; and many other particulars, which I will not tire you with relating" (*E*, 189). Evelina has no apparent sympathy for her cousin's frightening experience, even though she has known her physical terror. When Miss Biddy accuses her of being an "accessory" to her distress, Evelina is both bewildered and defensive, but Miss Biddy counters that merely by running away Evelina abetted her attackers (*E*, 189). Because Biddy Branghton belongs to a lower class and is thus ignorant of the polite (neoaristocratic) rules of society, Evelina refuses to pity her. It is clear that Evelina identifies more with members of the aristocracy (she laughs with Sir Clement) than with others of her sex. To speak up for the unfortunate or powerless (befriending Miss Biddy) would brand her as a radical, outside of proper status and gender boundaries. Burney urges her readers to see how a social order stratified by status can at once violate Evelina and subvert her moral priorities. Here it is hard not to recall Adam Smith's lament about the inevitable corruption of one's moral sentiments in a hierarchical society.

Mrs. Selwyn is the most controversial of the female guardians in *Evelina*, for she stands outside conventional gender limits. Evelina shares her concerns about Mrs. Selwyn with her friend, Maria Mirvan: "She is extremely clever: her understanding, indeed, may be called *masculine;* but, unfortunately, her manners deserve the same epithet; for, in studying to acquire the knowledge of the other sex, she has lost all the softness of her own" (*E*, 254). Her lack of gentleness marginalizes her further, since this "softness" is "so essential a part of the female character" (*E*, 254); in effect, Evelina feels less at ease with an outspoken woman than with an impertinent man. To gain male knowledge and the ability to protect young women like Evelina entails the loss of those qualities that define the proper lady.[33] When Mrs. Selwyn defends Evelina at Bristol Hotwells, her satiric voice and commanding air—those traits that defuse the possible attack—are quickly labeled unfeminine (*E*, 255–59). This scene occasions one of the novel's most ironic aphorisms, as uttered by an angry Lord Merton: "I don't know what the devil a woman lives for after thirty: she is only in other folk's way" (*E*, 257). His point, of course, is that female figures, like mothers and maiden aunts who protect women from male assault, are potentially effective guardians, but to be so they have to spurn orthodox notions of femininity.

But what of the fact that Mrs. Selwyn facilitates Evelina's recovery of her rightful place as the Belmont heiress? She solves the riddle of the mysterious other heiress, and she fearlessly confronts Belmont with the truth (*E*, 319,356). Yet in her heady self-confidence, reflected in her caustic voice, Mrs. Selwyn can cause even more trouble for Evelina. In fact, Evelina is forced into Sir Clement's arms out of a "dread of Mrs. Selwyn's raillery" (*E*, 311). While no harm comes of this incident, it points up the problems that Burney sees as inherent to the concept of female protectors. In a society in which women have little legal or social agency, the outspoken, satiric, and "masculine" woman is the only one who can shield herself verbally and physically without the help of a father, brother, or lover. In this way, Burney raises an ideological dilemma: for a woman to wield power in her society she must either be like a Mrs. Beaumont, who is inextricably entangled in the values of aristocratic ideology, or a Mrs. Selwyn, who, though marginal, can also sustain the inherent violations of male rule. Mrs. Selwyn is a satirist who, as Sir Clement observes, "breeds a general uneasiness among all who are in her presence" (*E*, 325). The irony, of course, is that his tongue is as unlicensed as hers; but his comment underlines one of the novel's most conspicuous themes: those who cause uneasiness violate the order and peace of their society. Women, as many feminist critics and historians point out, were expected to be the civilizers of society, especially during an era that experienced social upheaval.[34] Therefore, women like Mrs. Selwyn who renounced this pacific role were, at some level, more disturbing to Burney than men like Sir Clement. Mrs. Selwyn's independence is at odds with the social role she is expected to play. As Evelina remarks, her severity makes her many enemies; as a guardian, she poses as many problems as she solves (*E*, 275, 344).

Mme. Duval is perhaps the most complex member of *Evelina*'s triumvirate of possible female protectors. As I have shown, she is implicated in the kind of psychic violence that the Branghtons inflict. Her confrontations with Captain Mirvan expose Evelina to even more violence. Yet even if Mme. Duval can be violent in words and action (she slaps the servants a number of times), she is also the victim of one of the worst acts of cruelty in the novel: she is bound, gagged, and thrown in a ditch by the captain (*E*, 131–37). Evelina's narrative of this episode throws into relief the fact that women often fail to support each other. She lingers over Mme. Duval's appearance—"she hardly looked human"—and, recalling her response to Biddy Branghton, she has to stifle her laughter while her grandmother tells her frightening story. At times Evelina feels genuine sympathy, yet it is Mme. Duval's volubility that primarily holds her attention and provokes her thoughtless derision (*E*, 135ff). Mme. Duval knows no polite way of narrating such a horrific story; Evelina simply cannot look past her lower-class traits and her inability to use an aristocratic discourse. Evelina notes that Captain Mirvan calls such an incident "sport," attesting to the violence of a male vocabulary that will not even acknowledge the existence and horror of the abuse of women. That Madame Duval responds in kind, however, implicates her in the captain's violence. When she escapes from the ditch, she gives Evelina a "violent slap." Like Mrs. Selwyn, Mme. Duval only knows what we might call the language of men; both characters can be co-opted by the very institutions and ideas that repress women. As a possible means of replacement, then, the society of other women is necessarily hindered by the overwhelming fact of patriarchal hegemony.

## V

If these surrogate forms fail to fulfill the social function of an older system, then how can the more traditional aristocratic model be repaired to meet the exigencies of the modern world? Burney envisions a new society that depends

less on the sole criteria of prescribed status and more on the example of feminized and modernized aristocrats and a set of codes—manners—that, if successfully practiced, might mark one as a member of a "new aristocracy." We
should not be surprised, then, that in her first attempt to solve the problem of
women's safety, Burney links the self-protection provided by manners with the
external security offered by the feminized Lord Orville.[35]

The familiar reading of *Evelina* as a bildungsroman[36]—a chronicle of the
heroine's social maturation—provides us with a powerful perspective on the
problem of women's self-protection. In short, Evelina learns to be a more self-
dependent social performer. As I have shown, Sir Clement is one of Evelina's
most persistent and cruel tormentors. What marks his attacks are Evelina's
confused and largely passive reactions; she does not possess the tools to shield
herself from his aggression. But while Evelina is clearly physically weaker than
Sir Clement and can therefore never be inviolably safe, she does learn to fend
for herself in more powerful ways as her story progresses. At a dance early in
the novel, her ignorance of the rules and customs obliges her to "submit" to his
bold commands. Her description of his behavior eerily echoes the trauma of
rape: "You have tormented me to death; you have forced me from my friends,
and intruded yourself upon me, against my will, for a partner" (*E*, 33). But
these early experiences school her in forms of resistance; accordingly, at an
ensuing ball she is able to repel Mr. Smith's similar advances because she can
exercise her new knowledge to her obvious advantage (*E*, 209). In these examples, Burney uses the politics of the dance as an analogue for the larger
social and sexual negotiations (e.g., at Vauxhall) that women must master in
order to defend themselves.[37]

Such scenes show Burney flirting with the idea of creating a largely autonomous heroine, but she finally draws back from the more radical possibilities of her themes and language. What are the implications of this reticence?
We are left with the apparent fact that Evelina's marriage to Orville is a kind of
reward for her newly acquired social prudence—i.e., for learning "manners."
It is in Evelina's final scene with Sir Clement that we see this correlation most
fully. When Sir Clement corners her in the arbor and abuses her with his usual
menacing suggestions, she speaks and acts more confidently than she did in his
carriage: "I entreat you never again to address me in a language so flighty and
so unwelcome. You have already given me great uneasiness; and I must frankly
assure you, that if you do not desire to banish me from wherever you are, you
will adopt a very different style and conduct in future" (*E*, 326). As he so often
does, Orville happens upon this scene, but instead of her customary silent and
mortified reaction, Evelina calls out to him while demanding that Sir Clement
"release" her (*E*, 326). Gina Campbell has recently argued that Evelina's

"discourse" in itself cannot protect her; it is, nevertheless, a major precondition for Orville's protection.[38] While Campbell's observation is fundamentally true—Evelina grows more confident and this change secures her the protection of a new aristocrat—it might underestimate the extent of Evelina's newly gained assertiveness. Just as she was able to prevent McCartney from violence, so she obviates a potential duel between Sir Clement and Lord Orville by concealing the former's provoking letter from the latter; in fact, she seizes control of the situation by responding to Sir Clement herself (*E*, 370–71). Evelina's story may have a fairy-tale-like ending, but she has plainly learned to negotiate effectively some of the more dangerous dilemmas of the modern world.

If Evelina masters new ways of responding to violence, then Orville has always possessed this ability, as he embodies those values that Burney deems necessary to counter the ubiquitous cruelty of modern life. In Orville we find a singular example of a modernized and feminized aristocrat; he is often referred to as delicate, a feminized male (e.g. *E*, 247). Both Susan Staves and George Starr have noted the importance of his feminine attributes, and Staves in particular points out that the word "delicacy" suggests an awareness of the needs and sensibilities of others; it opposes cruelty.[39] In fact, Orville shows his sensitivity in potentially embarrassing situations by adapting and regulating his behavior for Evelina's needs. Twice in the novel he allows her to use his name (or their acquaintance) to escape from disconcerting or hazardous situations (*E*, 36, 231). The importance of this is obvious in light of the aristocratic father who refuses (or is too weak to grant) her the protective use of his name. Moreover, Orville is always courteous and gentle at moments when she has just experienced mental and physical trauma: "a politeness to which I have been sometime very little used" (*E*, 221, 223). Here Burney pointedly contrasts Orville's delicacy with Coverley's "unmanly rage" (*E*, 15); Orville exemplifies a newly defined masculinity. Evelina attributes her ability to be unrestrained with Orville to his delicate manners; she simply feels less embarrassed with him (*E*, 278). Like Adam Smith's ideal observer, Orville is able to sympathize with Evelina's predicaments, and this ability is tacitly linked to his feminine attributes. Whenever she meets him in public places, he seems to be with a "party of ladies" (*E*, 81, 228), and the joke among his fellow aristocrats is that he drives his phaeton "as careful as an old woman!" (*E*, 269). Villars suggests that Orville is an icon of a lost age of aristocratic idealism. Burney experiments here with a new notion of the hero, modified and feminized by various developments in the family, religion, and moral philosophy.[40] Yet Villars's suggestive comment reveals the ultimate futility of the politics of nostalgia in *Evelina:* Orville may be humanized, but he cannot plausibly exist in the modern world.

In the end, Burney endorses an aristocratic order whose corruptions are replaced by the values of sympathy and sensibility. That the Branghtons and

Mme. Duval are necessarily relegated to the margins suggests that Burney is not as yet ready to conceive of the participation of parvenus in this new community. In the last analysis, it is the ability to be sympathetic, delicate, and polite that distinguishes Orville and Evelina from the Branghtons. It is a commonplace of many eighteenth-century novels to locate a better society in a retired country setting where one can ignore the political and economic effects of a burgeoning class society.[41] This couple's retreat from the scene of social disorder is entirely consistent with an ideology that insists on the reestablishment of the social hierarchy on the basis of delicacy and politeness; Orville and Evelina represent a "new aristocracy" of manners. In his desire "to please and to serve all who are in his company," Orville re-enacts noblesse oblige in more modern ways (*E*, 61).

Thus Evelina's brusque statement to Orville that she is "ignorant" of the word *"settlements"* suggests how in some ways she is shielded from a world of harsh economic reality by her very ignorance; she trusts Orville to be a generous and kind husband. For this reason, it is not surprising that *Evelina* has frequently been read in the tradition of "Cinderella."[42] But in fact it might be more fair to say that *Evelina* is an often sophisticated critique of the aristocratic patriarchal order. *Evelina* adumbrates many of the socioeconomic issues that Burney will address throughout her career: the connections between the family (and its loss) and violence, the importance of sympathy and a feminized culture to counter or even dissipate this violence, the problematic values of a new capitalist nexus, and the new violations inherent in the rules of politeness and the male gaze (e.g., Orville's constant observation, or Sir Clement's ability to use manners to couch his intentions). At any rate, Evelina's wish for a "brother" has come to pass. That this small family (Evelina, Orville, and Villars) is sexualized indicates the extent to which it draws in upon itself, thus eluding the outside world. Now any highly-charged sexual relationship is tempered by familial unity and feeling. But in the later novels, this retreat will not be as simple. The decaying Gothic prison that is the patriarchal home in *Cecilia*, Delvile Hall, will serve as an even more powerful and indisputable symbol of the failure of the aristocratic world to sustain its power and moral authority.

## VI

With the anonymous publication of *Evelina* in 1778, Burney had made her own public entrance into the world, leaving the protective borders of her father's home. By concealing her novel from her father, the musicologist Charles Burney, she faced her own set of familial and social problems. My argument on the often volatile father/daughter dyad in *Evelina* provides a useful framework with which to investigate briefly Burney's entrance into public society as a published author. If the presence of the patriarchal family looms large in the story of *Evelina*, it perhaps looms even more so over its composition. In effect, those problems that Evelina struggles with—the imperious affective father and the violating consequences of a public entrance—greatly troubled her creator as well.

Feminist critics have long been intrigued with Burney's often ambivalent attitude towards her role as a published author, and her dedicatory poem to her father that prefaces *Evelina* has been widely recognized as a window on the complexities of her relationship with him.[43] This poem both gives witness to the delicate negotiations involved in Burney's decision to hide the novel from her father and also attests to the violations entailed in publication:

> Oh, Author of my being!—far more dear
>     To me than light, than nourishment, or rest,
> Hygeia's blessings, Rapture's burning tear,
>     Or the life-blood that mantles in my breast!
>
> If in my heart the love of Virtue glows,
>     'T was planted there by an unerring rule;
> From thy example the pure flame arose,
>     Thy life, my precept, — thy good works, my school
>
> Could my weak pow'rs thy num'rous virtues trace,
>     By filial love each fear should be repress'd,
> The blush of Incapacity I'd chace,
>     And stand, Recorder of thy worth, confess'd:
>
> But since my niggard stars that gift refuse,
>     Concealment is the only boon I claim;
> Obscure be still the unsuccessful Muse,
>     Who cannot raise, but would not sink, thy fame.
>
> Oh! of my life at once the source and joy!
>     If e'er thy eyes these feeble lines survey,
> Let not their folly their intent destroy;
>     Accept the tribute—but forget the lay.

The need to conceal her novel from her father suggests that, like the Rev. Villars, Charles Burney would have tried to prevent his daughter's attempt to express herself openly and freely.[44] That she so clearly deifies her father ("Author of my being") testifies to the power she associates with him, including his ability to reject. The first two lines of the third stanza capture Burney's fear of patriarchal censure. She cowers at the thought of naming herself as the author because of the reflection it would have on her father. As *Evelina* shows us, names signify a woman's bond with her father. Thus we can argue that Burney fears losing her place in her family by alienating her father (her mother is dead), and she is also alarmed at the thought of public humiliation; she would not "sink" his "fame." In fact, Charles Burney was desperately trying to circulate his family in elite society.[45] And while Burney claims that if she did have the gift to praise her father's worth, she would then acknowledge her authorship, we cannot ignore the fact that she plainly dreads his disapproval. Doody reads this poem as Burney's "apology" to her father.[46] But this description seems much too tepid, for it fails to account for the obvious fear and guilt that she feels for proceeding without his permission. If she were to reveal the truth, she would not apologize; she would stand "confess'd."

These rather opaque verses, therefore, suggest both a desire for and an anxiety of her father's notice. Like Evelina, Burney needs to venture forth from the security of patriarchal rule (which she labels "unerring" in line 6) to find her place in society—in this case as a published author—but she needs to return to the family, both accepted and protected. At the end of her career she would recall this poem, divulging to her father more explicitly that she had needed him to approve of her undertaking, but she had feared he would end her career before it began. His "blush" signifies his anger as much as his embarrassment:

> Little did I see the indulgence that would bring me forward! and that my dear father himself, whom, even while, urged by filial feelings, and yet nameless, I invoked, I thought would be foremost to aid, nay, charge me to shun the public eye; that He, whom I dreaded to see blush at my production, should be the first to tell me not to blush at it myself! [47]

In the end, her father did allow her to write, and yet his "indulgence" would be highly manipulative, as the story of the composition of *The Witlings* shows.[48] The fears expressed in the dedication to *Evelina* would eventually come to pass. Thus Burney's first publication is not so much a complete rejection of her father's authority as an independent act within the limits of his paternal rule.

Burney felt the need for protection because of the obvious potential for embarrassment or censure in any kind of public recognition. That she was painfully shy and insecure complicated her dilemma, since any direct public attention or acknowledgment both threatened and frightened her. Persistent staring especially made her feel violated and even attacked; like one of her heroines, she often had to flee the room (*DL* 1:97). In her dedication to the

authors of the "Monthly and Critical Reviews," Burney articulates her predicament: "Without name, without recommendation, and unknown alike to
success and disgrace, to whom can I so properly apply for patronage, as to those
who publicly profess themselves Inspectors of all literary performances?" Like
her heroine, Burney is wading into the often risky waters of public life without a
name, without a sign that at the very least promises a safe introduction; she has
no status as yet in polite circles and therefore has no patron to pave and secure the
way for her. She particularly dreads facing "censure or ridicule" because of her
sex (*DL*, 1:102). Hence she is appealing for their "protection," as she calls it,
since their critical reactions will help decide her authorial fate. In this way, the
male critic plays the same role as a father and brother do in a traditional paternalistic paradigm: he is expected to shield her literary, social, and sexual reputation.[49]

Once she had published her novel, however, Burney had begun the inexo-
rable journey towards a public life, although she insisted to Mrs. Thrale that
she assumed "the book would never be heard of" (*DL*, 1:97). Mrs. Thrale calls
Burney on her willful naïveté: "Poor Miss Burney! so you thought just to have
played and sported with your sister and cousins, and had it all your own way;
but now you are in for it! But if you will be an author and a wit, you must take
the consequences!" (*DL*, 1:96). Unlike Evelina, Frances Burney could no longer
hide in relative obscurity; she had to face the uneasy task of negotiating public
life (especially as a woman who could not have it "all [her] way"). Not only did
this mean a life away from the "safe" perimeters of her father's home. More
importantly, it also called for her entry into a volatile social and economic
arena. Burney seems to have had this development in mind in one of her early
journal entries: "I have an exceeding odd sensation, when I consider that it is
now in the power of any and every body to read what I so carefully hoarded . . .
[*Evelina*] may now be seen by every butcher and baker, cobbler and tinker . . .
for the small tribute of threepence" (*DL*, 1:23–24). Given the oft-noted correlation between the text and a woman's body, we might argue here that Burney's
"odd sensation" suggests the extent to which her entrance into the public arena
felt uncannily like the vulnerability of bodily exposure; anyone can now touch
and buy what had lately been held "in all privacy." If Frances Burney fears that
she (and her novel) have become a commodity in a money economy,[50] then the
wealthy heiress Cecilia Beverley similarly discovers that she is a commodity—
a token of exchange—for both her aristocratic and bourgeois guardians. It is
Burney's growing interest in the efficacy of the new capitalist nexus as a possible replacement for aristocratic patriarchal authority that finds a volatile representation in her next novel, *Cecilia*.

# 2

## *Cecilia*'s New Paternalism:
## The Promise of Women's Communities

L<small>IKE</small> Evelina, Cecilia Beverley is separated from her family; but her separation cannot be repaired. In *Cecilia* (1782) there will be no reconciliation with the father. Orphaned before the age of legal maturity, Cecilia must live with one of three male guardians chosen specifically by her recently deceased uncle to supervise her personal and financial affairs until she reaches her twenty-first birthday. Almost immediately her uncle's handpicked guardians force her to leave the home of Mrs. Charlton, "her benevolent friend" and "maternal counsellor," with whom she had been "content to dwell" until she could succeed to her sizable estate.[1] Removed from the reassuring ties of her youth, she is thrust into a world of social conflict, gambling, usury, dueling, and suicide. With this early sequence, Burney prepares her readers for one of the most disturbing elements of her second novel: Cecilia's guardians expose her to rather than shield her from the endemic violence of the modern world. They include Mr. Briggs, a bourgeois miser; Mr. Harrel, a dissipated and reckless gentleman who gambles away his income (and much of hers) and eventually his own life; and Compton Delvile, a haughty aristocrat who, despite his attenuating power, will subject her to the social violations congenital to traditional aristocratic rule. *Cecilia*'s readers will see that these men's apparent class differences hide some profound similarities, most central of which is their position of power in an overwhelmingly patriarchal culture.

But a conflict between these two classes will also prove to be a major source of violence in the novel. As a protobourgeois class slowly but assuredly becomes more powerful, the aristocratic order takes great pains to shore up its economic and cultural authority. And it is the means by which these two groups attempt to assert or maintain their power that cause a great deal of *Cecilia*'s violence. Some of these methods include the procedures of patriline repair and the means by which progressive men attempt to improve their social status, including uncontrolled consumption and a growing reliance on credit.[2] Burney shows us that a period of social conflict and status volatility ushers in a new era of increased violence and self-destructive behavior. Various means of self-violation like suicide and madness are often the individual's responses to these economic and cultural disputes. Suicide is at once an attempt to expel the poisons of aristocratic or bourgeois control and yet the result of succumbing to them as well.

Women, in particular, are the focus of violence in Burney's second novel. Cecilia and Mrs. Delvile, the hero's mother, will painfully discover that a patrilineal system of inheritance often confines them to limited roles of serviceability, to securing aristocratic male lineage. In other words, women are forced to sacrifice their money, their freedom, their identities, and almost their lives in order to help sustain and perpetuate the male line. In exchange, these women would putatively receive the gentry's protection. But it is implicitly understood that the gentry ensures social welfare and public safety in part for the purpose of protecting its own interests; thus in order to reap the benefits of this "protection," women cannot afford to threaten male rule.[3] With Mrs. Delvile, Burney takes up where she left off in *Evelina* by exploring more fully not only the motives but also the nearly fatal consequences of aristocratic women's complicity in those systems that can just as easily efface them. Yet *Cecilia* is also an experiment in the possibilities of a female community to counteract the violations of male authority: this community largely expunges aristocratic vice without sacrificing the best virtues of paternalistic rule. In the end, however, Burney's second novel registers a bitterly painful loss: we will see that as the bearers of moral authority, women could offer a restorative alternative to the decaying aristocratic order and the rising bourgeois nexus, but they face the stark fact that traditional aristocrats continue to wield a profound power even as they attempt to shore up their waning authority. Another way of saying this is that even in its decline, the aristocracy continues not only to present a menacing physical threat to women but also, through its laws, prevents them from using their moral strength to help transform the increasingly violent landscape of the modern world.

## I

*Cecilia* aims to expose the ways in which this aristocratic system requires great sacrifices of the women and men who are expected to uphold and maintain family continuity, especially during a period in which this order confronted severe crises in its socioeconomic authority. As the "only survivor of the Beverley family," Cecilia finds that her future choices are limited by the stipulations of her uncle's will: he "made her heiress to an estate of £3000 per annum; with no other restriction than that of annexing her name, if she married, to the disposal of her hand and her riches" (*C*, 5-6). Julia Epstein argues that the protection of Cecilia's maiden name undermines the very principles of "patrimonial succession."[4] But this reading seems more wishful than helpful. Far from containing what Epstein calls the "seeds of revolution," this provision illustrates that patrilineal assumptions are deeply embedded in the fabric of early-modern culture. Needless to say, Cecilia's uncle does not consider the Beverley name to be hers; rather, she is the conduit through which it will pass to another man. If she should die without children, the estate will be transferred to the next heir, Mr. Eggleston (*C*, 854). Cecilia's role is to produce a legitimate male heir, and in this way she is a valuable token of exchange for men. This situation is only complicated when Cecilia falls in love with Mortimer Delvile, a man whose father also insists on the perpetuation of his name and patrimony. Caught between her uncle's dynastic dreams and his father's similar aspirations, they confront the dangers entailed in sustaining such an untenable contradiction.

Compton Delvile, the hero's father, most fully enacts the social injustices endemic to the aristocratic system. His decaying ancestral home bespeaks his unhealthy nostalgia for a reigning epoch of aristocratic hegemony that is slowly but irretrievably crumbling:

> Delvile Castle was situated in a large and woody park, and surrounded by a moat. A draw-bridge which fronted the entrance was every night, by order of Mr. Delvile, with the same care as if still necessary for the preservation of the family, regularly drawn up. Some fortifications still remained entire . . . it was dark, heavy and monastic . . . but the decay into which it was falling rendered such remains mere objects for meditation and melancholy. . . . Festivity, joy and pleasure, seemed foreign to the purposes of it's [*sic*] construction. . . . (*C*, 457)

Here Burney alludes to the violence and social conflict contemporaries associated with the image of the Gothic prison.[5] Most specifically, we are reminded of the threat of forced marriages and the violent abduction of vulnerable heroines; and, indeed, Delvile will inflict a similar kind of domestic tyranny. But at the same time, we see the futility of his attempts to preserve aristocratic hegemony. In effect, he is entangled in a hopeless struggle to perpetuate his family line. Only the prospects of sterility or death seem likely in his lifeless, "monastic" home.

Mr. Briggs, Cecilia's bourgeois guardian, acerbically exposes the weakening of the ideology that underpins Delvile's illusions of authority. Briggs does not fear insulting "the name of Delvile," for it signifies little to a new bourgeois order that succeeds by virtue of individual talent and the accumulation of wealth. He pointedly asks, "will the old grandees jump out of their graves to frighten us?" (C, 454).

> Why all them old grandfathers and aunts you brag of; a set of poor souls you won't let rest in their coffins; mere clay and dirt! fine things to be proud of! a parcel of old mouldy rubbish quite departed this life! raking up bones and dust, nobody knows for what! ought to be ashamed; who cares for dead carcases? (C, 454)

The continuity of familial succession is now figured in the specter of "clay and dirt . . .[and] bones and dust." In Delvile we see evidence of Burney's increasing skepticism about the social utility of the aristocratic order. Briggs's contempt of Delvile's necrophilic interest suggests the former's utmost confidence that the demise of exclusive aristocratic rule is near. If in *Evelina* the past is associated with a paternalistic care that might yet be modernized for the purposes of solving new social problems, in *Cecilia* a traditional aristocratic past is often depicted as dead, beyond resuscitation in the modern world. The images of ruling-class power and authority (e.g., the castle and estate) are now only an ironic signal of the aristocracy's growing debility.

Yet despite the deterioration that surrounds him, Delvile holds on to the slippery illusion that he is safely removed and protected from the radical social changes taking shape outside his castle walls: "He was not, as in the great capital of the kingdom, surrounded by competitors, no rivalry disturbed his peace, no equality mortified his greatness; all he saw were either vassals of his power, or guests bending to his pleasure" (C, 458). Economic and political competition are utterly foreign possibilities in his isolated world. Delvile refuses to acknowledge that his way of life is slowly being replaced by the social innovations taking place in the "great capital of the kingdom." That he still has fortifications and a working drawbridge suggests that he feels the need to separate himself from these "inferior" parvenus who refuse to acknowledge his inherent superiority. Because Cecilia resists "bending to his pleasure," she upsets his aristocratic hauteur and apparent sanguinity (C, 458). Not only does she threaten to entice his son away from him; she also seeks to replace his ancestral name with the appellation of a family whose fortune is large (and could possibly repair his dilapidated estates) but whose genealogy is fairly recent (C, 362). It is somehow fitting, then, that it is at Delvile Castle—which one character recognizes as a Gothic "gaol" (C, 506)—that Cecilia simultaneously learns of Delvile's love and realizes the great strength of aristocratic (and patrilineal) customs. As we will see, it is Compton Delvile's harsh refusal to embrace change that wreaks havoc on Cecilia and his son.

Like Cecilia, Delvile is oppressed by familial demands. As the only son, he is expected to suppress his feelings in order to secure the preservation of the family; in short, the elder Delvile sees that "without [his son's] life and health the whole race would be extinct" (*C*, 462). Lady Honoria, a satiric character in the spirit of *Evelina*'s Mrs. Selwyn, claims that the Delviles care little about their son; their only concern is that he remain healthy enough to preserve the "old castle" (*C*, 489). As Lady Honoria jokes, he is merely a "puppet" for their dynastic ambitions (*C*, 484). The truth of her witticism is borne out: Delvile hesitates at first to declare his love for Cecilia because of what he calls the "unpleasant circumstance" of the name clause attached to her uncle's will (*C*, 477).

It is clear that the preservation of the aristocratic family depends upon the children's complete subjection to their father's will. Once Delvile discovers that Cecilia returns his love, however, he proposes a secret marriage. He soon reveals how he was indoctrinated into an aristocratic system that depends upon the imaginary value of elevated birth for its cultural authority: "Indeed almost the first lesson I was taught was that of reverencing the family from which I am descended, and the name to which I am born. I was bid consider myself as its only remaining support, and sedulously instructed neither to act nor think but with a view to its aggrandizement and dignity" (*C*, 562). "[I]nstructed neither to act nor think" in opposition to the family interest, Delvile has internalized the bitter lesson that his desires are a threat to larger familial goals. Mistaking "ambition for honour, and rank for dignity," as young Mortimer observes, his parents have long planned a "splendid connection" for him. Despite the fact that they have heretofore respected his "repugnance" to certain alliances, Delvile fears that they have lost patience; he concludes that he and Cecilia must marry at once in a secret ceremony. As in *Evelina*, the basic fiction of traditional aristocratic ideology—birth equals worth—is challenged.

Delvile's proposal of a clandestine marriage resonates with the progressive themes of the freedom of love and the violence of arranged alliances. But for Cecilia the question is how to accommodate individual wishes to the obligations of family. In turn, Delvile vehemently questions her caution:

> "But is there no time for emancipation? Am not I of an age to chuse for myself the partner of my life? Will not you in a few days be the uncontrolled mistress of your actions? Are we not both independant? Your ample fortune all your own, and the estates of my father so entailed they must unavoidably be mine?" "And are these," said Cecilia, "considerations to set us free from duty?" "No, but they are circumstances to relieve us from slavery." (*C*, 572)

Delvile's republican rhetoric only serves to sharpen the truth of Lady Honoria's belief that Delvile Castle is a "gaol." But at the same time, this couple will be the beneficiaries of the arbitrary prescriptions of tradition that Delvile so passionately vilifies. Because of the peculiar devices of English property law, Delvile is able to choose his own wife without surrendering his family's estates ("so entailed they must unavoidably be mine"). And Cecilia's fortune—part of her uncle's patrimony—will most likely be used to repair the estates. As these seeming contradictions suggest, *Cecilia* offers a partial challenge to aristocratic patriarchy: the father's harsh authority is loosened but not at the expense of upper-class privileges and the established social order (we will see a variation of this theme in the novel's depiction of female community). In turn, this larger problem highlights a more personal dilemma: Can the economic and emotional interests of marriage be reconciled?

*Cecilia* joins this debate by exposing how love does not solve the problem of women's legal subordination.[6] In order to back out of her clandestine plans with Delvile, Cecilia must travel alone to London, a singular sight that generates a lot of derisive speculation. One of the novel's most sardonic characters, Mr. Gosport, refuses to believe her claim that she has business in London: "[A]nd pray what can you and business have in common?" (*C*, 597). He insists that there can be only one possible motive for her trip—marriage. Using the discourse of English property law, he drolly notes that the community believes that Delvile has appropriated her body: "No, no; the place, they conclude, is already seized, and the fee-simple of the estate is the heart of the owner" (*C*, 597). His metaphor aptly, indeed frighteningly, summarizes her prescribed social role: a woman is a man's property, the vehicle by which he achieves his dynastic or financial aspirations. That her heart is the "fee-simple" of the estate—an estate in land belonging to the owner and his heirs forever—suggests that she is no longer an autonomous individual. In this way, Burney uses the term "heart" in both its literal and metaphoric meanings. Cecilia may have lost her heart (i.e., fallen for Delvile), but Gosport also presumes that she has surrendered her liberty. Such analogies call forth, despite their humor (indeed, Cecilia finds Gosport more vexatious than playful), a troubling ideological conflict: How was the notion of the freedom of love to be reconciled with the fact of a wife's legal and social nonentity in marriage? For many men the answer was simple: marrying for love naturally entailed their wives' sexual and social dependency.[7] As long as women remain legally and economically subordinate to men, love-based marriages cannot remedy these inequities.

For the moment, however, questions about the freedom and economics of love are put aside for the more pressing and seemingly impervious fact of Mr. Delvile's paternal rule. Cecilia fears that Delvile's scheme will damage her dignity and reputation; to enter a family without its consent would embarrass and even disgrace her (*C*, 556–57). The failure to obey the father's wishes—in this case Compton Delvile's—is akin to a mortal sin: "With such a weight upon the mind length of life would be burthensome; with a sensation of guilt early death would be terrific!" (*C*, 585). Mr. Delvile can wield psychological intimidation; to sin against the earthly father is to risk damnation. Even though Briggs has taunted Delvile about the impotence of his dead ancestors, it is evident in this scenario that Delvile poses a kind of mortal threat not only to his son but also to the beleaguered heroine.

Because she has internalized some of the most basic assumptions of patriarchy, Cecilia simply cannot gain liberty. She comes to the disheartening realization that her desire for autonomy is effaced by the psychological effects of learned dependence: "It seemed once more in her power to be mistress of her destiny; but the very liberty of choice she had so much coveted, now attained appeared the most heavy of calamities; since, uncertain even what she ought to do, she rather wished to be drawn than to lead, rather desired to be guided than to guide" (*C*, 621). Accordingly, she allows Delvile to guide her to church because her choice seems untenable: either she disobeys the father and marries Delvile, or she leaves him at the altar and faces the possibility of public scandal. Hence when the ceremony is interrupted by a mysterious woman who "glided out of the church with the quickness of lightning" (*C*, 626), we are not surprised that Cecilia instantly assumes that she is being visited by divine punishment for her defiant act against the father.

At the end of the novel, it is revealed that Monckton, Cecilia's revered male counselor, had sent this pew opener to disrupt the ceremony. What are the implications of this ironic turn of events? Cecilia may think that God has punished her for her apparent rebellion, but in truth she has been manipulated by an ambitious younger son of a noble family who sees her as a pawn in his sinister quest for power and wealth. Divine reproof is unmasked to reveal raw social ambition. Like many real younger sons, the fictional Monckton dreams of marrying an heiress to improve his fortunes and rank. Yet while he has been dispossessed because of the arbitrary device of primogeniture, he still has the power to manipulate and control Cecilia because he holds the social authority of gender.[8]

Monckton is a man whose actions are influenced by the values of a system that deems him expendable. By brutally exploiting women, he intends to attain what he tacitly believes is his proper and rightful role as a landed gentleman. His first step is to manipulate a dowager into marriage: "In the bloom of his youth, impatient for wealth and ambitious of power, he had tied himself to a rich dowager of quality, whose age, though sixty-seven, was but among the smaller species of her evil properties. . . ." (*C*, 7). One of Lady Monckton's most disturbing "evil properties," exacerbated by the fact that she knows her husband does not love her, is her "power" of "giving pain" to the beautiful young Cecilia (*C*, 721). In this way Lady Monckton reminds us of the cold and arrogant Mrs. Belmont of *Evelina*, who ignored the cruelties of the old women's race. But Lady Monckton is also like these old women, for she is a conduit for her husband's social aspirations. The men in this novel are irritated as well that women live past thirty:

> "I wonder when she intends to die," said Mr. Harrel. "She's been a long time about it," cried Sir Robert; "but those tough old cats last for ever. We all thought she was going when Monckton married her; however, if he had not managed like a driveler, he might have broke her heart nine years ago." "But an old woman has no sense of decency; if once she takes to living, the devil himself can't get rid of her." (*C*, 80)

This "brutal conversation," as Cecilia calls it (*C*, 80), signals once again that women are instrumental in this socioeconomic system but are ultimately expendable. Lady Monckton has already fulfilled her purpose; if she had any sense of "decency"—men's cruelty is couched in the language of decorum—she would quietly die and leave her money for the aggrandizement of her husband. By treating her harshly, this aristocratic system hardens Lady Monckton to others' feelings. In the meantime, Monckton eyes Cecilia's considerable inheritance and her youthful sexuality. Here the thirst for money and status is seen as coextensive with sexual lust; and in this case, forced marriage means the violent rape of Cecilia.

In the tradition of Sir Clement Willoughby in *Evelina*, Monckton is able to manipulate the heroine by invoking dominant cultural attitudes toward women. Doody argues that Monckton uses "social conventions as stalking horses for private desire."[9] But I want to suggest that these "social conventions" are not simply tools that individual men can exploit for their "private interest"; rather, these customs are inseparable from men's interests as a ruling class. Thus the codes that enjoin passive femininity exist in large part to maintain male rule. For example, Monckton can maneuver his way into one of Cecilia's trips to London because he can exploit the volatility of women's sexual reputation: "She knew he meant to insinuate that it would be conjectured she designed to meet Delvile, and though colouring, vext and provoked at the suggestion, the idea was sufficient to frighten her into his plan" (*C*, 720). He can "frighten" her into capitulation without resorting to physical force. Once again the rhetoric of protection (he claims that he is her only proper chaperon) barely conceals men's sexual violence. Although Cecilia is older, seemingly wiser, and more independent than Evelina, she shares the latter's distressing predicament: because a woman is subject to such scurrilous and potentially damaging gossip, she is forced to take shelter with dangerous men.

Ironically, Cecilia's happiness is dependent upon a system of inheritance that does not accommodate her desire for legal and social freedom. She struggles to establish an identity in a patrilineal order, but finds that she is expected to sacrifice her psychological needs for the benefit of men's economic interests. How, we must ask, can a woman be protected by an aristocratic system that, even in its decline, repeatedly victimizes her? *Cecilia* makes evident that the only protection that this order affords its heroine is the "gaol" of Compton Delvile; women's protection is indistinguishable from their imprisonment. It is not surprising, then, that Burney will seek to "replace" this older order with a newer, more progressive bourgeois one, a group that aspires to depose aristocratic domination.

## II

The Harrel's masquerade, which takes place soon after Cecilia leaves her childhood home, is an impressive episode that allegorizes, and at times even travesties, the theme of female dependence and male protection. Terry Castle argues that this masquerade "externalizes that fantasy of autonomy with which Burney's novel itself begins—the transgressive female aspiration after an unlimited power, the dream of the Heiress itself."[10] While I concur that one of Burney's enterprises is to explore the theme of female self-empowerment, I want to suggest that the tone of this episode is not one of feminist euphoria and defiance but one of violence and fear that seems more consonant with the generally repressive atmosphere of the novel. Further, this conventional eighteenth-century trope exposes the ways in which class differences are masked by the larger and more insuperable problem of female (dis)empowerment in an overwhelmingly patriarchal culture. The abuses of bourgeois power will be shown to bear a close relation to the injustices of aristocratic authority. Thus it would perhaps be more accurate to see the ways in which this cultural emblem of subversive desire cruelly mocks the dreams of female autonomy, which it also, if only fleetingly, enacts.

As Cecilia's trusted childhood friend, Monckton can ill afford to reveal his sinister sexual and economic designs. For this reason, the masquerade allows him the freedom to carry out his aggression and control in physical ways. Rather than granting Cecilia the liberty to choose her male companion, the masquerade reinforces, even aggravates, the male privilege of social and sexual control. In a devil's costume, Monckton uses his wand to prevent Cecilia from talking and moving at will: "Cecilia . . . felt no great delight in his guardianship, and, after a short time, arose, with intention to walk to another place; but the black gentleman, adroitly moving round her, held out his wand to obstruct her passage. . . ." (*C*, 107). Of course, the great irony here is that unbeknownst to her, his "guardianship" or friendship does indeed violate her boundaries and "obstruct" her desire for autonomy. And when some of the other masks attempt to free her, we are afforded a glimpse of Monckton's violent temper: "[T]he rage of Don Devil . . . seemed somewhat beyond what a masquerade character rendered necessary, he foamed at the mouth with resentment. . . ." (*C*, 111). During the evening, Monckton maintains his harassment of Cecilia by dogging her every move and repeatedly attempting to grab her hand (*C*, 116–24). So Monckton's daily role as a well-mannered gentleman and solicitous friend is a fiction as well. Burney's masquerade does not trumpet the subversive qualities we associate with this eighteenth-century topos. Rather, Burney is able to push against its familiar meanings to illustrate the extent and force of male power. Even the reputed images of female freedom cruelly reveal themselves to be slippery illusions; in other words, they contain the very signs of their own impossibility. It is not surprising, then, that Cecilia's male guardian is not threatened by the party's dynamics; only Cecilia is. Although she wishes to be a "free agent" (*C*, 110) at this masquerade, she finds that her "mind seemed almost as little at liberty as [her] person" (*C*, 112).

Mr. Briggs's arrival at the masquerade disrupts and destabilizes the decorous choreography, and thus we might expect that his energy would carry over into other kinds of categoric transgression such as the upsetting of gender hierarchies. Indeed, his chimney sweep's costume marks a sharp contrast with the gentry's elegant masks. But we soon see that his method of guardianship bears a close relation to the domineering protection of the aristocratic father:

> Every way he moved, a passage was cleared for him, as the company, with general disgust, retreated wherever he advanced. . . . As soon as he espied Cecilia, whose situation was such as to prevent her eluding him, he hooted aloud, and came stumping up to her; "Ah ha," he cried, "found at last;" then, throwing down his shovel, he opened the mouth of his bag, and pointing waggishly to her head, said "Come, shall I pop you?—A good place for naughty girls; in, I say, poke in!—cram you up the chimney." And then he put forth his sooty hands to reach her cap. (*C*, 117)

Covered with "dirt and filth" (*C*, 119), he reminds us of Compton Delvile's ancestors, who are now merely dust and bones. Thus Burney's masquerade serves a central purpose in the novel: to suggest that as a social replacement for aristocratic control, bourgeois patriarchy only extends the abuses of the system it seeks to replace and for which it has such contempt. With this in view, we see how Briggs's language infantilizes Cecilia; he threatens to cram this "naughty" girl up a chimney, where he can control both her and her money. Needless to say, he considers her a "naughty" girl because her inheritance gives her a certain amount of power. He gripes that her riches are wasted on her, for "girls [know] nothing of the value of money" (*C*, 181). Briggs's prison of ashes and dirt is disturbingly similar to Delvile's "gaol."

This correlation is only sharpened upon Cecilia's first visit to Briggs's home soon after the masquerade. In these passages, Burney urges her readers to see the cruel emptiness of the bourgeois belief that the home can somehow protect and nurture private feeling. Instead, Cecilia discovers that private feeling is inexorably affected by economic realities. She finds that Briggs's servants "get nothing to eat" but "old stinking salt meat" that "wold make a horse sick to look at" (*C*, 178). Such passages implicitly evoke a mythic past of paternalistic care when servants received the master's protection.[11] That is, in his attention to domestic economy, Briggs perpetuates the worst inequalities of a hierarchical society shorn of the comforting fictions of paternalistic care. In the modern world, the family is subject to the avarice of a capitalist businessman in whose home the value of money seems to overshadow individual needs.

Briggs's protection is predicated on severe bodily, emotional, and monetary regulation. Not only does he refuse Cecilia intellectual pleasures like reading—"all lost time; words get no cash" (*C*, 181)—but he also offers her a room designed more for thrift than for comfort: he "took her to a room entirely dark, and so close for want of air that she could hardly breathe in it. She retreated to the landing-place till he had opened the shutters, and then saw an apartment the most forlorn she had ever beheld, containing no other furniture than a ragged stuff bed, two worn-out rush-bottomed chairs, an old wooden box, and a bit of broken glass which was fastened to the wall by two bent nails" (*C*, 372). Ironically, Cecilia would have to sacrifice her physical comfort—perhaps even her safety—in order to receive the stingy guardian's dubious protection. In fact, she cannot breathe in Briggs's home; it can only extinguish her dreams of economic and psychological autonomy.

In this respect, Briggs's home is like Delvile Castle in that it advertises, even haughtily parades, its master's class-based form of patriarchal authority. The debilitating atmosphere at Briggs' home reminds us of the stifling environment at Delvile Castle, where the fortifications and moat also evoke a prisonlike aura. In effect, Delvile's preoccupation with his patrimony bears a close relation to Briggs's obsession with the value of money. Most important, both men share the singular objective of exploiting Cecilia in their separate quests for cultural and economic domination. When Cecilia chooses to live with Delvile instead of Briggs (each guardian is recompensed for her room and board), Briggs is angered because he sees his opponent reaping what should be his own fair "share" (*C*, 454). In short, Cecilia becomes the site of class conflict.

Briggs emerges as an upwardly mobile businessman who, in his criticism of landed rule and inherited wealth, obviously seeks to replace this older order. But the ascendancy of progressive ideas and capitalist practices also fuels the ambitions of men slavishly devoted to the making of money for the sole purpose of imitating the gentry and complicates their aim to replace the nobility by a desire to be absorbed by it.

As I have shown, *Cecilia*'s masquerade allegorizes the ways in which men of different social classes can perpetuate the underlying assumptions of patriarchal domination. Moreover, it is an emblem of excess, of unnecessary and wanton debts (*C*, 103). The fact that the masquerade takes place at the Harrel's home—their own private Vauxhall—seems entirely congruent with this theme; it highlights their socially ambitious attempt to model their homes on the excesses of the aristocratic estate. In essence, the Harrels cannot separate their private lives from their public desires, for their only concern is to be accepted and accredited by the gentry. To pursue such objectives they are forced to spend money unwisely, and it is about this improvidence that Cecilia tries to caution her friend, Priscilla Harrel: "Mrs. Harrel, with much simplicity, assured her *she did nothing but what every body else did,* and that it was quite impossible for her *to appear in the world* in any other manner" (*C*, 193).

What are the worst implications of this attempt at social assimilation? As we might expect, the Harrels incur a large debt, and it is in this striking section of the novel that we see most sharply how pecuniary (and emotional) embarrassment and suicide are two poles of a spectrum of self-abnegating behaviors. Mrs. Harrel imagines that unless she conforms to others' expectations, she will have to endure a cruel social death; but paradoxically to imitate others inevitably leads to financial death, a lesson her husband pays for dearly, as he spends his life gambling away his assets. In the eighteenth century, gambling was recognized as a sign of aristocratic decay; it was considered reckless and self-destructive.[12] Here we see how aristocratic indulgence and rashness are extended and preserved in the drive for accumulation.

Burney shows us that the other side of social assimilation is a dangerous, even fatal, self-mutilation. Most important, we see that like Monckton and even McCartney before him, Harrel is able to inflict violence on the heroine even as he is victimized himself. He is able to extort Cecilia out of a good deal of her inheritance by threatening suicide; he knows that she could never come to terms with the specter of his self-damnation: "[T]he moment I am informed there is an execution in my house, shall be the last of my existence!" (*C*, 266).

To Harrel, suicide is the only logical response to a financial "execution." If Delvile believes he is his own name and Briggs imagines himself inseparable from his cash, Harrel thinks his social rank is a mere reflection of his public image. Accordingly, if he cannot appear extravagant in public, then he is at best a social nonentity. He aims to mediate his status uncertainty by projecting the role of a wealthy gentleman. But in his attempts at aping the aristocracy, he soon discovers that he has lost the core of his identity.

If Cecilia's uncle sees her as an essential tool in his bid for patrimonial preservation, Harrel similarly views her as a vehicle for his own social aspirations. She is an object of exchange for both men, and this fact is apparent in their attempts to force her into marriages that would solidify their respective social ranks. As we have seen, her uncle hopes to find a man to bear his name and to preserve his estates. Likewise, Harrel is anxious to locate a wealthy aristocrat to finance his social ambitions. After Harrel's suicide, we discover that he had contracted a "debt of honour" with Sir Robert Floyer and had subsequently promised Cecilia's inheritance as remittance (*C*, 433). The aristocratic theme of forced marriage is redacted for the purposes of a progressive plot of social mobility and assimilation.

During Cecilia's stay at the Harrel's, it becomes increasingly clear that she is a commodity in their world. Harrel views his wife and his ward as tokens to be manipulated in his socioeconomic struggles. Not only do we learn that Mrs. Harrel has "been prevailed upon" to forfeit her marriage settlement to her husband (*C*, 270), but we also see him slowly divest Cecilia of her father's separate bequest of over £8000. As a result, she is forced into a hazardous relationship with a usurer; even worse, Monckton will eventually pay off her debts, thus insuring her obligation to him (*C*, 437–38). After Harrel has postponed the execution of his property by blackmailing Cecilia into paying his debts, he tries to persuade his reluctant charge to accompany him to the Pantheon: "But if we do not all go, we do almost nothing: you are known to live with us, and your appearance at this critical time is important to our credit" (*C*, 273). Here the word "credit" testifies to the idea that capitalist practices have converted people, especially women, into currency. Cecilia is Harrel's collateral, as it were, because he hopes that her appearance will allay the fears of his angry creditors. Reputational and financial credit are conflated in bourgeois ideology. Thus, in a capitalist society credit fulfills the same function that Delvile's name does in an aristocratic culture: both putatively signal one's honor and probity to the community. Ironically, instead of protecting Cecilia, as her uncle's will stipulates, Harrel compels her to protect him on his own terms.[13]

Some of *Evelina*'s most frightening moments of violence take place at Vauxhall, and I argued in chapter 1 that this is partly due to the volatile mixing of classes.[14] In *Cecilia* Burney again uses this public locale as a scene of violence, but here she investigates the ways in which class violence is internalized; appropriately, Harrel commits suicide at Vauxhall. The night of Harrel's death begins in violence. When his wife hesitates to accompany him, he "declared he would be detained no longer, and approached in great rage to seize her" (*C*, 397). His financial and social burdens drive him to commit violence, and women are the focus of his anger as the pressure to achieve social advancement intensifies. Once at Vauxhall, Harrel's creditors arrive en masse, like vultures smelling his impending death, to witness their victory.[15] When Harrel invites them to join his party, Mrs. Harrel is humiliated, and her response bespeaks the correlation between the pressures of assimilation and social, even physical, death: "'Are you mad, Mr. Harrel, are you mad!' cried his wife, 'to think of asking such people as these to supper? what will every body say? . . . I am sure I shall die with shame'" (*C*, 402). The irony, of course, is that Harrel will die because of "shame": pecuniary embarrassment and the ensuing public rejection.

That Harrel should kill himself in such an atmosphere of class hostilities underscores the ways in which violence is a pained response to the vertiginous experience of social upheaval. When the baronet Sir Robert Floyer arrives on the scene, he is incensed that Harrel expects him to eat and drink with laborers and businessmen: "'Why you don't fancy I'll sit down with a bricklayer?' 'A bricklayer?' said Mr. Harrel, 'ay sure, and a hosier too; sit down, Mr. Simkins, keep your place, man!'" (*C*, 410). This exchange leads one of the businessmen to defend his "place" in society: "I have as good a right to shew my head where I please as ever a member of parliament in all England" (*C*, 411). They almost come to blows. This dramatization of status vulnerability—the fear of losing one's social place—allows Burney to explore the ways in which physical death and social ruin become eerily conflated. That Harrel should suddenly insist that Sir Robert dine next to a hosier testifies to the burden he has been carrying; he has been trying to keep these two orders separate, aspiring to one and indebted to the other. But he is also refusing to uphold his social facade by continuing to deny his connection to the lower orders. So while his suicide is certainly a capitulation to the forces of the market and public opinion (he dies "from" bankruptcy),[16] it is a show of defiance as well in that he pays his bills *"with a BULLET"* (*C*, 430). He is eluding his creditors at the same time that he is exchanging his body for his debts.

In this respect, Harrel appears to have lost his sense of identity, and this seems compatible with social ideologies that figure the individual as a tool to be exploited for the purposes of accumulation or the preservation of a familial legacy. And this idea is sharpened by Burney's use of the figure of theater to depict Harrel's loss of self: one's social role is a mere fiction. He regrets that his wife is a spectator at his "parting scene," but he urges her to think of "it when

... tempted to such mad folly" as has ruined them (*C*, 398). And soon she hears the sudden "report of a pistol" and sees a waiter "passing . . . covered with blood" (*C*, 413–14). Later we learn that he lingered for twenty minutes, "quite speechless . . . [and] out of his senses" (*C*, 417). His body is a symbol of the menacing ramifications of an endless lust for money and social advancement. Just as he has cruelly used Cecilia to foster his economic hopes, Harrel becomes a mute victim of the arbitrary forces of the market.

When Cecilia hesitates to accompany the Harrels to Vauxhall on this fateful night, she makes a startling but honest admission about the futility of knowing when to conform to public codes that often seem improper and even immoral: "Oh Mrs. Harrel, I know no longer what is kind or what is cruel, nor have I known for some time past right from wrong, nor good from evil!" (*C*, 396). Like Delvile Castle, the structures of moral judgment are in danger of cracking at their foundations. Meadows, a stock character who emblematizes eighteenth-century cultural ennui, tells some frightening truths: "I hate public places. 'Tis terrible to be under the same roof with a set of people who would care less if they saw one expiring!" (*C*, 336).[17] Violence has become a familiar sight, the boring quotidian. Meadows's comments are especially true for Harrel who, because his relations were based solely on his debts, must die in a waiter's arms for lack of a real friend. Soon, his suicide becomes the fashionable joke: "A good man always wears a bob wig; . . . Ever see Master Harrel wear such a thing? No, I'll warrant! better if he had; kept his head on his own shoulders" (*C*, 453). Finally, his body is seized by his creditors because they want what's theirs, despite the fact that Harrel thought he could "blow out his own brains" to escape his debts (*C*, 447,463). Capitalists argue that "[w]hat's mine is mine" (*C*, 447), and they assume that a person's body is their exclusive property. The exchange metaphor becomes gruesomely literal.

## III

Up to this point I have explored the way bourgeois men sustain the violent excesses traditionally associated with the aristocracy, and one of the more disturbing ramifications of this absorption is the internalization of violence. Crucial questions remain, however, concerning issues of gender. Are women implicated in this same social model? And, if so, do they follow Harrel's self-destructive path? Or, are women able to offer a more plausible alternative to these male-dominated orders? More to the point, can women successfully counter the ubiquitous violence of the modern world in order to protect and empower other women? Burney's answers to these questions focus on violations structured by both an aristocratic and a bourgeois patriarchy. Even within a model of male domination, some women, instead of resisting this rule, continue to insist on regulating the lives of other women.

Burney begins her exploration of women's violence with Lady Honoria Pemberton, a character whose habitual displays of anger implicate her in the perpetuation of aristocratic social injustice and yet manifest her victimization at the hands of this same system as well. Placing Lady Honoria in the reductive category of "frustrated society women," critics have often accepted her as a simple stereotype.[18] For our purposes, it would be more useful to consider the ways in which her satiric voice contributes to the hostile atmosphere of the novel. Because Cecilia apparently accepts the legitimacy of aristocratic constructions of the passive and silent female, she is the frequent target of Lady Honoria's pointed remarks. Lady Honoria not only publicizes some of Cecilia's most private thoughts and feelings about Delvile but she is also oblivious to the embarrassment and pain this causes her. Mrs. Delvile castigates her for her inability to restrain her unlicensed tongue: "The rank of Lady Honoria . . . has yet given her a saucy indifference whom she pleases or hurts, that borders upon what in a woman is of all things most odious, a daring defiance of the world and its opinions"(C, 498). On the one hand, as a member of the aristocracy, Lady Honoria has obviously learned to detach herself from the anguish she causes. As a woman, on the other hand, she is chastened for a sardonic frankness that Gosport displays with impunity. Gentlewomen like Lady Honoria, we can conclude, have a "saucy indifference" to the pain they inflict because they are often treated with this same kind of brutal "indifference."

At the end of the novel, Lady Honoria candidly admits that her verbal tirades are an attempt to counter such "indifference":

> [T]he only thing that keeps me at all alive, is now and then making people angry: for the folks at our house let me go out so seldom, and then send me with such stupid old chaperons, that giving them a little torment is really the only entertainment I can procure myself. (C, 935)

Women become emotionally and intellectually vapid in the coercive environment of the aristocratic system; thus their anger is pivotal to their tenacity. While stuck in Delvile Castle, Lady Honoria jokes about suicide: "I really think I should pretend to lose my way, and instead of going over that old draw-bridge, throw myself into the moat" (C, 467). Her jocular attitude barely conceals her hostility. If she were to traverse the old drawbridge—that advertisement of Delvile's authority—she would seem to be tacitly accepting her abject status in this aristocratic order. Throwing herself into the moat, however, would be an act of defiance against and an escape from this system. Her "fashionable education" has schooled her in mentally and emotionally vacuous accomplishments (*C*, 464); her hostility is clearly a reaction against the lessons of her youth. While Cecilia suppresses her anger and frustration, Lady Honoria chooses to lash out against her victimization. In the end, Lady Honoria is able to mock aristocratic principles and those men and women who preserve and maintain them, for she has accepted the fact that these assumptions are more coercive than liberating. She welcomes the death of the old aristocracy.

Mrs. Delvile, on the other hand, is desperately trying to salvage the old aristocracy because it provides her with a social and familial identity; thus her son's choice of a wife becomes the focus of her intense efforts. Quite simply, his existence confirms hers. Forcibly married to her cousin Delvile, she has spent her life trying to curb her hostility; accepting his social, even sexual, will was the "hard study of her life" (*C*, 461). Because she shares the same family bloodline as her husband, she must contain her anger, for defaming or rejecting him would destroy her social and familial identities.[19] In their crossing of familial and sexual boundaries, however, the Delviles are shrouded by the shadow of incest. Indeed, the need to cement their lineage by inbreeding underscores the demographic and moral crisis confronting the aristocracy; its death seems ineluctable.[20]

Early in the novel, Mrs. Delvile cultivates a mutually satisfying friendship with Cecilia, but it is undermined by her stake in her family's preservation. Even Mortimer comments on their obvious affection for each other: "[S]he is sensible of your worth, she adores you, almost as I adore you myself! you are now under her protection, you seem, indeed, born for each other" (*C*, 518). But Mrs. Delvile's "protection" can be as tormenting and coercive as the custody of any of Cecilia's guardians. This point is consistent with a commonplace of sexual politics: women often prove to be more vociferous and persistent mouthpieces for patriarchal principles than even the father himself. Cecilia's love for her son is threatening to Mrs. Delvile's existence; she identifies more with her dead ancestors (recalling Mrs. Beumont's rejection of the elderly women forced to race) than with Cecilia. And yet women are ultimately effaced once they have produced a male heir. Mrs. Delvile fails to recognize that, like herself, Cecilia carries some of the heaviest burdens of patrilineal politics.

Given the fact that progressive men preserve and extend aristocratic vice, does it follow that women's implication in these abuses cuts across class lines as well? Burney explores this problematic mother/son relationship in a bourgeois family, the Belfields, whose story uncannily parallels that of the Delviles. Mrs. Belfield's sole ambition is to see her son become a gentleman even if this is to the detriment of herself and her daughter, Henrietta. Rejecting his father's linen-draper business, young Belfield unavailingly pursues the life of a gentleman: while focusing on his social aspirations, "he soon forgot the uncertainty of his fortune, and the inferiority of his rank" (*C*, 216). Because he bleeds his family's money supply dry, his mother and sister are often forced to live in financial distress. Henrietta bitterly complains about her mother's sacrifice: "[S]he used to deny both herself and me almost common necessaries, in order to save up money to make him presents" (*C*, 222). Here the word "deny" aptly signifies the self-sacrifice women are often required to endure for fathers, brothers, and sons. What's crucial, though, is that Burney condemns the mother rather than the son; he is unaware of their painful austerity. Like young Delvile, Belfield is often depicted as his mother's puppet, a vehicle in the service of her dreams.

It is no wonder, then, that Mrs. Belfield views her daughter as a poor substitute for her son: "But what is a daughter, madam, to such a son as mine? a son that I thought to have seen living like a prince, and sending his own coach for me to dine with him!" (*C*, 315). Her daughter is but an instrument for her son's aspirations; in fact, she assumes that Cecilia's friendship with her daughter is nothing more than a cover for the former's putative love for her son: "[I]t was rather an odd thing for such a young lady as you to come so often after Henny . . . especially when, to be sure, there's no comparison between her and my son" (*C*, 442). Once again class differences screen profound similarities. Like Mrs. Delvile, Mrs. Belfield is willing to support her son at the expense of all others. Hence Burney's subplot unveils a glaring truth: Mrs. Delvile's affluence, aristocratic manners, and elevated birth do not efface her similarities to what Cecilia calls Mrs. Belfield's common "vulgarity and selfishness" (*C*, 317).

Nowhere is Burney's exploration of the causes of women's self-violation more acute than in the scene of Mrs. Delvile's violent hemorrhage. In a letter to her surrogate father, Daddy Crisp, Burney wrote that she always imagined this scene as the apex of her novel. Accordingly, she is disturbed that he finds Mrs. Delvile's "violence and obduracy" to be "unnatural."[21] To Burney Mrs. Delvile's objection to her son's desire to marry Cecilia is disturbingly natural; it stems from her stake in the aristocratic order. The title of this chapter—"A Contest"—is congruent with Burney's sense of the crucial nature of this conflict. Mrs. Delvile's hemorrhage signifies the battle that has been brewing between the power of tradition and the progressive notion of the freedom of love. As the "representative" of her ancient family's "voice" and "opinion" (*C*, 638), Mrs. Delvile taunts her son with the image of his angry and embarrassed forebears: the "blood" of Delvile's ancestors will rise to his cheeks when he is called *"Mr. Beverley!"* (*C*, 677). Here blood is the figurative sign of patrilineal laws, status embarrassment, and violence.

Under such extreme pressure to prevent the obliteration of the Delvile name, Mrs. Delvile succumbs to her frenzied passions in what appears to be a final, bloody sacrifice to her family. When Delvile grabs Cecilia's hand from his mother, Mrs. Delvile senses her utter defeat: "[S]triking her hand upon her forehead, [she] cried 'My brain is on fire!' and rushed out of the room" (*C*, 680). They chase after her, only to find her "extended upon the floor, her face, hands and neck all covered with blood!" Delvile instinctively believes that she has attempted suicide: "[W]hat is it you have done!—where are you wounded?" She has internalized the prescriptions of a family that would sacrifice her to a cold, arrogant man. That she is speechless after this attack is only fitting, since it is as if her aristocratic ancestors have taken full control of her body; only blood comes out of her mouth. Here a woman's body becomes the symbolic territory for social conflict. Like Harrel, who ended up covered by his own blood, she has offered herself up to an unnatural system that refuses to recognize her separate identity; she is its mere "representative" (*C*, 638).

But her apoplexy also signifies a symbolic divorce from the aristocratic order. By this violent means, she is attempting to expel the oppressive will of her ancestors from her body; she severs the familial bloodline. And this is consistent with her subsequent effort to break the stranglehold of patriarchal domination by granting her "separate consent" to the marriage in the face of Mr. Delvile's continued objections. As a result, the couple separates, and Mrs. Delvile leaves for the continent (*C*, 815–19). Thus she breaks the familial line, challenges the exclusive rule of her husband, and leaves a country whose peculiar property and family laws undergird her subjection and sacrifice.

Lest we imagine that Burney has written a utopian work, however, we are left with the fact that while Mrs. Delvile may refuse to be used as a passive tool in this system, it is Cecilia—her surrogate daughter—who will now fulfill this sacrificial role. The Delvile name will be preserved and perpetuated because Cecilia will ultimately relinquish her inheritance. That she will obtain the same financial settlement as Mrs. Delvile is a disturbing sign that the aristocratic tradition, despite being in crisis, survives (*C*, 823). What Mrs. Delvile's actions undoubtedly accomplish, however, is a direct and powerful condemnation of the father's sole rule. By agreeing to marry Delvile with his mother's, but not his father's, consent Cecilia reinforces the progressive notion that a child's duty must be based on respect and affection: "With regard to his father, she left him totally to his own inclination; she had received from him nothing but pride and incivility, and determined to shew publicly her superior respect for Mrs. Delvile, by whose discretion and decision she was content to abide" (*C*, 809).

With Mrs. Delvile's defiant actions, it becomes increasingly obvious that for Burney moral authority now lies with the mother. And it is equally evident that the old-style aristocrat—i.e., Mr. Delvile—survives in spite of (or perhaps because of) the ascendancy of a new social group. Given these complex and contradictory conditions, *Cecilia* explores how the aristocracy might repair its own injustices while at the same time attempting to control the escalating violence

of an intense social conflict. New questions arise: How can women's superior
moral standing humanize this system? Can the progressive ideas that modernized and humanized Orville be used to support the domestic, perhaps even the
economic, empowerment of women? And, if so, can a self-supporting community of women replace the more traditional forms of social order and welfare?

In the course of the novel, Cecilia often dreams of establishing various
configurations of a female-dominated utopia to counteract the socially and
legally imposed seclusion and subordination she has painfully experienced. As
an heiress, she naively imagines that she has the same opportunities as any
male heir; accordingly, she fantasizes about the social prospects of her inheritance:

> [H]er affluence she therefore considered as a debt contracted with the poor,
> and her independence, as a tie upon her liberality to pay it with interest.
> Many and various, then, soothing to her spirit and grateful to her sensibility,
> were the scenes which her fancy delineated; now she supported an orphan,
> now softened the sorrows of a widow. . . . (*C*, 55)

Cecilia's dream is a feminist revision of aristocratic ideals; as we have seen, the
notion of being "contracted" with the poor has its roots in aristocratic ideology.[22] Thus her vision does not include the promise of a radical dismantling of
status hierarchy. Rather, Burney is experimenting with a modernized version
of the feudal obligation of charity. For example, Cecilia imagines taking care of
"widows" and "orphans"—those, along with the poor, who were historically
offered the reputed protections of paternalistic care. What is new and potentially subversive, however, is that women are now at the apex of this hierarchy.
The "old-style" aristocratic patriarch has clearly failed—or, more accurately,
has never fulfilled his expected social function—and thus Burney imagines a
woman as his successor.

And we do see some of the positive, hopeful effects of Cecilia's tenure as a
"paternalistic" landowner. Castle has argued that Cecilia's charity is an act of
"voluntary self-impoverishment."[23] But I want to suggest that practicing charity is the key to female self-empowerment in *Cecilia*. Women and the poor are
the recipients of Cecilia's charity; her guardians, on the other hand, are the
ones most threatened by the freedom with which she handles her money. Mrs.
Hill, the wife of a dying workman whom Harrel has refused to pay, is the object
of Cecilia's first charitable project. Consumption has claimed Mrs. Hill's son,
and her husband is slowly dying from the injuries he sustained after falling
from a ladder while working for Harrel (*C*, 86). Yet Mrs. Hill will be further
distressed because a widow is, as she laments, "always hard to be righted" (*C*,
86). Cecilia rescues Mrs. Hill from possible disaster by securing her a partner-
ship in a haberdasher's shop, where she works with "honest industry" and is

able to support her own children (*C*, 203). As the true bearers of moral authority, women supplant men as the most effective social patrons. Indeed, Cecilia heals some of the wounds of socioeconomic injustice. Thus charity enables women to help the poor while simultaneously empowering themselves. Of course, as we will see, they will need access to money and dominion over their own land.[24]

As Nancy Armstrong has shown most fully, women were expected to exemplify the virtues of self-regulation—monetarily, emotionally, and physically. Practicing charity was one way they could fulfill this social function.[25] As we have seen, Harrel is so preoccupied by the process of "emulative spending," to borrow a phrase from Harold Perkin, that he not only nearly decimates the entire Hill family but he also ends up giving his life to the forces of the market.[26] Cecilia intends to undo these class-bound wrongs, however, for she means to regulate the lusts that contributed to Harrel's tragedy. But Burney stresses that Cecilia needs power, money, and her own home to implement her ideas: "[T]he society she meant to form could not be selected in the house of another . . . these purposes demanded an house of her own, and the unlimited disposal of her fortune, neither of which she could claim till she became of age" (*C*, 56). And the day on which she finally does take possession of her estate, the impoverished tenants celebrate, for they regard it as "a day to themselves of prosperity and triumph" (*C*, 789). Cecilia wants to apply her own domestic values, which include a concern with the proper use of wealth, to the aristocrat's traditional role.

Cecilia's home epitomizes the kind of domestic household valued by many eighteenth-century conduct book writers. They argued that it was a woman's ability to practice self-regulation that gave her the capability to hold domestic responsibilities like the distribution of household monies. Cecilia masters such self-control because she has seen in Harrel how "external brilliancy could cover inward woe," and at Delvile Castle she had grown sick of "parade and grandeur" (*C*, 792). Her self-regulation is not the harmful self-repression that we associate with Briggs's parsimony. Instead, she prides herself on the alternative household that she offers: "Her equipage, therefore, was without glare, though not without elegance, her table was plain, though hospitably plentiful, her servants were for use, though too numerous to be for labour" (*C*, 792). While Burney may feminize the ethos of the Country House poems, she does not push the more radical possibilities of her vision. Her women's community reforms the corruptions and violations associated with aristocratic tradition, but does not subvert the aristocratic order itself; it is founded on the principles of rank and the ownership of land. That charity is its centerpiece buttresses this theme, since such methods of social welfare are an integral part of a system that relies on the principles of subordination for its preservation. If bourgeois men sustain aristocratic vice, then a women's community reinvigorates and regenerates aristocratic virtue.

Moira Ferguson has argued that the representation of female friendships in women's novels "reflected . . . resistance to patriarchal values, physical isolation, and emotional alienation, and most importantly, the exercising of personal choice in friendship."[27] In Cecilia's relationship with Henrietta Belfield we see the propitious effects of such a friendship. As I have shown, Henrietta endures the most basic wants because of her mother's idolization of her brother. But under the care and protection of Cecilia, she "tasted a happiness to which as yet her whole life had been a stranger," and "instead of being tyrannically imposed upon . . . [she was] treated with the most scrupulous delicacy" (C, 794). As we saw in Evelina, Burney used the word "delicacy" to describe the humanization of the older order in the figure of Orville. It is not surprising, then, that Cecilia is linked with this trait of sympathy and self-restraint, since she fulfills some of the same social and protective functions as Orville does. At Cecilia's most utopian moment, its heroine is relatively free to choose Henrietta as her closest companion and confidante (compare the stiff limits imposed on her marital choice). In fact, she finds in Henrietta an invaluable friend who "gave a new interest to her existence" (C, 794). In Burney's women's community, we see the obvious influence of the kind of Christian sisterhoods that Mary Astell and others proposed decades earlier: in their retreat from a hostile society, women were capable of instructing each other, performing charitable projects, and generally doing "good Works."[28]

Yet while Burney explores the utopian possibilities of this female-managed domestic project, she also finally acknowledges its implausibility in a world in which women have no political agency. English property laws were in place in part to obviate women from acquiring the freedom to wield the power and social leverage that were entailed in the ownership of land and other forms of moveable property.[29] In this case, Monckton is threatened by what he sees as Cecilia's "magnificent" and "unlimited" acts of charity, since he presumes that she is spending his future wealth (C, 794). As we have seen, all of her male guardians have attempted to control her financial power. Further, Cecilia's household never reaches its full potential because one of its residents, Mrs. Harrel, is still driven by the same values of "emulative spending" that had propelled her husband to his early, violent death; only luxury and excess can prevent her from falling into deep depression. Thus this community's possibilities are partly hindered by a woman who is still dazzled by the promises of bourgeois consumption.

It is the exacting laws of patrilineage, however, that irrevocably terminate Cecilia's auspicious tenure as a landowner. Once her secret marriage to the hero is revealed, her estate is seized by its new legal heir. Consequently, her marriage sabotages her attempts to solidify her female friendships and to continue her successful domestic enterprise. After the ceremony, with Delvile away in Europe, this heir, Mr. Eggleston, demands his rightful land and a refund of all the money she has spent since her marriage. Threatened with a lawsuit, Cecilia is again the object of male extortion: "It was easy to perceive that this man had been sent with a view of working from her a confession, and terrifying from her some money" (*C*, 858). No sequence in the novel illuminates the hypocrisy of patrilineal codes more, for not only is Mr. Eggleston not a blood relation of her uncle, who "had no particular regard for him," but he also has "extravagant and dissipated" sons who have accrued significant debts. It is clear that they will seize the estate and slowly bring it to ruin; even the poor envision their loss, and they soon expect to "be without bread" (*C*, 873). All of Cecilia's acts of charity and domestic economy are thus sacrificed to the idea of the male line. Here Burney condemns a system that valorizes the fiction of the male name to the point of social disintegration. The dreams of female community, or at the very least Cecilia's empowerment, turn out to be an ephemeral fantasy. We see the cruel limits of the social possibilities inherent in domestic ideology. Once again, then, we are faced with the prospect of an aristocratic marriage as the only viable, though by no means flawless, instrument of social welfare and women's protection.

## IV

Burney is clearly disenchanted—as she was in *Evelina*—with the more progressive alternatives for the replacement of old-style aristocratic social domination. But she is also more pragmatic and wary about the social instrumentality of this older form. The final chapters of the novel provide compelling evidence of Burney's increasing skepticism: her eponymous heroine suffers a violent emotional breakdown. Cecilia's marriage serves as the catalyst for one of the most violent sections in the novel. She discovers that as the owner of an estate, she had wielded a certain degree of socioeconomic power, but that as a wife she is a social nonentity.

Reading the last sections of the novel, we are reminded of Evelina's terrifying moments at Vauxhall. Like Evelina, Cecilia faces an implacable father. Because he believes his son's marriage to be a sham, Compton Delvile refuses to respond to Cecilia's pleas for help (*C*, 866–67), and Mrs. Delvile's "separate consent" is worthless. Cecilia decides that she must follow her husband to the continent: "[S]he resolved without delay to seek the only asylum which was proper for her, in the protection of the husband for whom she had given up every other" (*C*, 869). Marriage in a patrilineal culture not only effaces her social identity but limits the sanctuaries open to her as well. For the first time, she is essentially nameless and portionless. Mr. Hobson, a wealthy business-man, claims that a woman is a "nobody" until she marries, but she is also apparently a "nobody" once she weds (C, 877).

As a "nobody," Cecilia finds herself on the street, a felicitous metaphor for the vulnerability women face during a period of class upheaval. After discover-ing his wife alone with Belfield (she has sought out his advice), Delvile flies into a jealous rage. Fearing a duel, a panic-stricken Cecilia runs through the streets of London to prevent what she imagines will be a very bloody encounter (the hotheaded Delvile has already injured Monckton in a duel [C, 844–51]). But she is the one who meets with violence. While searching for her husband, Cecilia is suddenly "encircled" by a mob from which she "struggle[s] in vain to break away" (C, 895). As an archetypal Burneyan moment, this scene encapsulates a disturbing theme: growing class conflict, as suggested by this volatile mix of classes, is a real and immediate threat to women in a world where seemingly no social or familial constellation can adequately protect them. Moreover, this image of imprisonment serves as a fitting metaphor for a woman's dangerously circumscribed status. Even though Cecilia escapes, she succumbs to the pres-sure and violence:

> This moment, for the unhappy Cecilia, teemed with calamity; she was wholly overpowered; terror for Delvile, horror for herself, hurry, confusion, heat and fatigue, all assailing her at once, while all means of repelling them were de-nied her, the attack was too strong for her fears, feelings, and faculties, and her reason suddenly, yet totally failing her, she madly called out, "He will be gone! he will be gone! . . . he will die if I do not see him, he will bleed to death!" (C, 896)

Earlier in the novel, Cecilia had barely eluded a mob that had "encircled" her as criminals were being transported to Tyburn (C, 176). In this episode, Burney has carefully linked two key image patterns of the novel: the potentially violent mob and bleeding bodies. A member of this inebriated mob (a "gentleman") asserts that "he would himself take care of her," but his method of protection is to seize Cecilia's hand (C, 896). Both the violence endemic to class conflict and the violations intrinsic to the gentry's versions of social control finally over-power Cecilia's imagination.

Cecilia's madness has often been read as a symptom of her powerlessness. In a world in which she cannot act but can only be acted upon, she succumbs to madness; there is no other logical response to such helplessness.[30] Here mad-ness is the internalization of violence.[31] Because she cannot assert her will in her society, she is forced, like Harrel and Mrs. Delvile, to destroy herself.

Marriage, she soon discovers, can also be an act of self-annihilation: "I am married, and no one will listen to me. . . . Oh it was a work of darkness, . . . it has been sealed, therefore, with blood, and tomorrow it will be signed with murder" (*C*, 903). On one level, of course, she feels that she is being punished because of her secret marriage ("a work of darkness"). Disobeying the father brings violent consequences; Mrs. Delvile's warning about the father's curse was prophetic.[32] That no one will listen to her because she is married, moreover, reinforces the fact that a woman gives up her name and identity upon marriage. Only Delvile can publicly speak for her now.

Epstein argues that madness silences Cecilia, and this last example certainly attests to the plausibility of this reading.[33] But I would suggest, too, that madness allows her to speak the truth, for it breaks down the internalized barriers that mute women's voices. As *Cecilia* has shown, the other side of suicide is defiance. Like Mrs. Delvile, Cecilia refuses to allow her body to be used as a conduit for Delvile's bloodline. Madness, like the stroke, silences the ancestors' voices. Now we hear Cecilia's voice. When Delvile arrives—he saw her listed in the *Daily Advertiser* as an object to be reclaimed (a woman must be someone's property)—she cries, "Who are you? . . . If you do not mean to mangle and destroy me, begone this instant" (*C*, 906).[34] Cecilia imagines that Delvile is the villain, Monckton. We hear distressing echoes of the masquerade in her fearful question; in the surreal world of *Cecilia*, the protector and the persecutor are often indistinguishable. But Cecilia's madness frees her from the constraints of decorum, and she can now confront her fear of violence: "Cecilia resisted them with her utmost power, imploring them not to bury her alive, and averring she had received intelligence they meant to entomb her with Mr. Monckton" (*C*, 908). The thought of being buried alive is perhaps a woman's worst nightmare, for it captures well the twin fears of entrapment and powerlessness. That she particularly dreads entombment with Monckton reveals her fear of rape; as we have seen, he did plan to force her into marriage. No longer listening to her culture's prescriptions about women's silence, she is able to express those same fears that Evelina was forced to censor in Sir Clement's coach.

True, Cecilia soon recovers. But *Cecilia*'s denouement is decidedly less positive than *Evelina*'s. In fact, Burney strongly resisted both familial and public pressure to provide her readers with a happy resolution for her second novel.[35] We are faced, then, with the bleak picture of Cecilia ineluctably connected to Compton Delvile, who accepts her only to avoid public scandal. With her usual bluntness, Lady Honoria underlines what Cecilia has lost:

> [W]hat could ever induce you to give up your charming estate for the sake of coming into his fusty old family! I really advise you to have your marriage annulled. You have only, you know, to take an oath that you were forcibly run

away with; and as you are an Heiress, and the Delviles are all so violent, it will
easily be credited. (*C*, 933)

Cecilia has surrendered her power and freedom. Here Lady Honoria unveils
the truth about women's victimization. Given the fact that the Delviles face the
alarming specter of the termination of their ancient family, she knows that no
one would be shocked if they used force against a wealthy heiress for the selfish
purpose of preserving their estates. This final allusion to violence leaves an
indelible impression: it attests quite strongly to the fact that violence against
women is a familiar, even expected, sight in an aristocratic culture.

Despite Burney's stated refusal to pen a happy conclusion, she does seem
to offer a flimsy, even awkward, conciliatory gesture by having Mrs. Delvile's
sister, "dazzled" by Cecilia's "extraordinary sacrifice," bequeath her fortune to
Cecilia instead of to her nephew (*C*, 939). But Burney cannot pull back any
further from the grim ramifications of her story of loss and violence. In the
concluding paragraph, Cecilia quite honestly and frankly laments her misfortunes: "[A]t times she murmured herself to be thus portionless, tho' an HEIR-
ESS . . . she checked the rising sigh of repining mortality, and, grateful with
general felicity, bore partial evil with chearfullest resignation" (*C*, 941). *Cecilia*
leaves us with a melancholy image: an eighteenth-century heroine resigned to
a married life that requires her to give up her dreams of being an influential,
magnanimous landowner (an "evil" reversal), a role that would obviously have
brought her personal happiness and the power to begin to address the problem
of women's safety in a violent world.

# 3
## Mannerly Violence:
## *Camilla* and the New Patriarchy

In a journal entry dated 17 July 1786, Burney describes a short walk that she had taken with her father, of "not fifty yards," that uncannily evoked the frightening episodes of violence that had shattered the placid surface of her first two novels:

> We walked. . . . My dear father's own courage all failed him in this little step; for as I was now on the point of entering—probably for ever—into an entire new life, and of foregoing by it all my most favourite schemes [her literary ambitions], and every dear expectation of happiness adapted to its taste—as now all was to be given up—I could disguise my trepidation no longer . . . he would have slackened his pace, or have made me stop to breathe; but I could not; my breath seemed gone, and I could only hasten with all my might, lest my strength should go too.[1]

Burney was taking her first, reluctant steps towards what was to be a grievously lonely stay as deputy keeper of the robes at the court of George III and Queen Charlotte (July 1786–July 1791). Her position would require hours of attendance and exact a great physical and emotional price. The panicked sensation of gasping for breath that she experienced on this first day would become a near constant affliction by the end of her service. In the end, however, Burney's court experiences proved to be fruitful for the writer even as they nearly took the life of the woman.

In fact, the great social and cultural themes that preoccupied Burney in her fiction were also to be profound personal concerns during her years at court, and our reading of *Camilla* (1796) is deeply enriched and even challenged by these biographical episodes. Doody offers a compelling account of the ordeals Burney faced at court, but she stops short of exploring the connections between the often cruel hardships engendered by court ritual and the

representation of violence and self-violation in the novels.[2] My aim in the following pages is to read a selection of Burney's letters and journal entries from
this period as documents that explore in painful personal detail those themes
that find their conclusive development in the pages of her third novel. The
coerciveness of cultural institutions and the complex links between repression,
violence, and manners are issues that Burney personally struggled with in her
years at court.

As an unmarried thirty-four-year-old woman with no income and no apparent marriage prospects, Burney was an object of concern both to her family
and to her friends. To be offered a position at court was considered an honor,
and while Burney wished not to be made a social sacrifice, she capitulated to
her father's aspirations. As the above journal account suggests—and as would
later be made more explicit—Burney felt as if she were walking down the aisle;
her father had succeeded in "marrying" his daughter into the upper ranks of
society.[3] But once a member of this elite company, Burney would experience
most intimately the effects of strict behavioral codes on the individual. Indeed,
her responses to and interpretations of the conduct required at court help us
understand how Camilla Tyrold confronts a system of manners and codes of
female behavior that require her to fight against herself as if she were her own
worst enemy.

At court, Burney would be schooled in the bitter lesson that manners and
court ritual had a dark underside: if, on the one hand, these behavioral customs were pathways to social and royal acceptance, then, on the other, they
were the source of intense self-violation as well. Because the position of deputy
keeper of the robes was viewed as an aristocratic privilege—the single daughters of many aristocratic families coveted such an appointment—for a com-
moner to be offered this role was thought to be doubly honorable.[4] During her
years at court, Burney was always cognizant both of the honor bestowed upon
her and also of the powerful symbolic role the monarchy continued to play at a
time of social instability; the court in particular evoked the permanence and
solidity of an older world of status hierarchy. As status groups mixed and merged,
the intricate and practiced behavior required at court and in the royal presence
in many ways suggested a larger cultural anxiety about maintaining status distinctions. In fact, the contemporary belief that manners were an index to moral
character and a sign of respect for one's social "betters" partly originated in
court circles.[5] A royal servant had to accept rigid behavioral constraints if he or
she hoped to succeed at court and thus secure his or her social status.

Just before her entrance into court, Burney wrote her sister a satirical letter
in which she uses images of violence to decipher the conventional behavioral
customs (including self-scrutiny and self-regulation) required of the royal servant.
Burney had shown us in *Cecilia* that bodily and emotional regulation was part

of the process of domestication; Cecilia's brief role as an estate owner pictured the more progressive and utopian aspects of this ideology. But in her court letter, Burney investigates the darker side of such regulation. Titling her short narrative "Directions for coughing, sneezing, or moving before the King and Queen," Burney counsels self-annihilation: "[I]f you find yourself choking with the forbearance [preventing a cough], you must choke—but not cough" (*DL*, 2:353). Coughing, sneezing, and even moving—bodily functions that are natural and often uncontrollable—are considered unpardonable behavior in the royal presence. Burney equates the self-control required in such situations with a disturbing, unnatural self-violation. If you needed to sneeze, for example, you were expected to "oppose it, by keeping your teeth grinding together; if the violence of the repulse breaks some blood-vessel, you must break the blood-vessel—but not sneeze" (*DL*, 2:353). Both Doody and Epstein have read this letter as evidence of Burney's interest in propriety and the collateral theme of sudden bodily explosion; maintaining propriety can be self-wounding, especially for women.[6] But while Doody reads the particular image of grinding teeth and broken blood vessels as symptomatic of this self-wounding, I would argue that these images are violently aggressive as well. The vision of grinding teeth is a sign at once of repression and aggression. To be human in the royal presence—even if just to sneeze—is to declare a self, and to assert one's separate identity is judged as deliberately hostile behavior. Manners keep the more violent, angry self from emerging (certainly a self-protective function for a royal servant), but grinding teeth imply a barely contained fury, the irrepressible excess of an aggression turned inward, for the servant must bleed rather than disrupt the rigorous court etiquette. Hemorrhaging (as *Cecilia* taught us) can be symptomatic of one's capitulation to the values and principles of a hierarchical, aristocratic culture. At court a royal subject was strictly bound by her status and gender.

What are the consequences of repressing such intense feelings? The beleaguered subject responds to violence by further violating herself:

> In the third place, you must not, upon any account, stir either hand or foot, If, by chance, a black pin runs into your head, you must not take it out. If the pain is very great, you must be sure to bear it without wincing. . . . If the blood should gush from your head by means of the black pin, you must let it gush; if you are uneasy to think of making such a blurred appearance, you must be uneasy, but you must say nothing about it. If, however, the agony is very great, you may, privately, bite the inside of your cheek, or of your lips, for a little relief; taking care, meanwhile, to do it so cautiously as to make no apparent dent outwardly. And, with that precaution, if you even gnaw a piece out, it will not be minded, only be sure either to swallow it, or commit it to a corner

of the inside of your mouth till they are gone—for you must not spit. (*DL*, 2:353)[7]

The singular image of the black pin suggests external aggression, yet Burney purposely identifies no agent; likewise, the blood itself must be ignored as though it too has no observable existence. Thus it is not surprising that Burney does not depict the royal couple's reaction, both because signs of distress are to be disregarded and because they are self-censored. To this end, it is significant that the fictive subject worries more about her "blurred [read, bloody] appearance" than her obvious pain. Under these circumstances, only appearances are important; the pressure to conform to these judgmental spectators' expectations is immense. Epstein suggests that the hostile tone of this letter is indicative of Burney's "deep resentment of her powerlessness to resist this pet plan of her father's social vanity."[8] But Epstein's reading loses sight of the ways in which this letter also participates in a complex cultural discourse of manners that transcends the biographical. As Norbert Elias has taught us, manners can often function as signs of deference and, by this means, conceal those turbulent emotions that might cause disorder and violence.[9] In very graphic detail, Burney shows us the heavy burdens of this concealment.

The final, grotesque image of self-cannibalism—gnawing and swallowing one's own skin—suggests the degree to which the assumptions underpinning a restrictive code of manners and court ritual can be internalized. Burney suggests that some basic instincts of self-protection, such as caring for oneself during an illness ("If you have a vehement cold, you must take no notice of it," [*DL*, 1:353]) must be self-censored at court. By eating oneself, one is only literalizing the royal couple's expectations; in other words, an attendant should have no bodily or emotional presence. Hence, in order not to be summarily dismissed from court, the royal subject must violate her own body. This self-cannibalism is even governed by its own grisly code of conduct: she must "do it so cautiously as to make no apparent dent outwardly" (*DL*, 1:353). Self-inflicted violence becomes as ritualized and rule-bound as court customs themselves; in this case, the practice of manners seems indistinguishable from brutal acts of self-annihilation.

For Burney, the black humor of this letter would later seem to have been uncannily prophetic; during her years at court she wrote many angry accounts of the physical and emotional discipline demanded. For example, she soon realized that royal servants were assumed to have superhuman strength: they were expected to stand for long hours, go without food, or forget the life and friends they left in the world outside Windsor Castle (*DL*, 2:474–75, 469; 3:161). That a servant was not permitted to eat in the royal presence, moreover, is a suggestive commentary on the collateral subject of the laws for women's behavior

that Burney imaginatively explores in *Camilla*. Court rituals, like manners, offered a clear means of discriminating one's status, especially in unequal relationships.[10] To eat in the royal presence might be viewed as an assertive act
(satisfying an appetite), and it might also suggest an intimacy that was highly
inappropriate. Burney learns that public behavior becomes even more important as a sign for the inner self, for one's moral character. She also discovers
that women especially must walk an emotional tightrope in the public world, a
cultural dilemma that she will explore in *Camilla* and link thematically to the
phenomenon of psychological and physical self-violation, where the onus of
self-control and the responsibility for preserving public harmony will fall mainly
on women. From these compelling examples, we see how the position of the
royal servant can figure for the status of women in the public realm.

In her last year of service, Burney suffered a slow but unceasing physical
and emotional breakdown: "[L]anguor, feverish nights, and restless days were
incessant" (*DL*, 4:434). Burney had foreseen—perhaps even fantasized about—
this collapse almost three years earlier: "I must cherish no thought of retreat,
unless called hence, by willing kindness, to the paternal home, or driven hence,
by weakness and illness" (*DL*, 3:341). Like her heroines, she looks to the patriarch for rescue and safety; but if he refuses to respond, her only form of self-
protection is to will a serious illness. It is appealing to speculate that Burney's
sickness is a deliberate method of self-sabotage, unconsciously designed to force
her father's hand. As psychoanalytic thinkers have shown, women's episodes of
weakness and suffering (symptoms of masochistic behavior) function not only
as a means of reaching otherwise unattainable goals but also as a vehicle for
expressing what is perceived to be an inappropriate hostility. After all, Burney
needs permission from a formidable father who originally put her in this untenable position.[11] In May 1790, however, Dr. Burney finally did respond, giving his daughter permission to resign from service; but he left her to do it on
her own. Her subsequent experience with the monarch is curiously reminiscent of the fictional attendant who bleeds uncontrollably in the royal presence
and seems to elicit little attention or concern. Burney hopes that her illness will
abet her request for retirement, but she encounters an oblivious or perhaps a
stubborn queen: "It is true, my depression of spirits and extreme alteration of
person might have operated as a preface [for her request]; for I saw no one,
except my Royal Mistress and Mrs. Schwellenberg, who noticed not the change,
or who failed to pity and question me upon my health and fatigues" (*DL*, 4:434).
Asserting herself is so difficult that an act of self-violation—letting herself die—
might be her last, desperate chance for attention. Ultimately, she would rather
die than remain imprisoned at court.

Queen Charlotte was unable to read—or purposely misread—these signs
of distress. Burney's sickness throws into relief larger questions about her autonomy

at court: "[F]or though I was frequently so ill in her presence that I could hardly stand, I saw she concluded me, while life remained, inevitably hers" (*DL*, 4:437). The phrase "while life remained" suggests the tacit presence of suicidal thoughts or wishes. As Burney will teach us with the character of Camilla, self-violation (e.g., willing a deadly illness) may be a woman's only vehicle for escaping repressive cultural institutions. Here the servant is implicitly assumed to be a permanent possession of the queen, and thus her body and her life are not her own except through self-violation. Toward the end, in the privacy of her journal, Burney records that she cannot even breathe: "And so weak and faint I was become, that I was compelled to put my head out into the air, at all hours, and in all weathers . . . to recover the power of breathing, which seemed not seldom almost withdrawn" (*DL*, 4:436). Her vitality is sapped by the burdens of social ritual. Charles Burney had believed that this role would provide his daughter with a permanently safe home and obviate future economic troubles (a paternalistic fantasy in itself), yet the court that offers this kind of coercive protection nearly takes Burney's life. In this case, as in the fiction, a woman of privileged status, Queen Charlotte, sustains the violence engendered by oppressive cultural and political institutions.

Burney ultimately musters the courage to present the queen with a letter petitioning for her release: "I was half dead with real illness, excessive nervousness, and the struggle of what I had to force myself to perform" (*DL*, 4:439). As Burney had painfully discovered, her court post was "subversive" of her health, for she was forced to relinquish "peace," "ease," "freedom," "spirits," and "affections" (*DL*, 4:449). Burney finally left her court service on 7 July 1791; five years of her life had been spent in a lonely and restrictive role, but the experience was highly influential in coloring the texture of her next novel, *Camilla*. Here she would explore the links between physical violence, psychological torment, and the loss of autonomy. At the same time, she would expand her understanding of violence to include the notion that manners, although an often necessary and effective means of self-protection, can also be a source of women's self-abuse. Indeed, *Camilla* directs our attention to the way the smothering sensations that Burney experienced at court are a possible consequence of the unfailing observance of strict conduct and propriety.

## II

At first glance, Burney's third novel seems to be about a series of frustrating and complicated romantic entanglements. Its heroine, Camilla Tyrold, is the daughter of the Reverend Augustus Tyrold, the younger son of the house of Tyrold. Camilla's troubles first begin when Sir Hugh Tyrold, a wealthy baronet and elder brother of Augustus, mourning the fact that he never married, tries to compensate for his youthful mistakes by naming Camilla his sole heiress. But through his own carelessness, Sir Hugh exposes Camilla's youngest sister Eugenia to smallpox and soon after permanently cripples her during a childhood game. Consumed by his grief and guilt, Sir Hugh settles on Eugenia as his heiress, thereby subjecting her to a host of greedy suitors. In the meantime, Camilla's family hopes that she will marry Edgar Mandlebert, Mr. Tyrold's charge and the wealthy heir of "one of the first estates in the country."[12] It is Camilla's and Edgar's courtship, marked by frequent misunderstandings and miscommunication (often over would-be suitors like Sir Sedley Clarendel), that serves as the engine for Burney's larger social and political themes. In fact, Burney considered the term "novel" particularly unsuitable for her third work, since, as she wrote, "it gives so simply the notion of a mere love story. . . ." (*JL*, 3:117).[13] Rather than a "mere love story," *Camilla* is a harsh critique both of domestic ideology and also of the perils that a consumer and credit society create for single women like Camilla who live daily with economic uncertainty. As always in Burney's fiction, the couple's marriage serves as the paradigmatic gesture of closure; but before this conventionally happy denouement, Burney exposes the insidious violence congenital to early-modern courtship customs.

In *Camilla*, Burney once again takes up the issue of the rise of "domestic ideology," but she moves beyond and behind the progressive fantasy of *Cecilia*'s "women's community" to address the more troubling and problematic affinities between bourgeois domesticity and traditional forms of patriarchy. The domestic self-regulation that was offered as a positive replacement for an older paternalistic care in *Cecilia*, while still maintaining that structure's basic social function, is now the source of women's self-repression and even self-annihilation. In this way, *Camilla* poses new questions about this burgeoning ideology: How does the contemporary preoccupation with manners create new, more fearsome, and more unpredictable forms of violence? More specifically: Is this primarily self-inflicted violence, in the form of emotional, physical, and monetary repression, only an internalization of older, coercive patterns of aristocratic domination? In addressing these issues, *Camilla* poses a dialectical contrast to *Evelina*: in her first novel, Burney had advanced a more promising and liberating vision of women's auto-responsibility, but in *Camilla* she both ultimately resists and capitulates to modern definitions of the domestic woman, as she encourages her readers to see that the self-control and self-scrutiny required of this new woman have both crucial benefits and significant drawbacks. *Camilla* is a powerful account of the contradictory status of domestic ideology: the means of women's potential self-sufficiency can be used to convict them for instances of domestic or even public disorder.

Early in the novel, flush with optimism and passion, Edgar is intent on proposing to Camilla, but he receives some cautionary and inflammatory advice from his stern and studious tutor, Dr. Marchmont, that suggests the extent to which patriarchal ideas still dominate in a social climate that putatively promises free marital choice and greater autonomy for both men and women. Revealing a profound distrust of women's fidelity and moral rectitude, Marchmont counsels, even prods, Edgar to spy on Camilla, to test her virtue before disclosing his own feelings. Initially, Edgar recognizes the injustice of this advice— "[H]ow may I inquire into the state of her affections, without acknowledging her mistress of mine?" (*Ca*, 159)—but he is soon swayed by Marchmont's insistence that he examine her as if she were the object of a kind of quasi-scientific experiment:

> [Y]ou must study her, from this moment, with new eyes, and new thoughts. Whatever she does, you must ask yourself this question: "Should I like such behavior in my wife?". . . Nothing must escape you; you must view as if you had never seen her before . . . you must forget her wholly as Camilla Tyrold, you must think of her only as Camilla Mandlebert; even justice is insufficient during this period of probation, and instead of inquiring, "Is this right in her?" you must simply ask, "Would it be pleasing to me?" (*Ca*, 159–60)

Marchmont's disturbing counsel illustrates how new and more innovative violations are engendered by the rise of domestic ideology and by women's particular obligation to observe strict rules of behavior. From this example, we see that the rules for women's conduct are not based on a universal sex-blind code of "justice"—"Is this right in her"—but rather determined by men's own private desires and interests. Far from enjoying the freedom to circulate unchecked in public society, Camilla must suffer the violence of observation, the observation of a man not only counseled to be self-interested ("Would it be pleasing to me?") but also encouraged to be "positively distrustful" (*Ca*, 160). Moreover, it is tempting to suggest that Marchmont is exhorting Edgar to indulge in a kind of sadistic voyeurism. In this sense, Marchmont's implicit point is that Edgar might even find some pleasure in detecting Camilla's guilt; the pleasure of spying, needless to say, is in the wish that one will uncover scandalous secrets. By this means, his gaze violates Camilla's emotional and physical boundaries.[14]

As in *Cecilia* and *Evelina*, Burney again experiments with names to underscore women's appropriation by men, their victimization in a patriarchal culture. Marchmont urges Edgar to displace the real Camilla Tyrold with a fantasized version of his future wife, "Camilla Mandlebert." In other words, by naming her "Mandlebert," Marchmont expropriates Camilla for Edgar; she is simply an object of exchange between father and lover. In this case, however, the obliteration of Camilla's name does not explicitly serve to preserve and perpetuate a patrilineal legacy (as it does in *Cecilia*); rather it is a signal of how the seemingly ubiquitous male gaze sustains, even if in an altered form, women's continued domination by men. Here Camilla is symbolically subsumed under the surname of a man who presumes she is already his.

In such examples we see how the Burney of *Camilla* is more skeptical about the belief that a system of manners can function as a positive mode of self-protection for women. Unlike in *Evelina*, Burney is more interested here in investigating a necessary component for the success of this code: in short, Camilla needs her male audience to be respectful of and responsive to this modern form of protection. Another way of saying this is that Edgar must be a sympathetic spectator, willing to identify with Camilla's various public dilemmas. And thus the question becomes: What are the implications for women who attempt to practice manners if their audience is suspicious and judgmental? In answering this question, Burney explores the links between the rise of scientific discourse and experimentation and modern patriarchy's need to reimpose and bolster its attenuating authority in the face of eighteenth-century women's modest, but notable, gains. To this end, she uses the language of science to describe the early-modern innovation of the patriarchal gaze.[15] Indeed, Edgar will soon call his public scrutiny of Camilla his "experiments": like any experiment that is "deduced from false reasoning, and formed upon false principles, [Edgar's] was flattering in its promise, pernicious in its progress, and abortive in its performance" (*Ca*, 670–71). We are invited to see the affinities between the objectifying violations Camilla endures and the passive objects of scientific study. And for Edgar, Camilla's behavior is simply inscrutable. As his despair increases, he pleads with Marchmont to "explain, expound . . . this work [i.e., Camilla's behavior] of darkness" (*Ca*, 571). Like early modern scientists, Edgar and Marchmont use violent scientific discourse to help them in their encounters with the unknown: women are not unlike the domain of science. In fact, Marchmont's cynical reply to Edgar's plaint underscores his belief that Camilla can be tested, observed, and imagined as yet another enigma to be unraveled: "Ask me, my dear young friend, why the sun does not give night, and the moon day; then why women practise coquetry" (*Ca*, 571). As the narrator had observed, Edgar's testing of Camilla was formed upon "false principles." Edgar and Marchmont are exposed, not as careful scientists, but as essentialists: their subjective experiments are based on Marchmont's staunch belief that women are innately unfaithful.[16]

In a similar fashion, the increase in conduct books in the eighteenth century strongly suggests that certain social assumptions, particularly about women's behavior, needed to be widely and prominently disseminated during an era when an aristocratic system of patriarchy was being undermined. As Joyce

Hemlow noted over forty years ago, these manuals "attempted to resolve un-certainties about the position of women in society."[17] And more recently, Susan Staves has argued that the growth of secular material enjoining women's proper conduct bespeaks this culture's need to stem the tide of women's legal gains.[18] Burney joins this social and cultural debate by questioning the validity of this conduct-book gender ideology: *Camilla* will explain how the domestic obliga-tion of practicing a rigorous self-command and self-scrutiny (effects of the male gaze) often leads to women's self-abnegation and self-violation. Many critics have acknowledged the thematic similarities between eighteenth-century con-duct books and Burney's *Camilla*.[19] Hemlow, for example, argues that Burney's knowledge of this genre considerably weakens *Camilla*'s power. She maintains that Burney wrote *Camilla* specifically for court acceptance, as evidenced by its dedication to Queen Charlotte; a novel of manners would please the court.[20] Rather than an unambiguous offering to the queen, however, I would suggest that *Camilla* is in part an angry response to the rituals of court and their devas-tating effects on royal subjects. While many feminist critics want to distance Burney's novel from what they see as the restrictive nature of the conduct book analogy,[21] I would contend that Burney has purposely written an "anticonduct" book, for *Camilla* carefully explores and exposes the disturbing consequences to women of the advice and seemingly complacent certainties espoused in these homiletic manuals. As we have seen, Evelina longed for a "book of the laws and customs *a la modè*" (*Ca*, 72), a book which she hoped would teach her a code of manners that, once mastered, would function as an internalized means of self-protection. *Evelina* offers the most positive representation of this social replacement. *Camilla,* in contrast, presents a more pessimistic view, for it illus-trates how manners may not fully ensure respect, that they require a self-con-trol and self-violation that uncannily recall an earlier aristocratic domination.

Mrs. Arlbery, Camilla's most outspoken friend and an obvious descendant of the sardonic Mrs. Selwyn, offers the most biting commentary on the ways in which the attention on women's behavior is merely an altered, modern form of patriarchal domination. Mrs. Arlbery's driving ambition is to defy this control and regulation by subverting the rigorous code of manners. For example, she arrives at public functions alone, displays her keen cynical wit, and frightens Edgar especially because of her neglect of widely accepted social rituals: "She was guilty of no vices, but utterly careless of appearances . . . [and] had of-fended or frightened almost all the county around, by a wilful strangeness of behavior, resulting from an undaunted determination to follow in every thing the bent of her own humour" (*Ca*, 194). She is strikingly self-reliant, and Edgar sees her as a potential threat to his future plans, for she is the type of friend who could persuade Camilla of his unjust behavior and unreasonable expectations.

It is not surprising, then, that Mrs. Arlbery immediately exhorts Camilla to break the chains of this patriarchal authority: "You are made a slave in a moment by the world, if you don't begin life by defying it" (*Ca*, 246). Mrs. Arlbery recognizes how "formalities" and the "laws of politeness" (*Ca*, 247) can easily enslave women. Burney's purposeful use of the word "laws" here speaks to the cultural power and authority behind behavioral rules and customs. Generally speaking, it effectively underscores the connections between a more traditional system of patriarchy, in which the most basic social assumptions were tacitly understood (and some of which were codified in law), and a modern form of patriarchal rule that needs to make certain precepts of conduct explicit. Thus Edgar watches Camilla intently to capture her in the act of breaking these laws, and her association with Mrs. Arlbery only increases the likelihood that she will challenge his beliefs about women's proper roles.

Burney's novels consistently foster the view that female friendship has the potential to alleviate or even threaten the more rigid structures of male rule. Play-acting, fluid gender and status demarcations, and a defiance of many of the prevailing rules of behavior are the norm at Mrs. Arlbery's home, and Camilla is instinctively drawn to this subversive woman. It is at Mrs. Arlbery's, for example, that Camilla's brother Lionel, "accoutred in the maid's cloths," is momentarily transformed into a transvestite (*Ca*, 264). At the same time, he forces Ensign Macdersey to wear the coachman's wig. The ensign's anger at this breach of class boundaries threatens to ignite a potentially violent confrontation, but Camilla defuses the hostilities by emphasizing the "burlesque" possibilities of this scene; she whimsically places the coachman's wig on Lionel (*Ca*, 265). Her friendship with Mrs. Arlbery "re-animated" her spirits (*Ca*, 247), and as the narrator tells us, Mrs. Arlbery can elicit Camilla's true nature: "Gaiety was so truly the native growth of the mind of Camilla, that neither care nor affliction could chace it long from its home" (*Ca*, 546).[22]

*Camilla* is unique in the Burney canon for its depiction of the heroine's childhood; in this way, Burney can better underscore what is lost when women begin to experience the restrictions that the modern patriarchal gaze places on their behavior. Burney deftly employs the pattern of the bildungsroman to show how her heroine's development is not so much her journey to social and sexual maturation as her gradual subjugation to a patriarchal culture. G. A. Starr argues that the female-centered bildungsroman poses no "ideological challenge," since "the virtues demanded of her [the heroine] as a woman remain those prized in her as a child"; in other words, she is not required to renounce her childhood virtues—as her male counterpart must—because they "facilitate her integration into adult society" (i.e., marriage).[23] However, *Camilla* intimates a different view of female development: its eponymous heroine exhibits signs of self- confidence and intelligence that—if not stifled by cultural sanctions—might open up social possibilities other than conventional marriage. As a child, for example, Camilla "metamorphosed" her uncle Hugh into a woman, and gave him a doll to "nurse and amuse" (*Ca*, 18). At the same time, reveling in her ability to "govern and direct" her uncle, she boldly dons his wig (*Ca*, 18). Like Lionel's later merriments, this childhood game evokes the subversive dynamics of the masquerade. But patently unlike *Cecilia*'s masquerade, this moment of spontaneous play allows for a flexible range of social and emotional freedom. Camilla, like Mrs. Arlbery, is fascinated and excited by the crossing of the bound- aries of gender and class. The wealthy baronet is transformed not only into a woman but also into a nursemaid, and Camilla wields a power usually associ- ated with the baronet. If allowed to cultivate her imagination and use her intel- ligence, Camilla would not only learn how to take care of herself; she would also have the liberty to make her most important life decisions.[24]

Camilla's spontaneous and jovial spirit spills over into her early adulthood; while dancing with an impecunious child, it is obvious that she is not yet re- stricted by the repressive effects of male surveillance:

> To the gay heart of Camilla whatever was sportive was attractive; she flew to
> the little fellow, whose skin was clean and bright, in the midst of his rags and
> wretchedness, and, making herself his play-mate, bid the woman finish feed-
> ing her child, told the man to repose himself undisturbed, and began dancing
> with the little boy, not less delighted than himself at the festive exercise. (*Ca*,
> 110)

Dancing with this child, Camilla manifests not only her energetic, lively nature but her charitable instincts as well; the child's father is to be executed for steal- ing mutton to feed his family (*Ca*, 83). Here we see how her natural ability to express herself openly is diametrically opposed to the restrictive and silencing functions of a code of manners. In such exemplary scenes, we are directed to the stark contrast between Camilla's youthful autonomy and the growing limi- tations placed on her as she circulates in a patriarchal economy. And we see as well how this distinction also operates in the poor family's situation: if the man is guilty "according to the forms of law," then he was justified because of the "calls of nature" (*Ca*, 109). Burney throws into relief how the inequitable laws of property are bred from the same set of ideas that give birth to the codes of strict propriety that women are expected to maintain, even at the cost of the "calls of nature."

Unlike the more optimistic version of manners in *Evelina*, *Camilla* shows us the complex and frightening process by which the most restrictive cultural codes of silence and passivity are internalized. For at the same time that Edgar is spying on Camilla, her father instructs her to spy on herself, to detect and censor any outward signs of her love for Edgar; his counsel is an obvious counterpart to Marchmont's advice to Edgar. Calling his missive a "little sermon upon the difficulties and the conduct of the female heart" (*Ca*, 353), Mr. Tyrold poses a question that cuts to the heart of one of the most basic tenets of patriarchal domination—freedom of choice: "Since Man must choose Woman, or Woman Man, which should come forward to make the choice? Which should retire to be chosen?" (*Ca*, 358). Even though his daughter loves Edgar, he insists that she must first wait for him to declare his intentions. There is no free choice for women; Mr. Tyrold warns her that "where there are two parties, choice can belong only to one of them: and then let her call upon her feelings of delicacy, all her notions of propriety, to decide. . . ." (*Ca*, 358). "[N]otions of propriety," of course, dictate that it should be the man's choice. Tyrold asserts that "in theory" and "even in common sense" women should have the "equal right" of disposing of their affections, but eighteenth-century genteel society demands a woman's subordination. He defines the problem but ignores any responsibility for attempting to solve it. In the end, Camilla is circumscribed not only by her sex but by her social status as well; that is, because Edgar will soon become a wealthy landowner, Camilla's actions are further limited, since it is well known that she is wholly dependent upon her future husband for economic security. In fact, Marchmont has already warned Edgar to look for signs of Camilla's greed and social ambition.

Both Edgar and Camilla, therefore, have been counseled to conceal their true feelings, but their sex determines their culturally permitted reactions to this advice. While Edgar still has the autonomy to move freely in society and observe Camilla's deportment with impunity, she loses any independence she had and is forced to control her every look, word, or sigh. In a society that is deeply preoccupied with the relationship between one's conduct and one's inner worth, Camilla is forced to manipulate and disrupt this cultural sign system. Her behavior can never signify her inner feelings and beliefs because she has been instructed to conceal and resist these very emotions. Thus she helps others to misread her, unwittingly participating in her own abuse. Moreover, Dr. Marchmont has already written Camilla's story for Edgar: she will most likely follow the path of other fallen women, causing Edgar nothing but sorrow and humiliation. Armed with this traditional reading, Edgar is bound to read all of Camilla's behavior as shrewdly calculated and coquettish; she is frozen by his gaze.

Mr. Tyrold's homiletic epistle makes abundantly clear that the dilemma Camilla faces is a form of emotional abuse. He uses images of violence to force her to comply with the sanctions governing the behavior of the new domestic woman: "Struggle then against yourself as you would struggle against an enemy. . . . I can only require from you what depends upon yourself, a steady and courageous warfare against the two dangerous underminers of your peace and of your fame, imprudence and impatience. . . . Good sense will show you the power of self-conquest. . . . It will talk to you of those boundaries which custom forbids your sex to pass, and the hazard of any individual attempt to transgress them" (*Ca*, 358). True, Tyrold's language owes some of its power to the Protestant ethic of self-discipline that pertains to both men and women.[25] But just as importantly, Tyrold stresses that, with the rise of domestic ideology, women are now charged with preserving familial order.[26] For this reason, women are schooled in the distressing ideology that their own emotions and desires are their "enemy." Words such as "warfare," "self-conquest," and "hazard" bespeak the violating effects of this self-denial; if Camilla does not censor or subdue her own feelings, her reputation will be destroyed. To breach such rigid gender boundaries is ultimately to face expulsion from the community. Indeed, Tyrold cautions Camilla about her duty to the larger community, for her "discretion" in matters of the heart is tantamount to a civic and moral obligation; it is "the bond that keeps society from disunion" (*Ca*, 361). So the external force of social regulation remains. What is new is that Camilla's attention to manners internalizes an older method of policing women's behavior.

In this fashion, Burney reformulates some familiar terms and ideas of eighteenth-century moral philosophy for her own political ends. Tyrold's letter in particular echoes Adam Smith's carefully argued treatise, *The Theory of Moral Sentiments* (1759). Smith, too, contended that people govern their actions by internalizing the judgments and regard of imagined and real spectators. If the observer and the observed share corresponding sentiments, then it is "sufficient for the harmony of society."[27] Burney, though, sees the dangers implicit in such theories of moral spectatorship. She maintains that male spectators, armed with rigid expectations, can often violate a woman's integrity, especially since women do not hold cultural or political agency. Yet it is precisely women, as *Camilla* will show, who are held responsible for keeping a splintering society intact.

But, first, what of the women who refuse to play this pacific role? If Mrs. Arlbery can enliven Camilla's spirits, can she unwittingly or even knowingly contribute to Camilla's dilemmas as well? Significantly, it is Mrs. Arlbery who most clearly recognizes Edgar's motives. She rightly calls him a "watcher," terrified of a woman with financial and emotional sovereignty who might "curb his own will" (*Ca*, 482). In this case, the "watcher" (or spectator) needs the observed to internalize his expectations of her in order to be validated in his own character. Eventually Mrs. Arlbery imagines herself in a struggle with Edgar over Camilla's future. She wants to manipulate Edgar herself, to see him under her and Camilla's dominion: "'My resolution,' cried she, 'is fixt, either to see him at her feet, or drive him from her heart'" (*Ca*, 458). After all, Mandlebert reverences all that Mrs. Arlbery disdains: a careful regard for manners and customs and a strict adherence to culturally defined gender boundaries.

If the practice of manners offered a relatively unambiguous and efficacious means of self-protection for Evelina, then in *Camilla* we see the moral complications engendered by the doubleness of this behavioral code. In particular, Mrs. Arlbery's incessant attempts to defy these complex and rigorous standards ironically take a complicitous form. She advises Camilla to flirt in order to drive Edgar into a jealous rage, a strategy that is clearly doomed to fail; but it is nevertheless an attempt to register a protest against the gender conventions by which Camilla is so severely circumscribed. Women, as Tyrold makes explicit in his sermon, must differentiate between "discretion" and "deception," or coquetry. Yet Mrs. Arlbery uses sexual duplicity as an act of rebellion. In the end, however, she only serves to strengthen Edgar's power to gaze, for urging Camilla to be flirtatious confirms his deepest assumptions. On the one hand, we can argue that manners can only be transformed by parody or complicity. Mrs. Arlbery intends—perhaps naively—for Camilla to meet Edgar on his own terms, to turn his beliefs against him. On the other hand, Mrs. Arlbery reminds us of other Burney characters—like Mrs. Selwyn—who are also complicit in male-defined values and institutions. Burney urges her readers to see that in their attempt to use conservative conventions for more positive, liberating ends, women like Mrs. Arlbery can unwittingly do the work of a patriarchal culture.

In these examples, Burney exposes the contradictory nature of the principles of domestic ideology. By the same token, the new ethical and spiritual, even economic, responsibilities that might empower women in the home can be manipulated to condemn them for cases of domestic and public disorder. One of the deepest and most troubling ironies of *Camilla* is that its heroine is roundly criticized and blamed not only for instances of men's violence but for her own victimization as well. Thus the real test of Camilla's domestication is not determined in her private home but in the volatile public sphere. When Camilla travels to Southampton with Mrs. Arlbery, Marchmont explains to Edgar how he can discover Camilla's real motives with sly circumspection: "[B]e yourself of the party to Southampton, and there, a very little observation will enable you to dive into the most secret recesses of her character" (*Ca*, 595). Further, he will have an opportunity to "see her with other Sir Sedleys [i.e., dissolute aristocrats]. Public places abound with those flutterers after youth and beauty" (*Ca*, 595). Nowhere is the sadistic quality of spying more apparent than in Marchmont's instructions to his protégé: Edgar is not only allowed to search her secrets but is permitted to test her resolve, ultimately to watch her fail under external and internal pressure and then to reckon moral judgments. In effect, if those "Sir Sedleys" can have their way, Edgar can possibly even witness her rape. Thus, even as the rise of domestic ideology promises the possibility of an unprecedented privacy,[28] Burney exposes how male surveillance increases the likelihood for further intrusions into women's lives: Camilla does not gain privacy but experiences further exposure and a loss of control. She is slowly stripped of all personal boundaries in the interests of regulating her sexuality and thus securing Edgar's future home.[29]

Camilla's first public appearance at Southampton provides the paradigmatic instance of women's responsibility for not only sustaining "the bond that keeps society from disunion" but for provoking their own victimization as well. It is here that she innocently forms a relationship with Mrs. Mittin, a middle-class sycophant who makes herself indispensable to gentility: "To be useful, she would submit to any drudgery. . . . To please was her incessant desire . . . she would work . . .go of errands . . . be a parasite, a spy . . . keep a secret, or spread a report" (Ca, 688). A crowd of merchants and laborers quickly gathers to observe the two women as they ramble aimlessly through the streets of Southampton one afternoon. Eventually the mob lays wagers on the nature of the characters and motives of the two odd women: "Some supposed they were only seeking to attract notice; others thought they were deranged in mind; and others, again, imagined they were shoplifters, and hastened back to their counters, to examine what was missing of their goods" (Ca, 608). At this volatile historical moment, two women wandering the streets are considered fair objects for men's wagers or even their violence; a young woman like Camilla is deemed a loose woman or even a criminal if she appears in public without a suitable chaperon. Earlier, one of Edgar's titled friends had warned him about the possible dangers facing Camilla if she insisted on appearing in such public places: "A young woman is no where so rarely respectable, or respected, as at these water-drinking places, if seen at them either long or often. . . . If she is without fortune, she is thought to be a female adventurer, seeking to sell herself for its attainment; if she is rich, she is supposed a willing dupe, ready for a snare, and only looking about for an ensnarer" (Ca, 471). Women's social status is no deterrent against violence; in both of these scenarios, the women are held accountable for the men's negative perceptions of them. Edgar senses the threat when he witnesses Camilla meandering with her "vulgar" escort: "but her [Mrs. Mittin's] air and manner so strongly displayed the low bred society to which she had been accustomed, that he foresaw nothing but improper acquaintance, or demeaning adventures, that could ensue from such a connection at a public place" (Ca, 610–11). Edgar's fears speak to the gentry's growing cultural anxieties about their loss of power and control in the public sphere; as the Mrs. Mittins of the world become firmly established in polite society, violence (women's "demeaning adventures") threatens to shatter the polished surface of this previously encapsulated genteel culture. Because public places become associated with violence, crime, and sexuality, women (of the middle and upper classes) are pushed further into the domestic space.

How could Camilla be responsible—in Edgar's eyes—for the crowd's subsequent violence? By seeming to invite it. She sits in a public bathhouse, an apparently "willing dupe" (as Edgar's friend had warned) for these men's attentions: "She kept, therefore, her seat, looking steadily straight down the water, and denying herself one moment's glance at anything, or person, upon the beach: little imagining she ingrossed, herself, the attention of all who paraded it. . . . [H]er beauty, her apparently unprotected situation, and the account of the wager, seemed to render her an object to be stared at without scruple" (*Ca*, 613). Just as Edgar has watched and narrated Camilla's actions, so these upper- and lower-class men do the same. In this case, they interpret her "apparently unprotected situation" as their universal invitation to sexual attack. Thus it is no surprise when some gentlemen burst into the bathhouse and immediately surround Camilla: "Lord Valhurst, shutting the door, planted himself against it" (*Ca*, 614). Even though Lord Valhurst only professes the desire to see her home safely, he is disappointed "in losing the beautiful prey he believed just falling into his hands" when she is rescued by Edgar (*Ca*, 615). As we have seen, the innocent heroine suddenly and ominously encircled by menacing rakes who propose to "protect" her is a running motif in Burney's narratives.

How has this archetypical Burneyan moment altered since its first depiction in *Evelina*? When Evelina escaped from Sir Clement, Orville's reaction was largely one of palpable relief. In *Camilla*, however, Burney explores more critically the ominous implications of the new domestic ideology. Quite simply, Edgar admonishes Camilla for placing herself in such danger: "My whole intention is to remonstrate...can you pardon so plain a word? . . . against your appearing in public with a person so ill adapted to insure you the respect that is so every way your due" (*Ca*, 618–19). If she is obliged to ensure stability in the home, then she is also expected to calm public tensions. Implicit in Edgar's remonstrance is the idea that women must practice rigorous self-observation and self-control; otherwise they will incite men to violence.

Shortly after this frightening incident, Camilla finds herself lost in a maze of hotel corridors, separated from her party. Like Evelina in the dark and frightening woods of Vauxhall, Camilla runs wildly through the halls as men seem to materialize out of nowhere:

> While straying about thus, as far off as she could go without losing sight of Dr. Orkborne, a door she had just passed was flung open, and she saw young Halder, whose licentious insolence had so much alarmed her in the bathing-house, stroam [*sic*] out, yawning, stretching, and swearing unmeaningly, but disgustingly, at every step. Terrified at his sight, she went on, as she could not get to the Doctor without passing him; but the youth, recollecting her imme-diately, called out: "Ah, ha! are you there again, you little vixen?" and pur-sued her. . . . Camilla, then, too much scared to be aware she ran a far greater risk than she escaped, desperately sought refuge by opening the nearest door. . . . No one, however, could approach her so soon as the person of whose chamber she had burst; who was an old gentleman. . . . Yet when Halder, vowing he owed her an ill turn for which she should pay, would have seized her by the hand, he protected with his own arm, saying: "Fie, boy, fie! let the girl alone! I don't like violence." (*Ca*, 624–25)

The old aristocratic friend of Camilla's uncle Hugh rescues her here, but not before she is forced to run for her immediate safety. Whether it be in the dark walks of Vauxhall, the streets of London, or hotel hallways, all of Burney's heroines find themselves running for sanctuary. These mazelike passageways serve as metaphors for the larger social environment; Burney repeatedly in-vokes the paternalistic fear that young, single women who are thrust into a world of weakening aristocratic social domination are particularly vulnerable to assault. As in *Evelina*, the heroine is rescued by a familiar aristocratic guard-ian. But unlike Evelina, Camilla is also rebuked for her "thoughtlessness" and lack of "prudence" (*Ca*, 628). In essence, women are condemned for the fact that men of the upper classes are losing the ability to effect social control. But it is this very insistence on women's extreme self-observation and self-censor-ship—their "prudence"—that will lead Camilla to the brink of death.

Given the cultural preoccupation with the private and public effects of women's behavior, it is not surprising that Camilla experiences acute feelings of guilt when she is accused of inciting a duel between Hal Westyn and Lord Valhurst, the former defending and the latter attacking the honor and conduct of the young woman cornered in the public bathing house: "[S]he was the sole cause of this duel. . . . The inconsiderate facility with which she had wandered about with a person so little known to her, so underbred, and so forward, ap-peared now to herself inexcusable" (*Ca*, 636–37). Camilla's (mis)education is now nearly complete. She has internalized Edgar's stinging admonishments: in her wanderings with Mrs. Mittin, she not only leaves herself open to attack but she also unwittingly ignites larger social violence. The community would ultimately blame her if the duel were to result in fatalities (*Ca*, 637). In this way, we can see that this new ethical and domestic role which could empower women could also be utilized to accuse them of a new level of irresponsibility.

## III

Up to this point, I have shown the way a code of manners participates in the complex reordering of patriarchal control in the modern world; the violence of the gaze specifically intimates the shape that this altered form of domination will take. However, there is another set of dilemmas that Camilla must confront: those particular financial problems that coincide with the advent of commodity capitalism. Thus, we may ask, do new capitalist tools like financial credit and conspicuous consumption aggravate, extend, or ameliorate the specific violations created by the rise of domestic ideology? Most specifically: How does the growing importance of these seemingly unpredictable and unreliable economic developments affect the form that patriarchal domination will take in the modern world? Broadly speaking, *Cecilia* often showed us that patriarchal ideology came under assault as a consequence of a larger attack on aristocratic ideology and institutions. Similarly, Burney records in *Camilla* that patriarchy and female dependence are resolidified due in part to women's increasing economic vulnerability in a growing capitalist economy. Early in the novel, circumstances arise that lay the groundwork for Camilla's later serious financial distresses. Sir Hugh names Camilla's youngest sister Eugenia his sole heiress, and his improvident nephew, Clermont Lynmere, depletes the bulk of his wealth. Camilla's own brother Lionel, moreover, accrues substantial debts that require the Tyrold family, but especially Camilla, to be vigilant about expenses. Finally, Camilla loses her mother's advice and support when her mother must travel to the continent to secure Lionel's inheritance.

*Camilla* highlights one of the most fundamental economic obstacles specific to women in a patrilineal culture: the inequities created by this system's customs of inheritance can severely limit a woman's chance for an autonomous future. As a student at Oxford, Lionel attempts to pay off his growing debts by anonymously threatening his maternal uncle for the money. His explanation for his actions is remarkably dispassionate: "[I]t was only begging a little money, which he can afford to spare very well; and just telling him, if he did not come to a place I mentioned, he would have his brains blown out" (*Ca*, 225). In his second effort at blackmail, Lionel threatens to burn his uncle's house down with the entire family asleep in their beds (*Ca*, 226). That we know Lionel is basically good-natured does not mitigate the force of his obsession with violence; violent anger is a frequent response to sudden economic crisis and status uncertainty. As the son of a younger son, Lionel's future is dependent upon Mrs. Tyrold's wealthy country-gentleman brother; this Uncle Relvil must be appeased at all costs to obviate the "final ill consequences"—namely, Lionel's complete disinheritance (*Ca*, 229). Camilla, however, will be the ultimate victim of her brother's schemes. Not only must she face the most critical period of her life without her mother, but she must also practice monetary restraint because of her brother's frivolous machinations. Lionel's response to uncertainty is active and violent, while Camilla's reaction must be passive and censored. This brother and sister face a situation similar to that of McCartney and Evelina; the solutions available to them are determined strictly by their sex.

Not only do patrilineal assumptions severely circumscribe Camilla's prospects and require her own personal sacrifices, but also the unpredictable nature of some capitalist developments exacerbate her financial vulnerability. During her stay at Southampton, Camilla is on an ineluctable journey toward financial ruin and emotional breakdown bred of commodity capitalism. Because of the absence of thoughtful and financially savvy guardians, she must learn the harsh realities of the market economy from someone who thrives on its inequities, Mrs. Mittin. And Camilla is particularly susceptible to manipulation, for she, like Evelina, is innocent of the customs of the "ton," Burney's favorite term to describe the gentry. Therefore, Mrs. Mittin can convince her that she needs new cloaks and dresses in order to appear suitably attired at public functions, since even Camilla can see that her meager wardrobe is "out of date" (*Ca*, 689). Of course, that she is trying to impress Edgar aggravates the problem.[30] "[W]hen Camilla wanted cash for any of the very few articles she now allowed herself to think indispensable, instead of restoring it into her hands, she [Mrs. Mittin] flew herself to purchase the goods that were required, and always brought them home with assurances they were cheaper than the shopkeepers would let her have them for herself" (P.689). Repeatedly buying items on credit, Mrs. Mittin drives Camilla further into debt; indeed, since Camilla is never shown her accumulating bills, she inevitably loses track of her liabilities. Like her contemporaries, Burney conceives financial credit as a mysterious and highly undependable transaction that can ruin the improvident or the naive, and as scholars have noted, financial credit was depicted as female in the eighteenth century.[31] Because Burney's Camilla is a dependent woman, it is not surprising that the irony entailed in this cultural figure of financial insecurity and illusion is associated with someone more likely than any to suffer its consequences.

Just as Camilla must learn manners in a volatile public sphere, she is also expected to master the lessons of capitalism in this same environment. Camilla suddenly finds herself an easy mark for usurers, since Mrs. Mittin has spread a rumor that she is Sir Hugh's heiress. Ultimately, Camilla is forced into an unfair arrangement with a money-lender: "Mrs. Mittin, amongst her numerous friends, counted a Mr. Clykes, a moneylender, a man, she said, of the first credit for such matters with people of fashion in any difficulty" (*Ca*, 743). The myth of paternalistic care and charity has been replaced by a system that contains its own serious flaws: moneylending at exorbitant rates of interest. That Mrs. Mittin refers to Clykes as a man of "the first credit" is typical of Burney's irony. But in *Camilla*, the manifest distance between capitalist credit and aristo-cratic honor[32] cannot be taken to suggest that the latter has any real value or availability. We are left simply with the gap between credit as reputation and as shady financial dealing. Clykes is later described as one of Mrs. Mittin's most "useful" friends; the irony, again, demonstrates that the new capitalists "use" people as they utilize money—for profit and social gain (*Ca*, 785). Thus we can read *Camilla* as a narrative of the heroine's education, for she must come to differentiate between those with true "credit" and those who mean only to exploit her weaknesses.

Like its predecessor, *Camilla* underscores the correlation between conspicu-ous consumption and credit. In effect, Camilla accrues large debts partly be-cause she momentarily indulges an appetite for "emulative spending."[33] All of this prodigal capitalist activity, as the narrator pointedly cautions, thrives in the public domain: "She [Camilla] had repeatedly refused to borrow anything more of Mrs. Arlbery, always hoping every call for money would be the last; but she was too inexperienced to know, That in gay circles, and public places, the de-mands for wealth are endless and countless; and that economy itself, which is always local, is there lavish and extravagant, compared with its character, in private scenes and retired life" (*Ca*, 518). This passage suggests not only the social but also the gendered meaning attached to the separation of the spheres. A genteel public life necessarily demands expense, and a middle-class woman like Camilla must overextend herself in order to assimilate. Such troubling eco-nomic concerns, however, have supposedly not yet touched the "private" and "retired" life. Like the archetypal conservative plot that Michael McKeon has described, Burney's *Camilla* offers the secluded, domestic life as perhaps the only response to social corruption.[34] But Burney further complicates this con-servative pattern by locating the problems for an early-modern woman in this very retreat to the domestic home. To protect herself from economic viola-tions, Camilla must withdraw to the domestic sphere, but there she confronts the consequences of severe self-restraint and the concomitant loss of social free-dom. The form that male dominance takes in the modern world—imagined here through the complex discourse of manners and domesticity—poses a set of dilemmas that are only exacerbated by the rise of a capitalist economy.

In distinct but related ways, therefore, Camilla is subject to the manipula-tive powers both of a watchful suitor and of a shrewd, calculating capitalist speculator, Mrs. Mittin. The subtle similarities shared by these two otherwise distinct people (both, for example, have a penchant for spying) underscores the connections between the culture of patriarchal surveillance and the economy of capitalist speculators. Edgar and Mrs. Mittin share a desperate aim: they need to reckon returns in their relations with Camilla.[35] Edgar uses Camilla not only to validate his need for complete authority but also to allay his fears about the power of women's sexuality; as a kind of emotional capitalist, more-over, he threatens to withdraw sympathy and approval when he feels he has been defied. Likewise, Mrs. Mittin unfeelingly exploits Camilla in her quest to gain access to the world of gentility. Toward these two ends, both characters assert a tremendous amount of control: Camilla not only comes under the restrictive power of the gaze but is equally vulnerable to the forces of the mar-ket and the self-interested manipulations of her unscrupulous creditor. Rather than offering Camilla some kind of autonomy, bourgeois patriarchy and a capi-talist economy only aggravate her dependence.

Burney's insistent preoccupation with the largely public threat of sexual assault, however, continues to shape her third novel. At times it seems in fact to momentarily overshadow her ambivalence about the violations endemic to women's new domestic role. Sir Sedley Clarendel is Camilla's most menacing persecutor, for he can take advantage of her various misfortunes. In one exem-plary scene, Sir Sedley discovers that Lionel is pressuring Camilla to extort two hundred pounds from their already overextended uncle, Sir Hugh. Sir Sedley leaves the money for Camilla, but Lionel finds and keeps it, and thus Camilla is forced into Sir Sedley's debt. Immediately thereafter Sir Sedley proposes mar-riage (indeed, presumes it), and Camilla feels that she cannot refuse him, since she owes him money. In addition, Lionel balks at settling the transaction, a sure way of protecting his sister from Sir Sedley's designs. Lionel's language offers frightening testimony to the disturbing connections between sexual and financial exploitation: "No, my dear, no; you are the little debtor; so balance your ac-counts for yourself. . . ." (*Ca*, 523). Lionel's allusion is clear: marriage—in this case, sexual capitulation—is Camilla's only means for balancing her "accounts." In effect, Lionel is using her to avoid his own responsibility to pay Sir Sedley; she is ready currency for her brother.

Camilla simply cannot protect herself in a world in which she has little economic power. In one instance she is trying to refuse a supremely sanguine Sir Sedley "when Lionel, capering into the little apartment danced round it in mad ecstasy, chanting 'Lady Clarendel, Lady Clarendel, my dear Lady Clarendel!'" (*Ca*, 526). Just as Edgar was encouraged to think of her as "Camilla Mandlebert," so Lionel names and therefore appropriates Camilla for the would-be suitor; once more she is an object of exchange between men. His joyous prancing seems a bitter parody of Camilla's earlier dance with the small boy: now she is completely powerless. Soon Sir Sedley becomes even more pre-sumptuous because of Lionel's exhibition; as a result, Camilla "became . . . nearly frantic. She thought herself irretrievably in the power of Sir Sedley and by means so forced and indelicate. . . ."(*Ca*, 527). Her description eerily alludes to rape; to be forced into the power of Sir Sedley is like physical assault. Her heart, integrity, and perhaps even her body can be violated because men are able to manipulate women's economic vulnerabilities. In the end, Sir Sedley's method of violence, commonly associated with the aristocratic rake, shares some of the same violating features of the modern code of manners, as figured in the male gaze: both entrap women by violating either their physical or emotional boundaries.

## IV

Like its predecessor, *Camilla* is colored by the apprehension that women's search for protection is inseparable from moments of madness, self-destruction, and possibly even death. The final third of the novel relentlessly records how the violations posed by the self-censoring required in the practice of manners and the external threats created by a capitalist economy converge in the beleaguered heroine's hallucinatory, self-willed illness. When Camilla returns from Southampton, she is rudely greeted by the news that Lionel has incurred debts of nearly five hundred pounds; because he is under age, his father is held responsible for his liabilities. Nevertheless, Mr. Tyrold expects his daughters to sacrifice for their brother: "The painful result . . . was laying before his daughters the whole of his difficulties, and demanding if they would willingly concur in paying their brother's bills from their appropriate little store, by adopting an altered plan of life, and severe self-denial of their present ease" (*Ca*, 763–64). Once again Camilla is expected to endure "willingly" the pain of severe "self-denial." Moreover, this passage reveals the ways in which patriarchy is bolstered in the modern world: Mr. Tyrold's "demand" is followed by the more uncertain conditional phrase, "if they would willingly." As *Evelina* taught us, patriarchal power can be cloaked, and thus reinforced, in the language of affection and free choice: children, and particularly daughters, would be compelled to obey out of deference to these new bonds of affection with their fathers.

Shortly thereafter, however, Camilla's own bills come due, and her father is immediately confined to debtor's prison (*Ca*, 823). It is a bitter irony that Mr. Tyrold is imprisoned for his daughter's debts but not his son's. While her debits are much less serious than her brother's, her misjudgments have a potentially more destructive effect on the family. Burney encourages us to see that the new ideology of domesticity unfairly places the onus of self-control on women. If she had practiced self restraint, Camilla laments, then her father would not have been jailed. Just as she had suffered Edgar's reproaches for wandering the streets without a suitable protector, she feels the wrath of her parents' curses for her lack of financial control. She is even banished from her home: "I have become an alien to my family, and a burthen to myself! ordered from my home by my Father, lest my sight should be destructive to my mother" (*Ca*, 839).

Not only is Camilla putatively responsible for her immediate family's apparent ruin, but she also takes on the guilt for ostensibly destroying the exemplar of benevolent aristocratic rule, her uncle, Sir Hugh. When she travels to his home, she discovers a deserted, Gothic estate that slightly recalls Delvile Castle: "Nothing was in motion, no one was visible, not even a fire blazed chearfulness. . . . The stone passage was now nearly dark. . . . Everything looked desolate, all the family seemed to be vanished. . . . Terrified and astonished, she thought herself walking in her sleep. . . . Horrour crept through every vein of Camilla, in the explanation she awaited of this fearful mystery" (*Ca*, 850–53). She immediately takes the blame for her family's collapse: "My Father I have imprisoned!—my Uncle I have turned from his house and home!" (*Ca*, 853). Camilla's attempts to step out of her culturally prescribed role by momentarily indulging monetary and emotional appetites have all but impoverished her family. But this apparently conservative backlash (Camilla's "freedom" creates havoc and destruction) is challenged by the specter of the physical and emotional consequences it has on Camilla. So despite the fact that Burney settles her heroine in the domestic sphere, she clearly does not gloss over the serious drawbacks of this situation: the price can be women's brutal acts of self-wounding.

The climax of *Camilla* recalls the central crises of Burney's two previous novels: the heroine is in a desperate, perilous search for an asylum. Driven from her home because of her debts and finding her Uncle's house lifeless, Camilla's frightening dilemma is familiar to Burney's readers: "[W]hat asylum was any where open to her?" (*Ca*, 863). If she has been stripped of her only known supports, then—as the Burney of the court years taught us—her only available response may be suicide. In fact, Camilla's delirium is reminiscent of Burney's final illness at court, for both the author and her heroine were forced from their homes and compelled to deny their needs and desires.

If Camilla has been compelled to internalize Edgar's and Marchmont's expectations by censoring her emotions and behavior, then she has internalized the violations endemic to this external surveillance as well. After enduring her parents' anger and disappointment, helplessly watching her uncle and her father dispossessed, and desperately attempting to conceal her feelings, Camilla openly wishes for death. Like her tortured author at George III's court, Camilla endures a physical and emotional illness: "She was full of fever, faint, pallid, weak, and shaken by nervous tremors" (*Ca*, 868). In the first throes of her sickness, while housed at a roadside inn, she accidentally spies a corpse being carried in. She forces herself to view the cadaver, thereby facing what she claims most to desire: "Is not death what I am meeting?—seeking—desiring—what I court? what I pray for? . . . A cloth covered the face; she stood still, hesitating if she had the power to remove it: but she thought it a call to her own self-examination; and though mentally recoiling, advanced. . . . Yet she would not allow herself to retreat. She now put forth her hand; but it shook suspended over the linen, without courage to draw it aside" (*Ca*, 870–71). She does finally uncover the shroud, only to discover Eugenia's husband, dead by his own hand, a "ghastly figure," soaked with "large splashes of blood" (*Ca*, 871). He had unwittingly killed himself when threatening to kill his wife and then himself (*Ca*, 887). Facing the corpse of her brother-in-law is, she claims, her own "self-examination." Doody argues that Burney is here "exhibiting the death of the Father," the absence of law and authority.[36] But I think it would be more instructive to view this not as the death of a universal "Father" figure (for Bellamy is the "younger son of the master of a great gaming house" who through his lifetime has collected "debts of honor" [*Ca*, 892–93]), but as the death of a representative of an older aristocratic, primogenitural system. Bellamy had spent his life gaming, dueling, and manipulating heiresses like Eugenia. Through his bloody suicide, we are invited to consider how the vices bred from this system—dueling and gambling—lead to sure destruction. Camilla, too, has been victimized by this same inequitable system; thus it is not surprising that she is drawn to Bellamy's dead body, "seeking," "desiring," even "courting" his end. In this section of the novel, we see how the Burney of *Camilla* has grown even more skeptical and critical of the aristocratic father and his system of social authority.

If the adherence to a complex code of manners, as ideally conceived in *Evelina*, figures for the internalization of the social actor in the heroine, then it can also figure for the internalization of the male persecutor. That is, Camilla's wish for self-annihilation is a learned response, an internalization of the patriarchal gaze. In her hallucinations, the personification of Death eerily alludes to a menacing rapist: "Death, in a visible figure, ghastly, pallid, severe, appeared before her, and with its hand, sharp and forked, struck abruptly upon her breast. . . . She screamed—but it was heavy as cold, and she could not remove it . . . she shrunk from its touch. . . ." (*Ca*, 874). There is an inescapable aura of sexual danger in this passage; Camilla has internalized, as it were, what was formerly an external threat. And the phallocentric images in this scene (its powerful body and the heroine recoiling from its touch) imply that this internalization is a violent one, akin to the heroine's rape. His visibly powerful and sharp hand can be seen as a fetishistic displacement of the phallus. This apparition suggests the frightening similarities shared by the patriarchal spectator and the rapist: the male gaze ultimately objectifies Camilla as a sexual commodity, violating her boundaries and stripping her of all control. Indeed, she is clearly overpowered in this scene ("she could not remove it"); thus she finally fulfills Edgar's fantasy—she is a completely powerless, passive woman.

While Camilla's delirium is a frightening consequence of the male gaze, it just as forcefully testifies to her painful triumph over Dr. Marchmont's and

Edgar's reign of terror. During her feverish frenzy, a voice seemingly issuing from inside her (the male voice internalized) demands that she write her claims for mercy with a "pen of iron." "She wrote with difficulty . . . but saw that her pen made no mark! . . . the paper was blank!" (*Ca*, 875–76). On the one hand, it is not surprising that her pen leaves no mark, for she has repressed her feelings for so long that she simply cannot express herself. But, on the other, the blank page is a positive sign as well. Instead of signaling her abject dependency in a patriarchal culture, her inability to write with the phallic instrument is striking evidence of her refusal to capitulate to male expectations of expression.[37] Overwhelmed by "self-accusation," and "unlicensed by her will," she grabs the "iron instrument," but when finished, she found "no mark." While one recent critic argues that Camilla resists using this opportunity to make the pen her own, to speak for herself, it seems more fruitful to see the ways in which Camilla's silence is one of the most subversive tactics she can take in a culture that valorizes the male pen as the only valid instrument of expression.[38] Her language is not the discourse of the Dr. Marchmonts who demand that women visibly sign and prove their character and worth, and do so with male-controlled sign systems (i.e., the gender-specific language and behavior of female morality and self-control). She will not enter the prevailing discourse of authority; in fact, she has seized the pen "unlicensed by her will."

Camilla is yet again the object of judgmental spectators; the act of writing her claims for mercy suggests the tacit presence of a reader, most obviously the eyes of God. A voice demands that she read her doom, be a spectator to her own damnation, but her experience ends abruptly, the leaf of the book bursts, and she discovers it to be "only a vision" (*Ca*, 876). She has internalized Marchmont's conviction that she is a guilty, unworthy woman, and thus her imagination has explored and enacted this inner conflict; she was overcome with "self-accusation." The persistent strain of men's harsh judgments had pushed her to the brink of a self-willed death, but she struggles against this impulse and recovers. She refuses to be confined as the object of the male text; she will not certify her spiritual or moral "insufficiency" (*Ca*, 875). Restraint is regarded as the greatest virtue in Camilla's culture, but her illness breaks the coercive chains of self-denial, and in this way, she partially defeats the reigning cultural perceptions of women. As a result, Dr. Marchmont is compelled to acknowledge the "injustice," "narrowness," and "arrogance" of his misogynistic instructions to Edgar (*Ca*, 913).[39]

Once Camilla has recovered, she reads her illness as a metaphor for her status as a woman: she had thought herself "dead . . . to the world, its views, its hopes, its cares" (*Ca*, 878). She realized that a woman's worst nightmare is a social and economic death, and she has discovered the perils inherent in capitalist activity and in the prevailing cultural attitudes toward women. Yet at the same time that Burney exposes how the domestication of the heroine creates a new pattern of violation and abuse, she retreats, as it were, to the romantic closure first depicted in *Evelina*. Once again a young heroine returns to what she believes to be the safety of the paternal home: "Camilla, whose danger was the result of self-neglect, as her sufferings had all flowed from mental anguish, was already able to go down to the study upon the arrival of Mr. Tyrold: where she received, with grateful rapture, the tender blessings which welcomed her to the paternal arms—to her home—to peace—to safety—and primaeval joy" (*Ca*, 893). This passage resonates with some of the key terms that characterize the nostalgic idealizing myth of paternalism: "paternal arms," "safety," and "primaeval joy." There is a strong suggestion of infantilization here, and the reader misses the Camilla who laughed freely and often subversively with Mrs. Arlbery. True, Burney is willing to compromise the incipient possibilities in women's friendships or the development of a fully autonomous heroine for the ideological power she finds in the image of a modified aristocratic patriarchal family. Nevertheless, she does not back away from what is genuinely a contradictory story, and she brings her third heroine to the precipice of death. In the end, it is Mrs. Tyrold who articulates this paternalistic fantasy that Burney often turns to after exploring the ubiquitous violence facing women in the modern world: as Camilla's father tells her, it was her mother who "was sure Edgar Mandlebert could alone preserve you from danger" (*Ca*, 899). While the irony of this assertion partially detracts from its apparent optimism (after all, it is Edgar who put her in danger), Burney awkwardly leaves it as the least threatening of Camilla's limited options.

Yet *Camilla* suggests a movement toward liberation as well. Camilla's and Edgar's marriage is clearly patterned on a reformulated and modern paternalistic model. Sir Hugh, for example, is restored to his estate and fortune with Edgar's help. Thus the sentimental aristocrat is saved, and the impoverished tenants of the community rejoice at this marriage, for Camilla aims to be a charitable mistress (*Ca*, 906, 911). And so marriage provides the Burney heroine with safety and care, and it allows her to practice those activities like charity that were key to late-century paternalistic and domestic ideologies. Jacob, the family servant, had earlier foreseen this marriage not simply as an isolated event but as the cornerstone to the survival of the community: "all our hope is in you" (*Ca*, 771). In the end, Camilla finds a modicum of power and emotional freedom in marriage, as she can now be "candid" with Edgar (*Ca*, 902). There will supposedly be no more repressive silence.

Along with *Evelina*, *Camilla* is Burney's most penetrating exploration of the dynamics of domesticity. Unlike *Evelina*, however, *Camilla* illustrates that even as manners can be an effective means for women's self-protection, they can be self-violating as well because they oblige women to control and observe their own behavior. Thus, Burney's third novel shows us how promises of greater freedom and responsibility for women only serve to shore up patriarchal domination, and the new patterns of violence created by this reimposition of patriarchal control (most centrally, self-abuse) cruelly mimic this ideology of self-protection and autoresponsibility. Women now have the liberty, as it were, to violate themselves.

# 4

## *Evelina* Redux:
## *The Wanderer* and the Revolution

In 1812, when Burney and her young son were leaving Napoleonic France for her native England after a seven-year absence, she twice had to assure suspicious French authorities that the manuscript she was carrying—early work on her final novel, *The Wanderer; Or, Female Difficulties* (1814)—contained "nothing in it political, nor even National."[1] But in fact *The Wanderer* is one of Burney's most distinctly political novels. Its heroine, like Burney's Evelina, has no customary signs of gentility or even of simple respectability: she has no name, no apparent family, no money, and, in this case, no native country. I want to suggest that *The Wanderer* is a rewriting of *Evelina*, but this time Burney's putatively illegitimate heroine is a refugee in England, having escaped from France during "the dire reign of the terrific Robespierre, and in the dead of night."[2] Like Evelina, *The Wanderer*'s heroine, Juliet Granville, discovers that for a young woman, the modern world is a seemingly unending series of physical and emotional traumas, and her quest is also to find either a familial or social refuge. Yet the volatile political climate of the 1790s adds a new dimension to Burney's archetypal story of a lonely and unprotected heroine searching for physical and economic security. In *The Wanderer* Burney enters a decidedly feminist and revolutionary discourse that deeply influences her representation of violence and complicates and modifies as well her assumptions about the relative viability of the various social "replacements" for traditional aristocratic rule.

By using the French Revolution as her historical context, Burney enters an impassioned debate about the future of English society. Like many of her contemporaries, she feared the complete and violent demise of an older social order that symbolized a stable moral community. As we have seen elsewhere, the highly visible threat to aristocratic domination made it appear more attractive at a time when, as we remember Laetitia Hawkins protesting, women could not even safely negotiate a simple stroll down the street.[3] Edmund Burke lamented the fact that the Revolution had brought destruction to the "age of chivalry": "Never, never more, shall we behold that generous loyalty to rank and sex, that proud submission, that dignified obedience, that subordination of the heart, which kept alive, even in servitude itself, the spirit of an exalted freedom."[4] Burney certainly shares some of his sentiments. Yet at the same time, she envisions the incipient possibilities for women's freedom in this pivotal historical moment. For this reason, we see how *The Wanderer* is deeply informed and influenced as well by a feminist work like Mary Wollstonecraft's *A Vindication of the Rights of Woman*.[5] It is Burney's struggle to reconcile these two distinct political and social ideologies that accounts for the ambiguities and contradictions that we associate with *The Wanderer*.

In her final novel, Burney returns to one of the most important themes of her novelistic career: the potential of a community of women—or a group of female friends—to replace or at least to offer an alternative to male-dominated versions of authority and protection. Juliet Granville faces daily what Burney's previous three heroines experience only at critical moments: she literally wanders around England seeking an asylum. And it is an England that is profoundly suspicious of and hostile to a woman with no traditional signs of gentility. Significantly, each one of Juliet's temporary homes is governed by genteel women who sustain those violations that are an inevitable element of status-based institutions. They abuse Juliet by largely exploiting her vulnerability to social and pecuniary embarrassment. As I will show, one central motive for these women's abuse of a defenseless woman is their stubborn, even desperate, attempt to uphold the principles of a status society from which they derive apparent benefits. In this fashion, Burney seems to share Wollstonecraft's frustration with those constructions of passive and vacuous female behavior that hinder genteel women's capacity to use their reason and intelligence not only to improve their own situation but also to recognize their shared oppression with the less fortunate of their sex.

But there are other women who resist this violence embodied in cultural institutions, and they do their best to support Juliet during her wanderings. Elinor Joddrel, an obvious descendant of *Evelina*'s Mrs. Selwyn and *Camilla*'s Mrs. Arlbery, is Burney's most ardent spokeswoman for women's rights and the full-scale repudiation of aristocratic assumptions. She can be a powerful ally for Juliet; and yet Burney links her ardent feminism to her self-destructive behavior. In Elinor, Burney presents us with a character who possesses some of the more "conservative" inclinations affiliated with eighteenth-century female behavior—i.e., a susceptibility to feeling or "romantic" notions of love—but who has also internalized the liberating violence of the Revolution. Burney's most complex and forthright feminist ultimately suffers the consequences of attempting to break out of inhibiting gender constraints at a time when such behavior was especially frightening to English culture. *The Wanderer* powerfully reveals that women's attempt to forge a new identity in a radically changing modern world provokes the community's hostile reactions and, most alarmingly, women's internalization of this violence.

Burney explores in *The Wanderer* a new species of "replacement" that evolves out of both the concept of a women's community and the structures of bourgeois authority: female economic independence. Like the other means of self-protection that Burney has experimented with—i.e., manners—economic independence depends on a rationale foreign to aristocratic ideology. In other words, by attempting to climb the social ladder by her own talents, and thus achieve a respected and perhaps protective identity, Juliet challenges the notion of elevated birth as the only conduit of honor and integrity. But Burney will show that late-eighteenth-century England offers few opportunities for women to take the same path as the progressive hero. On this matter, *The Wanderer* not only enters into a dialogue with feminist works that address the problem of women's disempowerment in a growing capitalist society, but it also engages with perhaps the most noteworthy, male-centered progressive narrative of the century: *Robinson Crusoe*.

In the end, Juliet Granville, like Evelina, recovers her family name, her lost siblings, and her rightful inheritance, and, of course, she weds a suitable aristocrat. Burney stresses, however, that the other versions of social replacement have a vital role in the world she imagines, for both female friends and bourgeois protectors find a place in the aristocratic household of Juliet and her husband, Albert Harleigh. Thirty-six years after Burney first considered the question of female protection, she recognizes the importance of certain bourgeois principles in the fight for women's safety and independence.

## I

The real identity of *The Wanderer*'s heroine is a mystery both to the novel's characters and to its readers as well. For most of the narrative, we know her only as "Ellis," a name some women force upon her when they overhear her receiving a letter addressed with the initials, "L.S." (*W,* 83).[6] We soon learn, however, that Juliet is attempting to conceal her true identity. In the fourth volume, we discover that she is the legitimate daughter of Lord Granville, the son of the earl of Melbury, and Miss Powell, the daughter of an "insolvent man of business" (*W,* 640–41). Because he feared his own father's wrath at the news of his socially unequal union, Juliet's father never publicly acknowledged her. Her mother died during Juliet's infancy, and her father remarried, leaving her in the custody of a French Catholic bishop and his sister.

Lord Granville decrees in his will, however, that Juliet should inherit the same share as any other daughters that might issue from his second marriage. When he dies, his brother-in-law, Lord Denmeath, tries to protect the family name by refusing to recognize Juliet's legitimacy (*W,* 645). He promises that "she shall be portioned," provided that she remain in France (*W,* 645). The bishop is determined to "sustain the birth-right of the innocent Orphan" (*W,* 645), and hence he decides to take her to England. Unexpectedly, however, he is arrested by one of Robespierre's agents, who promptly blackmails Juliet when he discovers her true history; unless she marries him, the bishop will have to face the guillotine (*W,* 740–41). She fearfully complies. And so Burney's fourth novel opens with Juliet fleeing war-torn France and her brutal husband, vowing never to reveal her name or origin in order to safeguard the bishop's life. She escapes in a small boat with some English passengers who will be the main protagonists in her story: Elinor Joddrel, Mrs. Maple, Mrs. Ireton, and Juliet's eventual husband, Albert Harleigh. It is this complicated story that slowly unfolds while Juliet wanders through England.

Once Juliet lands at Dover, she feels that "female protection" is her most viable means of safety (*W,* 39). She assumes that women will want to care for a desperate and unprotected female, but she soon discovers that in their struggle to uphold those status assumptions from which they receive some significant benefits, genteel women willingly exploit the less fortunate of their sex. Just as the rakes in *Evelina* read that heroine's unprotected status as an opportunity for sexual assault and the easy assertion of their power, Juliet's three primary female guardians—Mrs. Maple, Mrs. Howel, and Mrs. Ireton—interpret her mysteriousness as an opportunity to abuse her and thereby to bolster their feelings of superiority.

These three women are defined by their status consciousness; in other words, they prove to be zealous spokeswomen for the gentry's arbitrary principles of rank. Mrs. Maple initially offers Juliet protection at the insistence of her radical niece, Elinor. But Mrs. Maple's preoccupation with Juliet's lack of traditionally respectable social signs hardens her to Juliet's plight. Needless to say, she fears that this lonely wanderer will upset her family's social position: "When the family assembled to breakfast, Mrs. Maple declared that she had not closed her eyes the whole night, from the vexation of having admitted such an unknown Wanderer to sup at her table, and to mix with people of rank" (*W,* 103). Her fear of public opinion testifies to women's precarious position in late eighteenth-century England. While the highly respected Harleigh, a peer's nephew, is able to aid Juliet without jeopardizing his status (for example, he insists that she be allowed to escape with them from France, [*W,* 11–12]), Mrs. Maple fears that she will be "ruin[ed]" for introducing a "poor wanderer" into her community (*W,* 111). Women of the gentry sustain their elevated status and its attendant power through reputation and the exclusion of other women. In this fashion, Mrs. Maple partly reminds us of *Pamela*'s Lady Davers, who fears for the preservation of her aristocratic position if Pamela is introduced into her "ancient and untainted" family. In other words, it is in her best interests if Pamela is excluded from her family, for Pamela undermines those aristocratic qualities that uphold Lady Davers's elevated status.[7] In both novels we see how any notion of female sorority is subsumed by genteel women's understanding of where they derive most of their authority. Unlike their male counterparts, for example, they do not hold land or political rights, and thus they are forced to hold onto their tenuous positions by acceding to the community's conception of proper behavior. Consequently, as Burney encourages us to see, those who sit at their dinner tables may threaten their already unstable status.

Burney creates a reputedly "bastard" heroine in order to examine and criticize her society's prejudices, for the majority of Juliet's persecutors uphold both "respectable" and patrilineal principles. Mrs. Maple labels Juliet an "illegitimate stroller" (*W*, 86), emphasizing not her solitude or need for protection but her lack of a proper name. These women reject Juliet's sincere assertion that she has no plans to deceive them: "Innocent? . . . without a name, without a home, without a friend?—Innocent?" (*W*, 133). By refusing to divulge her name and her family background, she is challenging the most basic assumptions of a patrilineal culture. And it is especially upper-class women who have the least tolerance for Juliet, since she threatens their social power, built as it is upon the assumptions of patrilineage and status. Indeed, Mrs. Maple refuses to speak in public "with a person of whom she had never seen the pedigree, nor the rent-roll" (*W*, 249).

Mrs. Maple and Mrs. Ireton presume that their rank and fortune allow them to be abusive; that is, they envision authority as acts of cruelty against their inferiors. Juliet comes to recognize Mrs. Ireton's obsessive need for domination: "She saw, too, that that lady was amongst the many, though terrible characters, who think superiour rank or fortune authorises perverseness, and legitimates arrogance; who hold the display of ill humour to be the display and mark of power. . . ." (*W*, 489). In this case, not name or fortune but harassment and violation mark the gentry's power. E. P. Thompson has argued that eighteenth-century ruling-class control largely depended on images of largesse or frightening displays of authority.[8] Here, we see a woman's inept attempt to assert this kind of cultural authority: images of power are merely blustering, empty displays of "ill-humour." Indeed, Mrs. Ireton's need to parade her authority publicly suggests not the secure possession of that power but its tenuousness. Because Juliet is embraced by many apparently honorable aristocrats— Harleigh, Lady Aurora Granville, and Lord Melbury (the latter two will be revealed as her half-siblings)—Mrs. Maple feels especially threatened. If the gentry accept a nameless "adventurer" with apparent respect, then the world that provides Mrs. Maple with her social identity and sense of superiority threatens to collapse. In a similar fashion, Mrs. Ireton reacts to Juliet's disobedience with fear and anger: "for you are a lady, no doubt! every body is a lady, now!" (*W*, 535). If women's class distinctions are blurred, then it becomes more obvious that they are all equally oppressed in an overwhelmingly patriarchal culture; Mrs. Maple and Mrs. Ireton envision a permanent loss of power and prestige.

"Ireton" is a fitting name for Juliet's female tormentor, for her incessant anger manifests her frustration at her inability to wield any lasting authority in her immediate circle. When Juliet tries to leave the room, Mrs. Ireton's indignant reaction testifies to her lack of significant power:

> Having constrained herself to hear thus much, Juliet conceived that the duty even of her humble station could require no more; she made, therefore, a slight reverence, with intention to withdraw. But Mrs. Ireton, offended, cried, "Whither may you be going, Ma'am?—And pray, Ma'am,—if I may take the liberty to ask such a question,—who told you to go?—Was it I?—Did any body hear me?—Did you, Lady Arramede?—or you, Miss Brinville?—or only Miss Ellis herself? For, to be sure I must have done it: I take that for granted: she would not, certainly, think of going without leave, after I have sent for her.". . . Sarcasms so witty, uttered by a lady at an assembly in her own house, could not fail of being received with applause; and Mrs. Ireton, looking around her triumphantly, regarded the disconcerted Juliet as a completely vanquished vassal. (*W*, 513)

The term "vassal" here alludes to the social relations of a feudal order. Certainly Juliet's role is that of a "vassal," if only because her extreme financial dependence leads Mrs. Ireton to demand the fealty and homage associated with this abject position; Mrs. Ireton expects Juliet to enact the ritual marks of allegiance and obedience. But the irony here is entailed in Mrs. Ireton's inflated sense of power; she is merely "a lady at an assembly in her own house." Her power is not derived from political might but from "[s]arcasms" or public displays of rudeness. Burney underscores the fact that women's desire to gain access to male-dominated political power is in the end solely a self-destructive wish. They would acquire little of men's tangible power—that Mrs. Ireton is nostalgically fixated on the authority associated with a lost feudal world underlines this fact—but they do internalize the tendency to exploit and abuse other women. Mrs. Ireton can only wield power in her own home in front of an audience of other similarly situated women. Moreover, her victims are only those weaker than she, namely, slaves and destitute servants.

What is most striking about Mrs. Ireton's and Mrs. Maple's absurd vision of themselves as "feudal" authorities is that they expect Juliet to uphold her end of this social contract but flatly refuse to perform the obligations incumbent upon them. I have shown that acts of charity often ease public hostility and correct social inequalities in Burney's novels. Juliet's female oppressors, however, are conspicuous for their lack of compassion and their suspicion of the charitable impulse. Mrs. Maple fears that granting Juliet a temporary asylum was a grave mistake: "[S]he could only quiet her conscience, for having been accessary, though so unintentionally, to procuring this favour and popularity for such an adventurer, by devoutly resolving, that no entreaties, and no representation, should ever in future, dupe her out of her own good sense, into other people's fantastical conceits of charity" (*W,* 212). Unlike Cecilia, who extols charity and uses her money and power to help women and the impoverished, Mrs. Maple and her fellow gentlewomen refuse to offer Juliet adequate help. In Mrs. Maple we are faced with a wealthy gentlewoman who views the obligation of charity as "fantastical," as a mere capricious whim. Not only does Mrs. Maple reject the obligations proper to her upper-class status, but she repudiates as well the more modernized version of charity as a mark of sensibility, a quality that supposedly crosses status boundaries. As one character argues, women's relationships should be based on gender rather than class or status identification: "[Y]et she [Juliet] is, at this time, without friends, support, or asylum: in such a situation, thus young and helpless, and thus irreproachably conducting herself, who is the female—what is her age, what her rank, that ought not to assist and try to preserve so distressed a young person from evil?" (*W,* 128). Here Harleigh seems to invoke the duties of the new "domestic" woman rather than the principles associated with older, more aristocratic notions of femaleness.

What specific forms does women's violence take in *The Wanderer?* While men can physically overpower Burney's heroines, women use verbal harassment to subdue and embarrass them. As Thomas Edwards argues, "Embarrassment conscripts its victim into a scene without allowing a choice of role; it is a blocking or barring of the freedom we claim for our selfhood . . . all social contact threatens embarrassment to those who are truly powerless."[9] Edwards's comments are particularly useful here: all social occasions are threatening for Juliet because they can jeopardize her simultaneous need to be protected and yet also to conceal her identity. She cannot reveal her name, for that disclosure would imperil the bishop's life, and yet she requires these women to protect her from public violence. In order to shield herself from the sexual and physical threats faced by a female wanderer, Juliet must submit to the loss of self entailed in these bitter women's ritualized social shaming. Juliet's choice is an untenable one, between the public, physical assaults of men and the more domestic, verbal violations of women.

As a form of violation, embarrassment depends upon perceived success. Mrs. Ireton must witness the signs of Juliet's distress in order to feel completely victorious. Here, as in *Camilla*, we see how the act of observation (i.e., the patriarchal gaze) can indeed function as a means of social control: Juliet seems no more to these women than an inert object of scientific study. In this case, her body is forced to display signs of its dependence and pain: "Juliet endeavoured to sit tranquil, and seem unconcerned; but her fingers were in continual motion; her eyes, meaning to look no where, looked every where; and Mrs. Ireton had the gratification to perceive, that, however she struggled for indifference, she was fully sensible of the awkwardness of her situation" (*W,* 516). If Juliet were openly to resist Mrs. Ireton, then their apparent status differences would collapse; indeed, it is Mrs. Ireton's ability to torment Juliet that sustains the distinctions between them.

The effects of such social abuse are discernibly similar to those experienced by a Burney heroine when she is physically or sexually threatened. She must find immediate protection: "'Ought I . . . to submit to treatment so mortifying? Are there no boundaries . . . ?' . . . Juliet could endure no more. The most urgent distress seemed light and immaterial, when balanced against submission to treatment so injurious. She walked, therefore, straight forward to the castle, for shelter, immediate shelter, from this insupportable attack. . . ." (*W,* 511, 550). Burney encourages her readers to see women like Mrs. Maple and Mrs. Ireton as violent persecutors, for they refuse to offer Juliet a surrogate familial home. Mrs. Maple, for example, threatens to turn Juliet out "in the dead of night"; Juliet labels such behavior "[v]iolence so inhuman" (*W,* 199). The phrase "in the dead of night" recalls Juliet's midnight escape from Robespierre's Terror (*W,* 11). If only obliquely, Mrs. Maple is linked with larger social violence and vicious tyranny.

In a similar fashion, we see how Mrs. Ireton upholds the principles of patrilineage and colonialism, in short, institutions that victimize the other. During her first visit to Mrs. Ireton's, Juliet witnesses a boy tormenting a small dog, an orphan waiting vainly for promised charity, and a slave, Mrs. Ireton's "most submissive" and thus favorite servant, "trembling" in fear of his mistress's rage (*W,* 479). Described by Juliet as wielding a "general tyranny," Mrs. Ireton takes obvious pleasure in threatening to return her slave to his native land to face brutal punishment: "'I will have you shipped back to the West Indies. And there, that your joy may be complete, I shall issue orders that you may be striped till you jump, and that you may jump,—you little black imp!—between every stripe!' . . . He dropt upon his knees to implore forgiveness; but he was peremptorily ordered to depart, with an assurance that he should keep up his fine spirits upon bread and water for a fortnight" (*W,* 482). Similar to a sadistic plantation mistress,[10] Mrs. Ireton smugly assumes that life with her would be more preferable to her slave than to return to his native West Indies. That the Somerset case of 1772 had made such a deportation illegal, moreover, offers us a tantalizing reading of Mrs. Ireton's position.[11] While it would be easy to presume that Burney is being careless with her historical facts here, it is more tempting to suggest that she is exposing Mrs. Ireton's empty illusions of power: the very foundations of her social identity (in this case, as an omnipotent slave owner) are slipping away, and it would be more to her benefit to embrace the virtues of charity and feminine benevolence that offer Burney's heroines their most significant amount of power and influence.[12]

As the watchful guardian of her "eldest brother's eldest son" (*W*, 495), Mrs. Ireton explicitly supports primogeniture as well. This little boy mimics an older rake by harassing and even hitting Juliet during her stay as Mrs. Ireton's paid companion (*W*, 498, 521, 536–37). Just as Mrs. Ireton revels in the thought of whipping her black servant, little Loddard, who is "evidently too wanton to find pleasure but in mischief" (*W*, 478–79), releases his anger on all those around him: "[N]o compliance, no luxury, no diversion could afford him more than momentary pleasure; while his passions were become also ungovernable, that, upon every contrariety or disappointment, he vented his rage, to the utmost extent of his force, upon whomsoever, or whatsoever, animate or inanimate, he could reach" (*W*, 494). As a kind of colonialist and defender of primogeniture—in other words, a surrogate for male interests[13]—Mrs. Ireton refuses to help Juliet gain her autonomy; rather, she subjects her to complete dependence. In fact, one character exclaims that Juliet is no more than a mere commodity: "What can rich people be thinking of . . . buying their fellow-creatures' liberty of speech and thought!" (*W*, 524).

It is obvious that Juliet is linked in these sections with the colonial other. As Orlando Patterson has argued, the archetypal slave was "stripped of his natal kinship ties, and to be so deprived in any kin-based society was to be socially killed."[14] By refusing her the use of the "Granville" name and legacy, Juliet's paternal family has stripped her of her birthright. Women's status in a patrilineal society is thus especially precarious, since their fathers have the power to annihilate them socially—to make them aliens in a male-dominated, kin-based society.[15] On the other hand, as Doody notes, Juliet's pseudonym "Ellis" contains the French pronoun for "she";[16] thus as "Ellis," Juliet is struggling not only to maintain but also to announce her essential, independent female identity and her right to exist in the face of the community's rejection. In other words, by using "Ellis" instead of her given name, Juliet is claiming possession of herself outside of all male-dominated familial structures. With no apparent husband or father, she threatens the principles of a kinship system that these women have internalized, and she is determined to survive even as they try to expel her from their society.[17] To those who attempt to uphold the status quo, Ellis/Juliet is connected with "class instability, natives, the colonized, and the potentially threatening, unassimilable other."[18] As one aristocrat exclaims in frustration, Juliet's namelessness makes her "[i]ndefinable, unconquerable, [and] unfathomable" (*W*, 629).

Juliet's parallel with the slave is apparent in her first appearance in the novel: when she boards the boat destined for England, her fellow passengers see "hands and arms of so dark a colour, that they might rather be styled black than brown" (*W*, 19). Consequently, they assume that she is either from the West Indies or from "somewhere off the coast of Africa" (*W*, 19). Not only is she presumably of African or West Indian descent, but she appears with her face partly bandaged as well (*W*, 20). Hers are the visible marks of servitude and victimization. As we might expect, her appearance as an adventurer is belied by her unmistakable noble characteristics. To the hero, her manners and language mark her as a proper gentlewoman (*W*, 75). And even Mrs. Ireton is astounded when she sees the metamorphosis of the "black insect" (*W*, 27): "a skin changed from a tint nearly black, to the brightest, whitest, and most dazzling fairness" (*W*, 43). Despite the fact that Burney evokes the romance trope of disguised nobility here,[19] she also explores how a dependent woman faces some of the same injustices as slaves and working-class laborers. Juliet's blackness not only links her with the colonial other but also with those classes from whom the aristocracy is differentiated by the whiteness of their skin. Of course, in some ways Burney is glossing over the problem of racial and social injustice in order to focus particularly on women's oppression. By borrowing from the discourse of colonial slavery, Burney is implicitly suggesting that women's abject condition is more significant than the lives of the colonized; after all, Juliet is transformed from "the blackest, dirtiest, raggedest wretch . . . into an amazing beauty," and thus she can escape her subjugation (*W*, 43). In the case of Mrs. Ireton, what is critiqued is her treatment of her slave—her moral lapse—rather than his lack of freedom.[20] Nonetheless, Juliet's linkage with the slave underscores the fact that both the domestic oppression of women and the exploitation and violence of slavery help maintain male political and economic power. *The Wanderer* quite strongly undermines the institution of paternalism with the visible presence of slaves and tormented servants. Rather than doling out charity, Mrs. Ireton—the closest figure to a paternalistic benefactor—sadistically punishes her social inferiors.

## II

In her search for alternatives to male-dominated forms of protection, Burney investigates a species of "social replacement" that she frequently refers to as "self-dependence" (*W,* 220, 275, 332). In *The Wanderer,* she advances the possibility that women can create a form of self-protection through their own industry. An important consequence of this formulation is that Burney reframes her narrative representation of both the bourgeoisie and women's communities. True, as they were in *Evelina, Cecilia,* and *Camilla,* parvenus are still portrayed as rude, garrulous, and overly obsessed with social assimilation; but in *The Wanderer* they prove to be potential models for Juliet in her struggle to be self-supportive. Female self-protection would develop out of the progressive premise that industry and self-improvement signal worth and maintain the regard for reputation that had previously been linked to elevated birth. Juliet's bid for self-dependence, however, fails for two manifest reasons: the failure of a female community to rally around her attempts to achieve sovereignty, and the refusal of a patriarchal culture to accept the threatening prospect of a single, working woman who does not fulfill the domestic ideal.

At the end of Juliet's story, when she is married to the aristocrat Harleigh, the narrator reflects on her heroine's difficulties, and in doing so she invokes the name of perhaps the most famous progressive literary hero of the century. She refers to Juliet as "a being who had been cast upon herself; a female Robinson Crusoe, as unaided and unprotected, though in the midst of the world, as that imaginary hero in his uninhabited island; and reduced either to sink, through inanition, to nonentity, or to be rescued from famine and death by such resources as she could find, independently, in herself" (*W,* 873). Unlike Crusoe, however, Juliet is not able to conquer her immediate social world or successfully achieve economic autonomy. Most obviously, Juliet does not have a slave at her disposal to help her attain her ambitious goals; as we have seen, Juliet is in fact linked to the colonial other in the treatment she receives from her female employers. Burney's engagement with Defoe's novel is not solely, as Doody reasons, a simple satiric reference to England's status as a desert island for the woman who strives to make a living;[21] rather, more substantially, Burney brings into high relief the ironic fact that Crusoe does not merely "make a living": he establishes a monarchy.[22] The social, legal, and economic avenues open to him are limitless. Juliet soon discovers that women find the progressive path blocked with impervious obstacles: "[H]ow insufficient, is a Female to herself! How utterly dependent upon situation—connexions—circumstance! how nameless, how for ever fresh-springing are her DIFFICULTIES, when she would owe her existence to her own exertions!" (*W,* 275). Juliet's protean and mysterious identity is a felicitous introduction to the theme of self-dependence; she is a nobody who must create herself by her own efforts.[23] She must find a home, friends, income, and protection until she can assume her real identity.

Juliet repeatedly comes up against the fact that women have great difficulty finding legitimate and satisfying work to meet their basic economic needs, and their ignorance of business procedures particularly hurts them at a time of bustling capitalist activity.[24] When Juliet attempts to earn her subsistence with her musical talents by teaching and performing, for example, her patroness, the genteel Miss Arbe, is determined to turn a "profit" by means of Juliet's musical talents (*W,* 208). Miss Arbe gathers students for Juliet, purchases a harp, and arranges benefit concerts, all in the hope of helping Juliet earn her living. But Miss Arbe's expensive schemes land Juliet in debt; in addition, Juliet's wealthy students refuse to pay their bills (*W,* 297–305). In the end, Miss Arbe proves only to be an "unprotecting patroness" (*W,* 319). One of Juliet's sole supporters, the radical Giles Arbe, scolds both Juliet's recalcitrant students and her indolent audience: "'. . . I think you should neither eat your meat, nor drink your beer, nor sit upon your chairs, nor wear your clothes, till you have rewarded the industrious people who provide them. Till then, in my mind, every body should bear to be hungry, and dry, and tired, and ragged!'" (*W,* 324).[25] Here we see how laboring work violates and debilitates the body. In their selfish use of Juliet's talents, these women are oblivious to her physical suffering. When she has a cold and cannot perform, they mock her weakness. Thereafter, she "sedulously" guards her body but soon grows "weaker" from both a lack of exercise and the excessive warmth of her closed apartment. Eventually, she is vulnerable to mental ills as well: "[S]he was shaken by every sound, and menaced with becoming a victim to all the tremors, and all the languors of nervous disorders" (*W,* 320–21). By attempting to please her female audience, she internalizes her external objectification as a performer. Only through self-violation can the servant seemingly fulfill her role. Hence laboring work, and in this case women's work in particular, is another form of cruelty. By limiting women to these physically and emotionally taxing jobs, their society finds a way to continue to control and abuse them.

Burney exposes the fact that because women are rendered weak and dependent by an aristocratic patriarchal culture, they become indifferent to others' pain; they embrace a conception of femaleness that codifies this callousness. Giles Arbe rails against this very fact when he argues that the musician—here allied with the working classes—often performs while in pain: "He sings, perhaps, when he may be ready to cry; he plays upon those harps and fiddles, when he is half dying with hunger. . . . And all this, to gain himself a hard and fatiguing maintenance, in amusing your dainty idleness, and insufficiency to yourselves" (*W,* 325). Not only are gentlewomen blinded to the difficulties of the poor, especially impoverished women, but their "idleness" and general "insufficiency" to themselves prevents them from developing the ability to take care of and protect themselves and others. They have internalized those aristocratic vices—indolence, intemperance, and privilege—that paradoxically sustain their oppression. They are especially overcome by an intellectual ennui.[26] Mrs. Ireton's summer home is filled with empty diversions—billiard tables, needlework, and chessboards—that bore and thus enrage her (*W,* 496–97). Because of this ceaseless tedium, they strike out at those women whom they consider to be their social inferiors. As Juliet sarcastically remarks, Mrs. Ireton needs no "lessons in the art of *ingeniously tormenting*" (*W,* 486).[27] The word "art" here is significant, for it seems tacitly to link Mrs. Ireton's harassment with the other hollow amusements that fill her time. Her brand of violence is as ritualized and predictable as a game of billiards.[28] The shortage of meaningful work and education for eighteenth-century women has not only forced Juliet to take a degrading position as Mrs. Ireton's "humble companion"[29] but also provoked the anger and frustration of the indolent women who abuse her. Thus these wealthy women are both victims and oppressors. One of the far-ranging implications of Burney's argument includes the notion that as long as women are unable to live on their own, they will have to rely on older, male-dominated forms of protection at the very moment that this means of safety is weakening and disappearing. Some of the violence against women, Burney suggests, will only cease when women have greater control over their lives.

In these episodes, we see how a new feminist discourse provides Burney with the language with which to explain and explore the motives behind women's violence against other women. Wollstonecraft, for example, argues that women's learned dependence makes them passive and weak. Here we see how Burney identifies this kind of passive weakness as one of the reasons why women are unable to respond sympathetically to each other and to unite in a common effort to improve their situation. Wollstonecraft complains that "riches and inherited honours" prove destructive to women, since unlike their male counterparts, upper-class women have no active outlet as soldiers or statesmen.[30] But she also argues that genteel women are in a position similar to that of aristocratic males in that they have certain "sexual privileges" granted them by virtue of their birth, and these "privileges" hinder them from "works of supererogation," works that would necessarily improve their status as "rational" and productive citizens.[31] We certainly hear Wollstonecraft's voice in the character of Elinor Joddrel (to whom I will return), Burney's revolutionary feminist, who argues that through their oppressive laws, men have rendered women "insignificant" (*W,* 399). Burney's Mrs. Maple, Mrs. Ireton, and Mrs. Howel exemplify the type of women that Wollstonecraft and Elinor criticize—women who have been taught to depend on men, uphold their social vision, and support the institutions of the status quo.

Because of her realization that the progressive path might offer opportunities for women, Burney seems more tolerant of the coarse behavior she has habitually associated with the middle and lower classes in her novels. Juliet gradually learns that she needs parvenus as much as she does her genteel female protectors. The fine discriminations of status begin to lose their luster for Juliet. The progressive belief that pride and honor rest in virtuous effort rather than in blood informs her attempt to gain economic and social autonomy: ". . . Ellis, who had no pride to support her present undertaking, save the virtuous and right pride of owing independence to her own industry, as readily accepted a proferred [*sic*] scholar from the daughter of a common tradesman, as she had accepted the daughter of an Earl. . . ." (*W,* 238). These tradespeople, furthermore, prove to be the "best paymasters" (*W,* 266). Juliet's friend, Gabriella, a member of an old aristocratic French family, who has had to seek asylum from the revolution, articulates this general critique of aristocratic ideology:

> Alas! whence I come, all that are greatest, most ancient, and most noble, have learnt, that self-exertion alone mark [*sic*] nobility of soul; and that self-dependence can only sustain honour in adversity. . . . Ah, Sir, the French Revolution has opened our eyes to a species of equality more rational, because more feasible, than that based on lands or rank; an equality not alone of mental sufferings, but of manual exertions. (*W,* 639)[32]

In the course of her novelistic career, Burney has gradually grown less skeptical of the possibility of women gaining protection, if not independence, from the rise of progressive ideology and practice. The revolution forces the aristocracy to adopt certain progressive notions if it hopes to sustain any of its power. And Juliet does indeed come to respect the middle and working classes; she appreciates the situation of working women in particular: she is "conscious that a dearth of useful resources, was a principal cause, in adversity, of FEMALE DIFFICULTIES" (*W,* 693).

Not only are women blocked from taking advantage of a whole range of employment opportunities, but when Juliet and Gabriella attempt to establish their own business, they discover that they lack the primary requisite for such an ambitious undertaking: sufficient capital (*W,* 403). Once again, Juliet and Gabriella must accept the "continual and vexatious delays of payment," since their genteel customers have "never known distress" (*W,* 404). Juliet and Gabriella are simply unable to withstand the caprices and power of the "insolent, vain, unfeeling buyer" (*W,* 428). In addition, the unethical subtleties of the "wary shopkeeper's code," of which Juliet is wholly ignorant, prevents her from holding her own with the tradespeople with whom she is forced to do business. That is, not understanding that one must set "an imaginary value" for "whatever is in vogue, in order to repair the losses incurred from the failure of obtaining the intrinsic worth of what is old-fashioned" (*W,* 623), Juliet is the victim of what many of Burney's contemporaries saw as the mysterious and hazardous code of exchange value.[33] In these sections of the novel, Burney urges her read-ers to see that women need to learn the procedures of the new capitalist system so that they might "owe [their] existence to [their] own exertions" (*W*, 275). While Juliet clearly laments the loss of a system that valued the "intrinsic" worth of property and goods, her notion that this ideology is "old-fashioned" paves the way for a more willing, even if only necessary, acceptance of a new capitalist order.

How does Burney's detailed and at times sympathetic exploration of progressive and capitalist developments affect her narrative representation of violence and protection? Evelina had often chosen to accept the dubious "pro-tection" of Sir Clement Willoughby rather than subject herself to the public embarrassment of being seen with Mme. Duval and the Branghtons. In a scene that recalls Evelina's escape from her relatives at the opera into the menacing confines of Sir Clement's carriage, Juliet is abducted by Sir Lyell Sycamore. Under the ruse of being called to a female friend's house, Juliet finds herself trapped in a moving carriage, pursued by an apparent highwayman. Suddenly, Sir Lyell, the mastermind behind this deception, jumps into the carriage and his exchange with Juliet echoes that of Evelina's with Sir Clement: "Quit the chaise, Sir Lyell . . . instantly, or you will compel me to claim protection from those two men! 'Protection? you pretty little vixen! . . . who should protect you like your own adorer?'" (*W*, 458). Like Evelina, Juliet tries desperately to spring from the moving carriage; the threat of rape, moreover, is palpable in this pas-sage (*W*, 457–60). But in an important reversal of Burney's first rendering of this scene, the heroine chooses the protection of a parvenu; Mr. Tedman pro-vides "immediate safety" (*W*, 460). And, in fact, Sir Lyell's discourse in some ways proves to be more offensive and glib:

> Sir Lyell looked on, visibly provoked; and when they were driving away, called out, in a tone between derision and indignation, "Bravo, Mr. Tedman! You are still, I see, the happy man!" . . . Mr Tedman angrily muttered, "The quality always allows themselves to say any thing!" (*W*, 461)[34]

If only tentatively, Burney explores the possibility that bourgeois authority is a feasible alternative to exclusive aristocratic rule. While the Branghtons were obviously absent from Evelina's retirement with Orville to Berry Hill, Mr. Tedman is noticeably present at the conclusion of Burney's final novel. He is invited to the aristocratic seat, Harleigh Hall, "where, with no small pride, he received thanks for the first liberality he had ever prevailed with himself to practice" (*W*, 871–72). He is still the object of Burney's social satire—his chari-table feelings are not instinctual—but his willingness both to protect Juliet and provide her with much-needed money reforms his crude exterior and supports the hypothesis that bourgeois and aristocratic authority must reach something like a rapprochement to create the kind of protective and compassionate society Burney envisions.

## III

Up to this point, I have tried to suggest that Juliet is vulnerable to violence and economic distress in large part because of genteel women's attempt to uphold the standards of a hierarchical society that would of necessity reject a nameless female wanderer. At the same time, Juliet is prevented from taking the same progressive routes to economic success and autoresponsibility as her male counterparts. Both of these social problems were the insistent concerns of contemporary feminists. In *The Wanderer*, Burney creates a bold, outspoken figure, Elinor Joddrel, both to articulate the most radical notions of contemporary feminist and revolutionary thought and to illustrate what she fears are the most hazardous repercussions of this potentially anarchic agenda. In Elinor we see a woman who repudiates all of the time-honored, established institutions, yet at the same time will try to kill herself because of her unrequited love for the aristocrat, Albert Harleigh. In many ways, Elinor contains all of the complexities of Burney's experimentation with the notion of female independence, most central of which is the fear that women's efforts to achieve self-protection and develop a new social identity can lead to madness, violence, and even death.

Like *Camilla*'s Mrs. Arlbery, Elinor assails the rigorous code of manners that is at the very core of a new bourgeois patriarchy. Not only does she see manners as a code of behavior that requires an uncompromising self-scrutiny and self-repression. She also views the suspicion of women's public appearances enjoined in the new domestic ideology as a hindrance to their desire for self-reliance. It is this new cultural construction of the domestic woman that she identifies as Juliet's greatest impediment. Early in the novel, Juliet displays genuine talent as an actress and as a musician (*W*, 74–75, 94), and Elinor believes that she should take full advantage of her natural abilities in order to support herself. But Juliet dreads such public exposure. As Harleigh has warned her, echoing *Camilla*'s Edgar Mandlebert, her public performance imperils her as-yet unacknowledged family (i.e., his) and her value as a future wife and mother: "If, then, there be any family that you quit, yet that you may yourself desire should one day reclaim you; and if there be any family—leave mine alone!—to which you may hereafter be allied, and that you may wish should appreciate, should revere you . . . for such let me plead! Wound not the customs of their ancestors, the received notions of the world, the hitherto acknowledged boundaries of elegant life!" (*W*, 343). It is this domesticating idealization of women that Elinor disdains because it obviates their attempts to attain economic autonomy: "Oh woman! poor, subdued woman! thou art as dependant, mentally, upon the arbitrary customs of man, as man is, corporally, upon the established laws of his country! . . . And you, Ellis, you . . . endowed with every power to set prejudice at defiance, and to shew and teach the world, that woman and man are fellow-creatures, you, too, are coward enough to bow down, unresisting, to this thraldom?" (*W*, 399). The customs and manners enjoined in bourgeois patriarchy are tantamount to "established laws." Needless to say, Elinor and Harleigh are articulating two widely opposed ideologies here: Harleigh's "acknowledged boundaries of elegant life" quite obviously represent the strict confines of a hierarchical society. He is tacitly suggesting that if Juliet should perform—that is, work and attain independence—the larger social ordering (i.e., the genteel family) would be undermined. But it is just this effect that Elinor hopes for when she exhorts Juliet to break the chains of this social and familial "thraldom."

It is hard not to hear the influence of Wollstonecraft in Elinor's impassioned plea to Juliet to break the fetters of dependence. In *A Vindication of the Rights of Woman*, Wollstonecraft writes that all women "want to be ladies. Which is simply to have nothing to do, but listlessly to go they scarcely care where, for they cannot tell what."[35] In other words, Wollstonecraft, like Elinor, is incensed at the fact that women are taught to be dependent on men and, hence, never become rational, productive members of society: "Taught from their infancy that beauty is woman's sceptre, the mind shapes itself to the body, and, roaming round its gilt cage, only seeks to adorn its prison."[36] Both Wollstonecraft and Elinor see women confined in a debilitating "prison" or "thraldom." But at the same time, in the end Wollstonecraft, as Mitzi Myers has argued, settles mainly for a feminized bourgeois ethic that focuses primarily on women's potential empowerment in the domestic sphere;[37] they can be, if given the chance, "more observant daughters . . . more faithful wives, more reasonable mothers."[38] Here we see Burney depart from Wollstonecraft, if only because Elinor pleads with Juliet to take greater chances in the public sphere and not simply to hope for significant autonomy in the domestic realm.

Elinor represents the contradictory extremes we have seen entailed in Burney's various representations of women's communities. Elinor recognizes and encourages Juliet's evident abilities to challenge the "thraldom" of patriarchal attitudes and values, yet she stops short of providing real aid; in fact, she is the one who suggests the job as a humble companion (*W*, 400). Janet Todd expresses disappointment over the fact that Burney did not explore more fully and accept more willingly the possibilities inherent in the two women's friendship.[39] But Todd misses Burney's point that this relationship cannot flourish because of Elinor's selfishness, which is born of her own secure economic position; Elinor is oblivious to the humble companion's victimization. Thus she does not fully reject all of the assumptions entailed in her aristocratic rank.

As Juliet muses, moreover, Elinor is powerless to help because she refuses to pursue her ideas within the limits of the prevailing structures of society: "Ah, why, to intellects so strong, a heart so liberal, a temper so gay, is there not joined a better portion of judgment, a larger one of diffidence, a sense of feminine propriety, and a mind rectified by religion,—not abandoned, uncontrolled, to imagination?" (W, 401). Here is strong evidence of Burney's genuinely contradictory attitude towards the use of revolutionary tenets to help alter women's defenseless and dependent position. On the one hand, Burney is certainly suspicious of—to use a term of Wollstonecraft's—"blind propriety" in women, for it hinders, as we have seen with Juliet's female guardians, their chance to express themselves in rational thought and action.[40] On the other hand, Burney is equally frightened by the specter of a total lack of "female propriety" that seems to her to be an inevitable trait of the revolutionary feminist. So while even the more cautious Harleigh notes that change is eventually necessary, he duly advises that restraint is the only means of effective reform: "[T]he general laws of established society" must be "ameliorated, changed, or reformed, by experience, wisely reflecting upon the past," for they can never be "wholly reversed, without risking a rebound that simply restores them to their original condition" (W, 206–7). Hence the very revolutionary steps that promise women's greater liberation might paradoxically result in a reimposition of the status quo, the continued abject dependence of women.[41]

We see this paradox most vividly in Elinor. Her outspoken refusal to adhere to the principles of feminine propriety is explicitly tied to her self-destructive impulses. If a too rigorous attention to a code of manners entails violations associated with the male gaze and its self-mutilating internalization, then a blind disregard of these social strictures threatens to dismantle both external and internal forms of protection. Because Elinor spurns the inveterate codes of "proper" female behavior, she loses all sense of boundaries. As we have seen, much of the violence in Burney's novels is closely associated with the breakdown or deliberate violation of personal and social boundaries. In *The Wanderer*, all forms of violence are implicitly or explicitly linked to the anarchy of the revolution. Here we see how suicide mirrors the revolutionary impulse toward utter chaos. While Elinor can speak eloquently and forcefully for women's freedom—"How tenacious a tyrant is custom. . . . We are slaves to its laws and its follies, till we forget its usurpation" (W, 174)—she also appears to be a conventional victim of excessive romantic love. To be sure, she ventures to break the "laws" of "custom" by openly declaring her love for Harleigh. However, Burney's readers need only recall Mr. Tyrold's sermon to Camilla about self-censorship

to see the dangers inherent in Elinor's behavior. We see a genuinely contradictory theme in Burney's novels here: the increasingly creative and defiant struggle
for female self-protection is an enterprise that Burney fears is the inescapable
path to self-mutilation or death. For women to find protection from the hostilities of the modern world often requires subjection to institutions that entail
their own violating features; and yet Burney palpably fears that a quick and
total repudiation of traditional structures might place women on a self-destructive path.

Elinor's suicide attempts are a daring public gesture of defiance. Doody
has only tepidly agreed with this formulation: "Yet the female suicidal gesture,
though it seems defiant, original, and liberating, is an obedience to social commands. . . . The customary command for woman is that she be unobtrusive,
slender, and quiet."[42] Doody's comments conflate what are really in fact quite
different female attempts at self-destruction in Burney's novels. Camilla, for
example, does wish for death as a response to the scrupulous passivity required
in the code of manners; and Mrs. Delvile's stroke dramatizes her reaction to
the enactment of aristocratic and patrilineal principles. But Elinor is committing
suicide in the open, not calmly slipping away in private; her act is unblushingly
rebellious. Both the hero of the novel and the social demands that organize this
society require that she not express her love or her atheism. Elinor acts boldly
on her feelings by both openly declaring her love for Harleigh and developing
a plan using Juliet to detect his true feelings. She takes as much pleasure in her
actions as she does in her passion: "My design, as you will find, in making you
[Juliet] speak instead of myself, is a stroke of Machievalian [*sic*] policy. . . ." (*W*,
161). It is not so much her love for him but the way she resists custom that
defines her character; her passion for Harleigh can at times seem like a vehicle
for her revolutionary principles. (In fact, she refuses to adopt her culturally
constructed role in the courtship plot. Harleigh blames her self-mutilating impulses and seemingly irrational behavior on "these fatal new systems" and the
growing disillusionment with religion entailed in the new revolutionary enthu-
siasm [*W*, 184, 191, 204]). In Elinor's characterization, we see Burney's apprehension that an explosive break with the institutions that provide women with
a routinely violating mode of protection may only facilitate a liberation that is
also self-destructive.

One particular episode illustrates well how Elinor's defiance and fierce
independence are wedded to acts of self-annihilation. Juliet is reluctantly performing at a small concert in order to support herself; Elinor deems it a perfect
opportunity to attempt a public suicide, for Harleigh will be in attendance.
Elinor appears dressed as a "deaf and dumb" man while Juliet is making her
entrance: "[A] strange figure, with something foreign in his appearance, twice

crossed before the chariot, with a menacing air, as if purposing to impede her passage. . . ." (*W*, 356). Significantly, it is Elinor's uncontrollable passion for Harleigh, and thus her jealousy of Juliet, that in fact does "impede" Juliet's "passage," her attempts to achieve self-dependence. Appropriately, however, Elinor disguises herself as a man; crossing gender boundaries allows her freedom from the same customs that Harleigh has invoked to castigate Juliet for her public appearance. As a "deaf and dumb" man, moreover, Elinor is able to mock, rather than adhere to, her culture's insistence on women's silence.

During her performance, Juliet suddenly spies a "glitter of steel" in the stranger's hands. When Juliet suddenly realizes that it is Elinor, she immediately faints; Harleigh rushes to her aid. By losing consciousness at a moment of intense fear, Juliet typifies the culturally constructed notion of the female. Elinor's attempted suicide, on the other hand, is an atypical response. Paradoxically, she refuses to be "deaf and dumb"; she uncovers the outspoken woman:

> The large wrapping coat, the half mask, the slouched hat, and embroidered waistcoat, had rapidly been thrown aside, and Elinor appeared in deep mourning; her long hair, wholly unornamented, hanging loosely down her shoulders. Her complexion was wan, her eyes were fierce rather than bright, and her air was wild and menacing. "Oh Harleigh!—adored Harleigh!—" she cried, as he flew to catch her desperate hand;—but he was not in time; for, in uttering his name, she plunged a dagger into her breast. The blood gushed out in torrents, while, with a smile of triumph, and eyes of idolizing love, she dropt into his arms, and clinging round him, feebly articulated, "Here let me end! . . ." (*W*, 359)

Elinor's behavior here underscores the fact that female suicidal behavior is anything but a simple capitulation, as Doody argues, to men's desire that women be "unobtrusive, slender, and quiet." To be sure, Elinor hyperbolically plays the role her society might expect: that of a woman swept up by her emotions, succumbing to the irrational power of romantic love. Indeed, she names herself his "willing martyr."[43] But as Epstein points out, Elinor might also be exaggerating her role in order to "lampoon" her society's conventions and demands.[44] This scene also suggests that a woman's need for the aristocratic lover and protector is inextricably linked with self-mutilation. Her suicide is sexualized as she plunges the knife into her breast at the instant she utters Harleigh's name.[45] Her "idolizing love" brings only death. Elinor, however, is definitely not the object of Burney's scorn here; as Claudia Johnson has shown, many women writers of the period created a "ridiculously caricatured," "freakish feminist" in order to (seemingly) adhere to reactionary ideology.[46] But it is clear that

Elinor is not simply a caricature, for she offers insightful commentary on the precarious position of women at a dangerous and volatile cultural moment. Rather than mocking her, Burney sees Elinor as the victim of historical circumstance.

That Elinor's second suicide attempt takes place on an altar reinforces Burney's contention that the extreme dependence and loss of reason entailed in conventional forms of "romantic" love can easily lead to violence and even self-violation. Elinor's clothing suggests the figure both of the corpse and the bride: "Startled, [Juliet] looked more earnestly, and then clearly perceived, though half hidden behind a monument, a form in white; whose dress appeared to be made in the shape, and of the materials, used for our last mortal covering, a shroud. A veil of the same stuff fell over the face of the figure...." (*W*, 579). Elinor puts a pistol to her temple, but Harleigh manages to prevent her destruction. This scene eerily mirrors the story of Juliet's marriage, when she is forced to wed one of Robespierre's most brutal agents in order to save the life of her affective father—the bishop—who is about to be beheaded. The scaffold and the altar become nearly indistinguishable; here marriage is the product not of love but of violence. When the bishop is standing on the scaffold, a completely horrified Juliet witnesses the executioner display the "ghastly, bleeding head of a victim" (*W*, 743). She stays the execution of the bishop by relinquishing her sovereignty: she is "dragged" to the site (i.e., the altar) of her own "execution" (*W*, 745).

That Elinor is finally unable to kill herself suggests the ways in which she is constricted, despite her best efforts, by the force and power of a resisting culture. She is left in a "state of shame and despair" from her "conscious failure" (*W*, 580, 584). But the point here is not, as Doody contends, that Elinor submits to her society's demands by trying to kill herself. Rather, Burney encourages us to see that Elinor is never allowed the traditional heroic death associated with those literary figures who are wholly committed to their heartfelt principles. As Elinor laments, "I am food, for fools,—when I meant to be food only for worms!" (*W*, 580).[47] She can never fully communicate or convince Harleigh of the relevance of her iconoclastic ideas. After she recovers and is trying to help Juliet gain self-dependence, however, she reveals her shrewd understanding of her society: "If I were poor myself, I would engage to acquire a large fortune, in less than a week, by advertising, at two-pence a head, a sight of the lady that stabbed herself" (*W*, 400). If women are to be public spectacles, then she will learn to profit by selling herself and managing her own objectification.[48] To the end, Elinor insists on challenging and flaunting her culture's most deeply rooted beliefs about women.

## IV

At the outset of this chapter I suggested that *The Wanderer* is a rewriting of *Evelina*. One of the most arresting features of this revision of *Evelina* is that by comparing these two works, we can most effectively see Burney's growing skepticism about the viability of any form of aristocratic rule. In a much more malicious way, John Wilson Croker, in his review of *The Wanderer*, makes this same comparison: "The Wanderer has the identical features of Evelina—but of Evelina grown old; the vivacity, the bloom, the elegance, 'the purple light of love' are vanished; the eyes are there, but they are dim; the cheek, but it is furrowed, the lips, but they are withered."[49] Perhaps Croker is impugning the physically older Burney. But I would also propose that he is contemptuous of *The Wanderer* for the very fact that it deals more openly with radical questions than *Evelina*. There is no way to overlook or conveniently ignore Burney's sharp attack here on traditional ruling structures. As I have shown, *Evelina* is partly shaped by a nostalgic myth of paternalistic care, a myth Burney invoked as a corrective formulation: she offers there a vision of society that might possibly be preserved by feminizing and modernizing the aristocracy. Lord Orville is the embodiment of this largely conservative social replacement for traditional rule. Thirty-six years later in *The Wanderer*, however, deeply and profoundly affected by both the revolution and a developing feminist dialogue, the hope for a modernized aristocracy seems all but gone. While the novel's denouement presents us with another aristocratic couple, it is greatly tempered by the fact that the aristocratic hero has been largely ineffectual in protecting Burney's most beleaguered and molested heroine.

In her final novel, Burney at once parodies "traditional" aristocrats and sharply questions whether a modernized aristocracy has any real serviceability or value in an increasingly violent modern world. First, the "old-style" aristocracy is portrayed in its dotage. Sir Jaspar Herrington, an old, withering bachelor, often proves to be troublesome and even abusive to Juliet. As a bachelor, what he calls an "unnatural character" (*W*, 540), he has failed to sustain his patrilineage; his estate is entailed on his next of kin (*W*, 631). In a last futile effort to preserve his honor and his estate, he proposes to Juliet; the image of the old, doddering aristocrat inflamed by Juliet's youth and vitality conjures up only ridicule (*W*, 634). When Sir Lyell grows increasingly angry over Sir Jaspar's involvement with Juliet, for example, the latter is ready to "parry" Sir Lyell's "broad sword" with his "stoutest of crutches." Sir Lyell declines the challenge and sneers that old men like Sir Jaspar "ought not to meddle with affairs of which they must have lost even the memory" (*W*, 504). The sexual joke, of course, is obvious. But in this tacitly allegorical episode, we see the ways in which the "old-style" aristocracy continues to persist even in the face of its inevitable demise. Sir Jaspar's crutches, for example, are signs of his—and the aristocracy's—growing debility and impotence; and yet they serve as menacing weapons as well. Quite simply, he still has the ability to express his sexual and social authority. In fact, his first intimated proposal is nothing short of frightening: "Confused, and perplexed how to understand him, Juliet was rising . . . but Sir Jaspar fasten[ed] her gown to the grass by his two crutches. . . . Forced either to struggle or remain in her place, she sat still. . . ." (*W,* 546). Ironically, while Sir Jaspar can barely protect Juliet from Sir Lyell's "broad sword," he is still able to molest and unsettle her. This paradox allows Burney to underscore quite effectively how traditional aristocratic "protection" is, in the end, more violent than protective.

Harleigh is the novel's version of a more modernized aristocrat; like Lord Orville, he declares his love for the heroine even before he knows about her aristocratic roots (*W,* 868). His love for the putatively "bastard" heroine in itself entails a critique of traditional aristocratic beliefs. But he, like Sir Jaspar, proves to be an inept protector; he can do very little to help Juliet in her frantic search for sanctuary. Lord Orville demonstrates strength when he seizes control from the intractable Captain Mirvan in the final scene of *Evelina;* he throws the monkey out of the room, thereby ending the captain's successive stream of violent practical jokes. But Harleigh is a mere helpless spectator when Juliet's French husband takes "diabolical delight" in abusing her: "The man roughly gave her a push, seeming to enjoy, with a coarse laugh, the pleasure of driving her on before him" (*W,* 727). Harleigh can only watch helplessly as the working women of the inn shield Juliet from her husband's brutal treatment: "He was then again at his window; where he saw a second chambermaid administering burnt feathers, which had already recovered her from the fainting fit; while the mistress of the house was presenting her with hartshorn and water. . . . But Juliet was saved from his grasp by the landlady; who humanely, upon seeing her almost expiring condition, had entered the carriage, during the dispute, with a viol of sal volatile" (*W,* 733–34). Sir Jaspar is helpless because he is devoid of "strength," while Harleigh lacks "courage" to offer assistance; he will not interfere with what he sees as the legal husband's indisputable right to force his wife to return back with him to Robespierre's France (*W,* 736).

Moreover, Juliet initially finds herself in such desperate straits because her aristocratic father had lacked the "courage" to confess his exogamous union; he suffered from an "unfortunate indecision of character" and was unable to foresee that his refusal to acknowledge his daughter would inevitably lead to her "endless distresses" (*W,* 869). While Harleigh blames these "endless distresses" more on the unanticipated revolution than on the father's flaws, Burney throws into high relief the failure of the aristocratic father. In fact, the patriarch, unlike Sir John Belmont, is dead when the story begins. As opposed to

*Evelina, The Wanderer* offers no redemption for the guilty father. In this way, we see how a long history of aristocratic rule has only served to place Juliet in grave jeopardy: it has never offered her inviolable or even adequate protection.[50]

Given Burney's final disenchantment with all forms of aristocratic rule, the tableau at "Harleigh Hall" that concludes the narrative is noteworthy not for the presence of the aristocratic couple and their son, which seems at this point merely a matter of convention in a Burney novel, but for those friends who are included in the new home. Not only is Mr. Tedman there, Juliet's bourgeois protector, but also Dame Fairfield, a peasant woman who gave Juliet refuge while she was fleeing from her brutal husband in the New Forest (*W,* 722, 871). Once she is married, Juliet is able to exercise her newfound "power" by sending for Dame Fairfield (*W,* 871), using her authority in the domestic household to empower and protect another woman. And many of the poorest cottagers who had aided Juliet in her wanderings are visited "with gifts and praise" (*W,* 872). Significantly, Juliet's three female persecutors—Mrs. Howel, Mrs. Ireton, and Mrs. Maple—are excluded from Harleigh Hall, for they are considered the outsiders of this new community. Women will eventually have to find protection from violence, Burney suggests, in a community that crosses class and gender boundaries. All of Burney's experimental "replacements"—a reformed aristocracy, bourgeois protectors, a community of women, and various forms of self-protection (manners and industry)—are part of the solution. To this end, Burney has used the principles and terms of eighteenth-century social and political conflict—i.e., those of progressive ideology (with its emphasis on affective bonds and manners) and domestic ideology—to explore the best means for restructuring society and women's position in it.[51]

In the social world captured by Burney's novels, these several replacements for traditional aristocratic rule especially depend on affective bonds; even self-protective measures like manners and industrious conduct are subject to the acknowledgment and support of the surrounding community. Sir Jaspar Herrington's explanation of his sister-in-law's (Mrs. Ireton's) cruelty and his relative kindness testifies to the large gap that exists between legal and affective bonds: "She is my sister-in-law, to be sure; but the law, with all its subtleties, has not yet entailed our affections, with our estates, to our relations. . . ." (*W,* 504–5). Juliet's stepsister, Lady Aurora Granville, would "blush to be of the number of those who want documents, certificates, to love and honour you!" (*W,* 554). Honor is less dependent upon the "documents" of birth than it is upon character, manners, and moral rectitude. Affective bonds ideally should replace the legal fictions of aristocratic rule; and in this way, feeling can cross the boundaries of both class and gender.[52] In the end, the institutions of patrilineage and primogeniture are rejected; and yet the replacement of these older systems is inevitably associated with violence and violation. In this fashion, Burney propounds the necessity of liberating women from the violating "protections" of aristocratic rule, but she seems resigned to the fact that change will inevitably involve its own forms of violence.

Not only are aristocratic assumptions like patrilineage undermined by revolutionary principles. Traditional patriarchy itself is also jeopardized by the same rebellious fervor.[53] As I have shown, the father in Burney's novels is a central figure in large part because the heroine is always in some ways separated from her family. In *The Wanderer*, however, not only is the legal patriarch dead; the affective father is powerless. Juliet must endure a forced marriage (though never consummated) and wander England subject to poverty and people's scorn in order to save the Bishop's life. Roles are reversed, and, ironically, the "more than daughter" (*W*, 741) must save and transform the family system in order to benefit from its protective features. The patriarchal guardian is helpless in the face of social hostilities; indeed, the bishop, or holy father, has been stripped of his rank by the revolutionaries (*W*, 616). The documents that finally legitimize Juliet and secure her the protection and social identity she requires (and that prove the mother's honor) are brought to light by Admiral Powel, the lately discovered brother of Juliet's mother (*W*, 839–40). The original documents, in the possession of the affective father, were consumed in the fires of the Revolution (*W*, 646). So it is the maternal and not the paternal inheritance, as it were, that ultimately saves Juliet. The mother's honor, born of integrity rather than status, replaces male protection.

After their marriage, Harleigh and Juliet live in France with the bishop, Gabriella, and Gabriella's mother until "it became necessary to return to their home, to present, upon his birth, a new heir to the enchanted Admiral" (*W*, 871). Unlike Evelina, who finds a home with both Lord Orville and the Reverend Villars, Juliet supplants the affective father with the mother's brother. In this way Burney encourages us to see that patriarchal forms are undergoing reform; she imagines a society less strictly dependent on an unadulterated patrilineal model of the family. In essence, the birth of the heroine's son signals the continuation of the mother's family.

Despite the customary fortuitous denouement, the narrative representation of female protection finds an uneasy final expression. Before Burney pairs her heroine with the proper aristocratic hero, this heroine decries her limited means of physical and emotional protection: "Alas! . . . is it only under the domestic roof,—that roof to me denied!—that woman can know safety, respect, and honour?" (*W*, 666). A contemporary of Burney's argued that the domestic sphere is indeed the safest place for a woman: "The whole world might be at war, and yet not the rumor of it reach the ear of an Englishwoman— . . . and still she might pursue the peaceful occupations of her home; and her natural lord might change his governor at pleasure, and she feel neither change nor hardship."[54] We might hear slight echoes of the Burney of *Evelina* in Laetitia Hawkins's words, but the Burney of *The Wanderer* recognizes that an English-woman not only hears about "war" but is also inevitably affected by it. The answer to Juliet's question, nevertheless, is a reluctant affirmative, for only un-der the "domestic roof," and with an acknowledged social identity, does a Burney heroine find any semblance of safety and respect. To be sure, one of the costs entailed in this domestic safety is a dangerous self-repression, as *Camilla* illus-trates. But Juliet's life outside the "domestic roof" is that of a wanderer, and there is as yet no safety for such a woman: "but she had severely experienced how little fitted to the female character, to female safety, and female propriety, was this hazardous plan of lonely wandering" (*W,* 671).

Yet the figure of the wanderer may prove to be an appropriate metaphor for what is most hopeful in Burney's social vision. Even if women's lives are filled with innumerable difficulties, they still have the inner strength to perse-vere:

> Yet even DIFFICULTIES such as these are not insurmountable, where mental courage, operating through patience, prudence, and principle, supply physi-cal force, combat disappointment and keep the untamed spirits superiour to failure, and ever alive to hope. (*W,* 873)

Four Burney heroines make an entrance into the world ostensibly to find the proper husband, but the countless episodes of physical and psychological vio-lence that punctuate Burney's novels tell us that their story is about much more than this. Early in her final novel, Burney poses the following suggestive ques-tion: "What is woman unprotected?" (*W,* 344). The four novels that span thirty-six years tell us that this "unprotected" woman's story is about the painful struggle to find, define, and inhabit a new social identity that may conform successfully to the radically altered and often violent landscape of the modern world.

# Notes

## INTRODUCTION. SOCIAL TRANSFORMATIONS

1. Quoted in *The Journals and Letters of Fanny Burney, 1791–1840*, ed. Joyce Hemlow (Oxford: Clarendon Press, 1972–84), 7:234 n. 3.

2. Walter Allen, for example, is chagrined by Captain Mirvan's stunts and the old women's race in *Evelina*. See his *The English Novel: A Short Critical History* (New York: E. P. Dutton, 1954), 98. J. M. S. Tomkins complains that some of these scenes are "distressing to read"; consequently, Burney "offends" the reader's sensibilities. See *The Popular Novel in England, 1770–1800* (London: Constable & Co., 1932), 134–35. Such assumptions persist even today: in his mostly favorable review of Julia Epstein's recent work on Burney, John Richetti honestly admits that before reading Epstein's work, he had "dismissed" these scenes of violence as "simply a lack of narrative control and an eighteenth-century sensibility rougher than our own." In his candor about his "limitations" as a reader, however, Richetti acknowledges the importance of the feminist reappraisals of Burney's work. See "Recent Studies in the Restoration and Eighteenth Century," *Studies in English Literature* 30, no. 3 (summer 1990): 538.

3. Margaret Anne Doody, *Frances Burney: The Life in the Works* (New Brunswick, N.J.: Rutgers University Press, 1988).

4. Julia Epstein, *The Iron Pen: Frances Burney and the Politics of Women's Writing* (Madison: University of Wisconsin Press, 1989), 4.

5. Ibid., 7.

6. Other readings that I have found beneficial include Kristina Straub, *Divided Fictions: Fanny Burney and Feminine Strategy* (Lexington: University of Kentucky Press, 1987); Patricia Spacks, "Dynamics of Fear: Fanny Burney," in *Imagining a Self: Autobiography and Novel in Eighteenth-Century England* (Cambridge: Harvard University Press, 1976), 158–92; idem, *The Female Imagination* (New York: Alfred A. Knopf, 1975); Susan Staves, "*Evelina*, or Female Difficulties," *Modern Philology* 73 (1976): 368–81; and Judith Lowder Newton, *Women, Power, and Subversion: Social Strategies in British Fiction, 1770–1860* (Athens: University of Georgia Press, 1981), 23–54. Both Staves and Newton recognize the social forces at work in these episodes of violence, but neither critic acknowledges the complexity of this social context. Newton, for example, claims that the men of the lower orders "lack social and political consequence," and therefore Evelina can dismiss them (*Women, Power, and Subversion*, 47).

139

Further, Newton criticizes Burney for being an apologist for the rule of the landed gentry; she argues that Burney idealizes marriage as the only "lasting" protection open to women. I will argue that Burney's attitude toward the aristocratic patriarchal order is more ambivalent and historically nuanced than Newton's argument allows.

7. Michael McKeon eloquently observes that "the history of male dominance may be understood to entail a general continuity complicated by specific and divergent discontinuities." Too often, he argues, the category of "patriarchy" has been used ahistorically in an attempt to explain "an implausibly universal human nature." See "Historicizing Patriarchy: The Emergence of Gender Difference in England, 1660–1760," *Eighteenth-Century Studies* 28, no. 3 (1995): 295.

8. For historical accounts of the legal status of married women, see Susan Moller Okin, "Patriarchy and Married Women's Property in England: Questions on Some Current Views," *Eighteenth-Century Studies* 17, no. 2 (1983/1984): 121–38. Amy Louise Erickson, *Women and Property in Early Modern England* (New York: Routledge, 1993). Lawrence Stone, *The Family, Sex, and Marriage in England, 1550–1800* (New York: Harper and Row, 1977), 332; and idem, *The Crisis of the Aristocracy, 1558–1641* (Oxford: Clarendon Press, 1965), 591. Janelle Greenberg, "The Legal Status of the English Woman in Early Eighteenth-Century Common Law and Equity," *Studies in Eighteenth-Century Culture* 4 (1975): 171–81. Greenberg argues that the legal system of equity, administered through the Court of Chancery, allowed married women a modicum of legal rights and freedoms ("Legal Status," 176–77).

9. Quoted in Elizabeth Bergen Brophy, *Women's Lives and the Eighteenth-Century English Novel* (Tampa: University of South Florida Press, 1991), 159.

10. Sir William Blackstone, *Commentaries on the Laws of England*, 19th ed. (New York: W. E. Dean, 1841), 355.

11. For a cogent discussion of the legal and social reasoning behind this law, see Bridget Hill, *Women, Work, and Sexual Politics in Eighteenth-Century England* (Oxford: Basil Blackwell, 1989), 196–99.

12. Susan Staves, *Married Women's Separate Property in England, 1660–1833* (Cambridge: Harvard University Press, 1990), 227. See also Peter Laslett, *The World We Have Lost Further Explored*, 3d ed. (New York: Charles Scribner's Sons, 1984), 76.

13. Staves, *Married Women's Separate Property*, 86.

14. E. P. Thompson, *Customs in Common* (New York: New Press, 1991), 47.

15. Edmund Burke, *Reflections on the Revolution in France* (1790), in *Edmund Burke: Select Works*, ed. E. J. Payne (Oxford: Clarendon Press, 1877), 2:55.

16. Stone, *Crisis of the Aristocracy*, 283, 591. See also E. P. Thompson, "Eighteenth-Century English Society: Class Struggle Without Class?" *Social History* 3, no. 2 (1978):133–65.

17. Harold Perkin, *The Origins of Modern English Society, 1780–1880* (London: Routledge and Kegan Paul, 1969), 49.

18. Thompson, *Customs in Common*, 136. Thompson offers a very helpful and thought-provoking discussion of the various complications that arise in our use of the term "paternalism"; he notes, for instance, that it often forces us into "confusions of actual and ideological attributes" (24).

19. Ibid., 21. Thompson also makes the important point that the gentry maintained its mystique and cultural hegemony not through a careful attention to daily responsibilities but through the occasional dramatic gesture; for example, during times of severe shortage, they might make substantial donations to charity (46).

20. Quoted in ibid., 23. Thompson observes that no matter how far we go back in time, we would find that the ideal of paternalism always seemed to belong to a mythic past (23–24).

21.  Raymond Williams, *The Country and the City* (New York: Oxford University Press, 1973), 59, 165. See also Don E. Wayne, *Penshurst: The Semiotics of Place and the Poetics of History* (Madison: University of Wisconsin Press, 1984), 8–9, 76.

22.  Burke, *Reflections on the Revolution in France*, 60.

23.  Michael McKeon, *The Origins of the English Novel, 1660–1740* (Baltimore: Johns Hopkins University Press, 1987), 131–32, 150–53. "Patriline repair" is a term used by Peter Laslett, *World We Have Lost*, 211–13. See also Lawrence Stone and Jeanne C. Fawtier Stone, *An Open Elite? England, 1540–1880* (Oxford: Clarendon Press, 1984), 69–72.

24.  On these various inheritance practices, see Stone and Stone, *An Open Elite?*, 5–6, 83–104.

25.  McKeon, *Origins of the English Novel*, 154.

26.  Staves raises similar questions; see *Married Women's Separate Property*, 203–4; see also Eileen Spring, "The Family, Strict Settlement, and Historians," *Canadian Journal of History* 18 (1983): 379–98. Spring contends that spelling out the rights and provisions of younger children before birth was an effective means of preventing their future claims or threats (393); and Eileen Spring and David Spring, "The English Landed Elite, 1540–1879: A Rejoinder," *Albion* 17 (1985): 393–96.

27.  Erickson, *Women and Property*, 150.

28.  As Staves observes, men wanted women to have enough to survive, "but not enough to exercise the power that comes with a significant accumulation of property . . . women [were] considered incompetent to exercise" such a large degree of power. See *Married Women's Separate Property*, 35; see also, 4, 60, 84, 221–22.

29.  Mary Wollstonecraft, *A Vindication of the Rights of Woman* (1792; reprint, edited by Carol H. Poston, New York: W. W. Norton, 1975), 65.

30.  William Hayley, *A philosophical, historical, and moral essay on old maids. By a friend to the sisterhood* (London: T. Cadell, 1785), 1:7.

31.  Wollstonecraft writes about her harsh experiences in "Thoughts on the Education of Daughters" (1786/87). See *A Wollstonecraft Anthology*, ed. Janet M. Todd (Bloomington: University of Indiana Press, 1977), 33.

32.  Leonore Davidoff and Catherine Hall, *Family Fortunes: Men and Women of the English Middle Class, 1780–1850* (Chicago: University of Chicago Press, 1987), 308–15.

33.  Hill, *Women, Work, and Sexual Politics*, 85, 95–96; Peter Earle, "The Female Labour Market in London in the Late Seventeenth and Early Eighteenth Centuries," *Economic History Review*, 2d ser., 42, no. 3 (1989): 344. Earle notes that in 1851 the primary occupations for women still consisted of domestic service, the needle trades, laundry, and nursing (341).

34.  Hill, *Women, Work, and Sexual Politics*, 229. In her research on the issue of eighteenth-century women's work, Hill notes that wives who were shut out of their husbands' growing public businesses could still perform what was viewed as their most important purpose: bearing children. Thus single women were seen as thoroughly useless.

35.  Ibid., 229–30.

36.  Ibid., 185. See also Christopher Lasch, "The Suppression of Clandestine Marriage in England: The Marriage Act of 1753," *Salmagundi* 26 (1974): 99.

37.  Erica Harth, "The Virtue of Love: Lord Hardwicke's Marriage Act," *Cultural Critique* 9 (1988): 154.

38.  Staves, *Married Women's Separate Property*, 4

39.  Staves's perspective on contract ideology and its implications for married women's legal and social status is largely congruent with my own: "Contract ideology was used in the eighteenth century to legitimize the husband's power over his wife and so was part of a

process of mystification." The idea that separate maintenance is strong evidence of the weakening of patriarchy, she argues, is much "too simple" a conclusion. See ibid., 166–67.

40.  Lawrence Stone has argued that "the hardest evidence for a decline in the near-absolute authority of the husband over the wife among the propertied classes is an admittedly limited series of changes in the power of the former to control the latter's estate and income." *Family, Sex, and Marriage*, 330. See also Stone and Stone, *An Open Elite?*, 73–75, and Staves, *Married Women's Separate Property*, 143–47; 168–70.

41.  For other contributions to this controversy, see Okin, "Patriarchy"; Eileen Spring and David Spring, "The English Landed Elite, 1540–1879: A Review," *Albion* 17 (1985): 149–66. For the position that women did gain independence with these prenuptial contracts, see Lawrence Stone, *Family, Sex, and Marriage*, 300–303; Randolph Trumbach, *The Rise of the Egalitarian Family: Aristocratic Kinship and Domestic Relations in Eighteenth-Century England* (New York: Academic Press, 1978), 71. For Staves's views on pin money, see "Pin Money," *Studies in Eighteenth-Century Culture* 14 (1985): 47–77.

42.  Mary Astell, *Some Reflections Upon Marriage* (London: John Nutt, 1700), 39.

43.  Stone, *Family, Sex, and Marriage*, esp. chaps. 6–8. See also Trumbach, *Rise of the Egalitarian Family*, 71.

44.  Staves, *Married Women's Separate Property*, 224.

45.  Ibid., 222–30. For other negative reactions to Stone's argument, see Okin; Eileen Spring claims that it "is not love that is incompatible with patriarchy; it is equality and freedom that are incompatible with patriarchy." See "Law and the Theory of the Affective Family," *Albion* 16 (1984): 17. Alan MacFarlane counters Stone's hypothesis with anthropological evidence that people loved spouses and their children in preindustrial societies. He takes exception to the notion that love suddenly appeared in the eighteenth century as a primary characteristic of family life. Alan MacFarlane, review of *The Family, Sex, and Marriage in England, 1500–1800*, by Lawrence Stone, *History and Theory* 18, no. 1 (1979): 103–26.

46.  Erica Harth argues persuasively that when studying the history of personal and emotional life, what is key is expectations rather than practice. In this case, what is important is that by the eighteenth century people believed one should marry for love. See "Virtue of Love," 124.

47.  For an analysis of this debate, see ibid., 125–40.

48.  Stone, *Family, Sex, and Marriage*, chap. 7, esp. 270–74.

49.  Ibid., 272–81, 316; Staves argues that the rhetoric of "free choice" was in large part an illusion because it only made women psychologically dependent on their husbands; the fear of disinheritance, of course, always loomed large. See *Married Women's Separate Property*, 214–15, 224.

50.  Perkin, *Origins of Modern English Society*, 24–30. Peter Laslett agrees with a nineteenth-century rise, but he delineates eighteenth-century society as a one-class model; according to Laslett, the aristocracy was the only legitimate and viable class (*World We Have Lost*, 22–23).

51.  R. S. Neale, *Class in English History, 1680–1850* (Totowa, N.J.: Barnes and Noble, 1981), chap. 1. See also McKeon, *Origins of the English Novel*, 166; J. G. A. Pocock offers an excellent analysis of the conflict between the "landed" and the "monied" interests as articulated by contemporaries like Swift and Bolingbroke. See *The Machiavellian Moment: Florentine Political Thought and the Atlantic Republican Tradition* (Princeton: Princeton University Press, 1975), chap. 13, esp. 446–61.

52.  McKeon, *Origins of the English Novel*, chap. 4, esp. 153, 162–63, 167–69.

53. Keith Wrightson, "The Social Order of Early Modern England: Three Approaches," in *The World We Have Gained: Histories of Population and Social Structure*, ed. Lloyd Bonfield, Richard M. Smith, and Keith Wrightson (Oxford: Basil Blackwell, 1986), 201.

54. Perkin, *Origins of Modern English Society*, 49.

55. Thompson, *Customs in Common*, 44.

56. Wrightson makes this point ("Social Order," 199).

57. J. G. A. Pocock, *Machiavellian Moment*, 463–64. See also his *Virtue, Commerce, and History: Essays on Political Thought and History, Chiefly in the Eighteenth Century* (Cambridge: Cambridge University Press, 1985), 48–50.

58. Pocock, *Machiavellian Moment*, 452–56. See also McKeon, *Origins of the English Novel*, 204–5.

59 John Brewer, "Commercialization and Politics," in *The Birth of a Consumer Society: The Commercialization of Eighteenth-Century England*, ed. John Brewer, Neil McKendrick, and J. H. Plumb (Bloomington: Indiana University Press, 1982), 211, 213. Brewer notes that a "rival, a disagreeable client, a begrudging partner or personal enemy could all be hamstrung or even driven out of trade altogether by an action for debt" (211).

60. Isaac Kramnick deftly analyzes the conservative reaction to the rise of public credit: these conservatives, mostly those belonging to the Bolingbroke school, saw these new capitalist forces as undermining what they perceived to be the values and structures of a more "traditional" society. See *Bolingbroke and His Circle: The Politics of Nostalgia in the Age of Walpole* (Cambridge: Harvard University Press, 1968). On the other hand, as I will show, Burney is not so much concerned with turning back the clock as she is with assessing the future implications of these changes on the already oppressed and vulnerable women of the early-modern period.

61. See Harth, "Virtue of Love," 134–35.

62. J. H. Plumb, "The Commercialization of Leisure in Eighteenth-Century England," in *Birth of a Consumer Society*, 282–85.

63. Perkin, *Origins of Modern English Society*, 92–93; 96.

64. Quoted in Paul Langford, *Public Life and the Propertied Englishman, 1689–1798* (Oxford: Clarendon Press, 1991), 462–63.

65. Langford notes that pin money and dower were the subjects of much criticism; see *Public Life and the Propertied Englishman*, 503.

66. Pocock, *Machiavellian Moment*, 465–66. In this case, social morality seemed to be divorced from a new personal code: excessive self-interest.

67. Mitzi Myers, "Reform or Ruin: 'A Revolution in Female Manners,'" *Studies in Eighteenth-Century Culture* 11 (1982): 203–4.

68. This passage is from Sarah Cowper's unpublished diary and is quoted in Brophy, *Women's Lives and the Eighteenth-Century English Novel*, 179.

69. Nancy Armstrong, *Desire and Domestic Fiction: A Political History of the Novel* (New York: Oxford University Press, 1987), 69, 72.

70. The aristocracy, Lasch argues, had to adopt a "thoroughly 'middle class'" attitude towards the management of the estate, child rearing, marriage, and education; see "The Suppression of Clandestine Marriage in England," 102–3.

71. Stone and Stone, *An Open Elite?*, 324.

72. Armstrong, *Desire and Domestic Fiction*, 92, 153.

73. Ibid., 66; Mary Poovey, *The Proper Lady and the Woman Writer: Ideology as Style in the*

*Works of Mary Wollstonecraft, Mary Shelley, and Jane Austen* (Chicago: University of Chicago Press, 1984), chap. 1.

74. J. C. D. Clark, *English Society, 1688–1832: Ideology, Social Structure, and Political Practice during the Ancien Regime* (Cambridge: Cambridge University Press, 1985), 106–7. J. H. Plumb argues that like their French counterparts, these English gentlemen shared "the same grotesque extravagance, the same heightened class consciousness, the same feckless attitude to the crises in politics or society." See *England in the Eighteenth Century* (New York: Penguin Books, 1950), 84–85.

75. Donna T. Andrew, "The Code of Honour and its Critics: The Opposition to Duelling in England, 1700–1850," *Social History* 5, no. 3 (1980): 434.

76. For further treatment of these issues, see Poovey, *Proper Lady*, 27; Armstrong, 79–89; and Anna Clark, *Women's Silence, Men's Violence: Sexual Assault in England, 1770–1845* (New York: Pandora Press, 1987), 117. Clark's study offers a good general overview of the problem of violence against women in the early-modern period.

77. Staves, *Married Women's Separate Property*, 224.

78. Ibid.

79. This ideology was a key element in the parliamentary debates concerning Hardwicke's Marriage Act. See Harth, "Virtue of Love," 146.

80. James Fordyce, *Sermons to Young Women, In Two Volumes* (London: A. Millar and T. Cadell, 1766), 227.

81. Laetitia Hawkins, *Letters on the Female Mind, its Powers and Pursuits. Addressed to Miss H. M. Williams, with particular reference to her Letters from France* (London: Hookham and Carpenter, 1793), 2:194. For a discussion of Hawkins's work, see Poovey, *Proper Lady*, 33.

82. On the various definitions of manners, see the *OED*.

83. Norbert Elias, *The Civilizing Process*, trans. Edmund Jephcot (New York: Urizen Books, 1978), 187.

84. Quoted in Donna T. Andrew, "The Code of Honour," 427.

85. Adam Smith, *The Theory of Moral Sentiments* (1759; reprint, New York: Garland Publishing, 1971), 38. David Marshall has argued that Smith's use of the metaphor of the theater to delineate this paradigm of social relations illustrates the importance of spectatorial sympathy as a tool of socialization. See *The Figure of Theater: Shaftesbury, Defoe, Adam Smith, and George Eliot* (New York: Columbia University Press, 1986), 187.

86. Andrew, "The Code of Honour," 420–22.

87. Julia Epstein writes: "*Evelina* is more than merely a comedy of manners and errors" (*Iron Pen*, 95). Epstein's formulation is reductive, for it limits the possible definitions of manners to no more than a concern with trifling errors in polite etiquette. Thus by apparently rescuing Burney from what she sees as a naive or useless categorization, Epstein blinds herself to the argument that Burney's attention to manners and behavior testifies to her acute recognition of her era's social dynamics.

88. James R. Kincaid, "Anthony Trollope and the Unmannerly Novel," in *Reading and Writing Women's Lives: A Study of the Novel of Manners*, ed. Bege K. Bowers and Barbara Brothers (Ann Arbor, Mich.: U.M.I. Research Press, 1990), 87–90. Kincaid also notes a basic paradox of manners: they are highly sophisticated forms of behavior yet are often believed to be instinctual (90).

89. For a suggestive and powerful use of this metaphor, see McKeon's argument about the replacement of drama by narrative. *The Origins of the English Novel*, 125–28.

90. Claudia Johnson, *Jane Austen: Women, Politics, and the Novel* (Chicago: University of Chicago Press, 1988), 26–27.

## CHAPTER 1. *EVELINA* AND THE POLITICS OF NOSTALGIA

1. *Diaries and Letters of Madame D'Arblay 1770–1840*, ed. Austin Dobson (London: Macmillan, 1904), 1:22. This edition is hereafter cited in the text as *DL* with volume and page numbers given parenthetically.

2. Fanny Burney, *Evelina; or, The History of a Young Lady's Entrance into the World* (New York: Norton, 1965), 294. All future references are to this edition, abbreviated *E*, and page numbers will appear parenthetically in the text.

3. On the ideology of paternalism see above, introduction, 17–18.

4. Recently, feminist critics have established the importance that names play in Burney's novels. See Margaret Anne Doody, *Frances Burney: The Life in the Works* (New Brunswick, N.J.: Rutgers University Press, 1988), 40–41, 45; Julia Epstein, *The Iron Pen: Frances Burney and the Politics of Women's Writing* (Madison: University of Wisconsin Press, 1989), 3, 96–98; Patricia Meyer Spacks, *Desire and Truth: Functions of Plot in Eighteenth-Century English Novels* (Chicago: University of Chicago Press, 1990), 141; Joanne Cutting-Gray, *Woman as "Nobody" and the Novels of Fanny Burney* (Gainesville: University of Florida Press, 1992). Cutting-Gray devotes her study to the ways in which Burney's heroines attempt to resist the "patriarchal sense of identity" (3).

5. Irene Tucker also argues that Villars is able to appropriate Evelina as his daughter because her legal father has disowned her. See "Writing Home: *Evelina*, the Epistolary Novel, and the Paradox of Property," *ELH* 60, no. 2 (summer 1993): 425. Tucker reads *Evelina* in the context of contemporary debates about authorial rights (specifically for letter writers), property, and representation.

6. Doody, *Frances Burney*, 40.

7. Mary Poovey, *The Proper Lady and the Woman Writer: Ideology as Style in the Works of Mary Wollstonecraft, Mary Shelley, and Jane Austen* (Chicago: University of Chicago Press, 1984), 26. In her history of sexual assault in England from 1770 to 1845, Anna Clark documents that women who were raped were caught in a legal and social vise: if they explicitly described their assault, then the jury would most likely assume that they were unchaste, and, thus, had willingly engaged in sexual intercourse. The alternative, of course, was painful silence. See *Women's Silence, Men's Violence: Sexual Assault in England, 1770–1845* (New York: Pandora Press, 1987), 64, 67.

8. Vauxhall, along with spa sites at Bath, Tunbridge Wells, and Brighton, was a wildly popular spot for the growth of leisure activities that brought together the gentry and the leisured middle class. One of the most notorious such pastimes was "that favourite eighteenth-century sport of sauntering to ogle girls." See J. H. Plumb, "The Commercialization of Leisure," in *The Birth of a Consumer Society: The Commercialization of Eighteenth-Century England*, ed. Neil McKendrick, John Brewer, and J. H. Plumb (Bloomington: Indiana University Press, 1982), 283. On a further discussion of the commercialization of leisure, see above, introduction, 26.

9. Thomas R. Edwards, "Embarrassed by Jane Austen," *Raritan* 7 (1987/88): 65.

10. Recent feminist critics have read this scene as symptomatic of the consequences of a transhistorical patriarchal rule; see, especially, Kristina Straub, *Divided Fictions: Fanny Burney and Feminine Strategy* (Lexington: University of Kentucky Press, 1987), 44–45; Doody, *Frances Burney*, 56; Epstein, *Iron Pen*, 114–15. For an alternative view, see Earl R. Anderson, "Footnotes More Pedestrian than Sublime: A Historical Background for the Footraces in *Evelina* and *Humphry Clinker*," *Eighteenth-Century Studies* 14 (1980): 56–68.

11. Of which see above, introduction, 20.

12. Straub, *Divided Fictions*, 45.

13. In a fascinating discussion of the role of clubs and fraternal societies and organizations in eighteenth-century England, John Brewer notes the institutionalization of aristocratic violence, especially against women and the lower orders. Stories were legion of young aristocratic rakes perpetrating violence; one such tale tells of rakes who "slit watchmen's noses and rolled old ladies down hills in barrels full of nails." See "Commercialization and Politics," in McKendrick, Brewer, and Plumb, *Birth of a Consumer Society*, 218.

14. See above, introduction, 22–23.

15. Mary Poovey, "Fathers and Daughters: The Trauma of Growing Up Female," *Women and Literature* 2 (1982): 56.

16. On the incest prohibition as a basic ordering principle that undergirds the preservation of the social group, see Claude Lévi-Strauss, *The Elementary Structures of Kinship*, trans. James Harle Bell, John Richard von Sturner, and Rodney Needham (Boston: Beacon Press, 1969), 32, 51, 489. See also Salvatore Cucchiari, "The Gender Revolution and the Transition from Bisexual Horde to Patrilocal Band: The Origins of Gender Hierarchy," in *Sexual Meanings: The Cultural Construction of Gender and Sexuality*, ed. Sherry B. Ortner and Harriet Whitehead (Cambridge: Cambridge University Press, 1981), 40.

17. Irene Fizer's excellent essay on the theme of father-daughter incest in *Evelina* addresses many of the same concerns. She specifically explores Belmont's sexual threat to Evelina. My argument complicates rather than contradicts Fizer's thesis. Most centrally, Fizer's premise (that Burney critiques the legal/biological father) obliges her to downplay and gloss over the emotional and sexual threat posed by Villars. In fact, she argues that Villars wields little significant power; his is a "maternal paternity." I see Burney's critique of patriarchy (involving both the aristocratic and affective fathers) as much more historically nuanced. See "The Name of the Daughter: Identity and Incest in *Evelina*," in *Refiguring the Father: New Feminist Readings of Patriarchy*, ed. Beth Kowaleski-Wallace and Patricia Yeager (Carbondale: University of Southern Illinois Press, 1989), 78–107.

18. The terms "husband," "father," "lover," and "friend" had strong affective connotations in the eighteenth century, especially in sentimental fiction. See Janet Todd, *Sensibility: An Introduction* (New York: Methuen, 1986), 2. On the gradual development of the affective implication of the category "friend," see Lawrence Stone, *The Family, Sex, and Marriage in England, 1550–1800* (New York: Harper and Row, 1977), 97–98.

19. This is a familiar theme in the work of recent feminist critics. See Poovey, "Fathers and Daughters," 46; and Straub, *Divided Fictions*, 74–75; Doody reads against this commonplace of Burney criticism to suggest that Orville is Evelina's "temptation, her challenge, not her Mentor" (*Frances Burney*, 64).

20. To some degree, the father/son paradigm here reflects what Carol Pateman has argued is a critical shift in modern patriarchy from the exclusive rule of the father to the liberation of the son, who, in a civil bond with his other "brothers," nevertheless maintains the subjection of women. Thus modern patriarchy is fraternal in form. See *The Sexual Contract* (Stanford, Calif.: Stanford University Press, 1988), chap. 4.

21. Patricia Meyer Spacks observes that Evelina's "search for intimate association produces multiplication rather than substitution" (*Desire and Truth*, 141–42). Spacks argues that this doubling allows Evelina to combat more effectively her many difficulties. I want to suggest, however, that this multiplication is also a means of revealing the underlying persistence of a harsh patriarchal order.

22. Doody, *Frances Burney*, 65.

23. Doody argues that Evelina experiences embarrassment as a real threat to the stability of her identity (ibid., 60).

24. *Memoirs of Dr. Burney, arranged from his own Manuscripts, from Personal Recollections. By his Daughter, Madame D'Arblay* (London: Edward Moxon, 1832), 3:283–84.

25. Ronald Paulson, *Satire and the Novel in Eighteenth-Century England* (New Haven: Yale University Press, 1967), 266–67. On the novel of manners see above, introduction, 30, 31–32.

26. Burney, *Memoirs*, 125–26. Of course, the "elegant connections" that Caroline Evelyn provides are originally derived from Belmont. I will soon discuss, however, the role of women in Evelina's quest for social and familial acceptance.

27. It is a commonplace of Burney criticism to label Evelina a snob because of her contradictory attitudes toward the Branghtons and Sir Clement. Toby Olshin reads her actions as an indication of a lack of "moral growth." See "'To Whom I Most Belong': The Role of the Family in *Evelina*," *Eighteenth-Century Life* 6 (1980): 29–42. Judith Newton suggests that Evelina is too easily blinded by Sir Clement's "courtly language." See *Women, Power, and Subversion*, 33–38. But what of Evelina's final rejection and even defeat of Sir Clement? Neither critic fully recognizes how both social orders (as represented by Evelina's cousins and Sir Clement) are formidable, often violent forces and have a significant effect on her future social possibilities.

28. Adam Smith, *The Theory of Moral Sentiments*, ed. D. D. Raphael and A. L. Macfie (Oxford: Oxford University Press, 1976), 61. For further discussion of this theme see David Marshall, *The Figure of Theater: Shaftesbury, Defoe, Adam Smith, and George Eliot* (New York: Columbia University Press, 1986), 186–88.

29. Doody, *Frances Burney*, 40.

30. Claudia Johnson, *Jane Austen: Women, Politics, and the Novel* (Chicago: University of Chicago Press, 1988), 25.

31. Lawrence Stone claims that the gendering of leisure activities generated closer relationships between women; in fact, the bonds between them could sometimes be closer than those between husband and wife. See *Family, Sex, and Marriage*, 402–3.

32. Doody, *Frances Burney*, 53.

33. On the many strictures placed on women's behavior, see Poovey, *Proper Lady*, 3–47.

34. On women as the civilizers of society see above, introduction, 29–30; Jayne Lewis, "Compositions of Ill Nature: Women's Place in a Satiric Tradition," *Critical Matrix* 2, no. 2 (1986): 31–69; and George A. Starr, "'Only a Boy': Notes on Sentimental Novels," *Genre* 10, no. 4 (1977): 501–27.

35. As Paul Langford has argued, one of the most anxiety-producing fears about a corrupt aristocracy was the "example it set and the guidance it provided." See *Public Life and the Propertied Englishman, 1689–1718* (Oxford: Clarendon Press, 1991), 548–49. In this case, Orville is a reconstructed aristocrat who offers a last-ditch attempt to reform the attentuating aristocratic order. His virtue is as important as his hereditary status, or indeed even more important.

36. On *Evelina* as a bildungsroman, see Starr, "'Only a Boy,'" 523–27; James P. Vopat, "*Evelina*: Life as Art—Notes Toward Becoming a Performer on the Stage of Life," *Essays in Literature* 2 (1975): 42–51; Huang-Mei, *Transforming the Cinderella Dream: From Frances Burney to Charlotte Brontë* (New Brunswick, N.J.: Rutgers University Press, 1990), 39–47.

37. On the subject of manners see above, introduction, 30–32.

38. Gina Campbell, "How to Read Like a Gentleman: Burney's Instructions to her Critics in *Evelina*," *ELH* 57 (1990): 577.

39. Susan Staves, "*Evelina*; or, Female Difficulties," *Modern Philology* 73 (1976): 372–73; Starr, "'Only a Boy,'" 526.

40. On the political and religious background of sensibility, see Todd, *Sensibility*, 10–31; and John Mullan, *Sentiment and Sociability: The Language of Feeling in the Eighteenth-Century Novel* (Oxford: Clarendon Press, 1988).

41. Janet Todd discusses this theme in the context of the rise of sensibility and senti-ment (*Sensibility*, 96).

42. See, for example, Huang-Mei, *Cinderella Dream*, 31–53; Martha G. Brown, "Fanny Burney's 'Feminism': Gender or Genre?" in *Fetter'd or Free? British Women Novelists, 1670–1815*, ed. Mary Anne Schofield and Cecilia Macheski (Athens: Ohio State University Press, 1986), 29–39. Edward Copeland argues that Evelina's inheritance is a sign of "grace" rather than a mark of economic reality. "Money in the Novels of Fanny Burney," *Studies in the Novel* 8 (1976): 24–37.

43. See Epstein, *Iron Pen*, 25–29; Patricia Meyer Spacks, "Dynamics of Fear: Fanny Burney," in *Imagining a Self: Autobiography and Novel in Eighteenth-Century England* (Cambridge: Harvard University Press, 1976), 158–92; Katherine Rogers, "Fanny Burney: The Private Self and the Public Self," *International Journal of Women's Studies* 7 (1984): 110–17. Doody sees this poem in particular as evidence of Burney's "elopement," for she "went into the world without her father's knowledge" (*Frances Burney*, 25).

44. Doody notes that Charles Burney would often withdraw affection if his children faltered or disobeyed him; he was adept at emotional blackmail (*Frances Burney*, 24).

45. Ibid., 39. Irene Tucker has suggested that the anonymity of the dedication is not so much a sign of a daughter's fear of paternal disapproval but of Burney's attempt to imagine a kind of authority that is not "based upon the model of possession." That is, if there is no recipient of a letter (or in this case, an epistolary novel), then the author maintains owner-ship. The blank in the text ("To ———") reminds Tucker of Evelina's early refusal to sign "Anville" in her letters to Orville ("Writing Home," 434–35). While I would agree that Burney is attempting to establish her own voice away from her father and his authorial career, I would suggest that the language of the poem points more to her fear, as even she would later tell her father, than to any desire to break completely free of his parental "own-ership."

46. Doody, *Frances Burney*, 32.

47. Fanny Burney, *The Wanderer; Or, Female Difficulties*, ed. Margaret Anne Doody, Rob-ert L. Mack, and Peter Sabor (Oxford: Oxford University Press, 1991), 3.

48. On Charles Burney's efforts to suppress the production of Burney's comedy, see Doody, *Frances Burney*, chap.3.

49. In her article on the role of the critic in *Evelina*, Gina Campbell shares some of my concerns. She makes the interesting point that if male critics are expected to be protective of feminine innocence, then they will also hold the power of moral mentors, possibly censoring the female author's ideas ("How to Read," 580–82).

50. Felicity Nussbaum notes that the published self (through the vehicle of women's autobiographies) was often considered property in a capitalist economy. See *The Autobio-graphical Subject: Gender and Ideology in Eighteenth-Century England* (Baltimore: Johns Hopkins University Press, 1989), xiv.

## CHAPTER 2. *CECILIA*'S NEW PATERNALISM

1. Fanny Burney, *Cecilia, Or Memoirs of an Heiress*, ed. Margaret Anne Doody and Peter Sabor (Oxford: Oxford University Press, 1988), 6. All future references are to this edition, abbreviated *C*, and will appear parenthetically in the text.

2. On these several means, see above, introduction, 19, 26–27.

3. On the ideology of paternalism, see above, introduction, 17–18.

4. Julia Epstein, *The Iron Pen: Frances Burney and the Politics of Women's Writing* (Madison: University of Wisconsin Press, 1989), 157. For a similar view, see Terry Castle, *Masquerade and Civilization: The Carnivalesque in Eighteenth-Century English Culture and Fiction* (Stanford, Calif.: Stanford University Press, 1986), 267. According to Castle, the terms of Cecilia's legacy are "a direct affront to masculine hegemony."

5. Gary Kelly has written that such prison images were often used in late-eighteenth-century novels to protest "against what was seen . . . as a social and political hegemony still unjustly exercised by a decadent aristocratic chivalric and feudal culture." See "Jane Austen and the English Novel of the 1790s," in *Fetter'd or Free: British Women Novelists, 1670–1815*, ed. Mary Anne Schofield and Cecilia Macheski (Athens: Ohio State University Press, 1986), 286.

6. On such questions, see above, introduction, 22–23.

7. Erica Harth has questioned whether the ideology of love-based marriages was solely a progressive notion. She argues that this ideology is consistent with a conservative view that visualized love-based alliances as a deterrent to adultery: such unions would most likely guarantee the smooth transition of property. "In the social complex of marriage, property, and money, love functioned as an instrument of social control." See "The Virtue of Love: Lord Hardwicke's Marriage Act," *Cultural Critique* 9 (1988): 136.

8. On the status of younger sons, see above, introduction, 19.

9. Margaret Anne Doody, *Frances Burney: The Life in the Works* (New Brunswick, N.J.: Rutgers University Press, 1988), 112.

10. Castle, *Masquerade and Civilization*, 270.

11. On this aspect of paternalism, see above, introduction, 18.

12. On which see above, introduction, 28.

13. Miranda J. Burgess has also noted that Burney plays with the moral and financial definitions of "credit." This can best be seen, Burgess argues, when Burney invokes the "credit of sensibility" (e.g., tears as signs of one's sensibility) as a way that her heroines must "purchase" a husband (i.e., tears as coin), and, thus, moral and economic meanings become conflated. Where I strongly disagree with Burgess is in her curious claim that Burney uses these terms in order to embrace an older version of marriage as a private agreement between father and suitor, the implication being that women are only commodified, for Burney, in a capitalist culture. See "Courting Ruin: The Economic Romances of Frances Burney," *Novel: A Forum on Fiction* 28, no. 2 (winter 1995): 131–53.

14. On which see above, chap. 1, 40.

15. For a discussion of the complex relationship between creditor and debtor, see above, introduction, 25.

16. For similar reflections on the role of consumerism and credit in Harrel's actions, see D. Grant Campbell, "Fashionable Suicide: Conspicuous Consumption and the Collapse of Credit in Frances Burney's *Cecilia*," *Studies in Eighteenth-Century Culture* 20 (1990): 131–45.

17. Campbell notes that Meadows's conversation teems with references to "nothingness," illustrating that, like paper credit, the Vauxhall milieu is based on the imaginary and not the real. Ibid., 139. For this contemporary understanding of credit, see above, introduction, 25.

18. Epstein, *Iron Pen*, 171. Doody's reaction is typical: Lady Honoria is an "impertinent rattle to whom the author delegates the work of uttering some truths more cutting than the heroine can utter" (*Frances Burney*, 125). Jayne Lewis, on the other hand, sees satiric female characters as spokespersons for Burney's own angry observations; with them she can

"confront her own satiric proclivities . . . without destroying herself in the bargain." Jayne Lewis, "Compositions of Ill Nature: Women's Place in a Satiric Tradition," *Critical Matrix* 2, no. 2 (1986): 68–69. Such readings tend to ignore the complex social and psychological motivations of these kinds of satiric characters.

19.  Jayne Lewis has argued that women in the eighteenth century were reluctant to criticize social institutions because to malign them "would be to attack their own socially defined identities" ("Compositions of Ill Nature," 42).

20.  Compare instances of threatened incest in the Belmont clan. See above, chap. 1, 44, 45–46. On the demographic crisis in the aristocracy, see above, introduction, 19.

21.  *Diary and Letters of Madame D'Arblay, 1778–1840*, ed. Austin Dobson (London: Macmillan, 1904), 2:127. Future references to this edition will appear in the text as *DL*, with volume and page numbers given parenthetically.

22.  On which see above, introduction, 17–18.

23.  Castle, *Masquerade and Civilization*, 278. For the view that Cecilia's dreams are in the spirit of an Augustan tradition that exposed such ambitious fantasies as grandiose illusions, see Doody, *Frances Burney*, 117–18.

24.  A landowner who derived his income wholly from his rents was considered the "embodiment of the independent gentlemen [*sic*]." See Paul Langford, *Public Life and the Propertied Englishman, 1689–1798* (Oxford: Clarendon Press, 1991), 63. Burney draws on this most recognizable contemporary understanding of the concept of independence in order to formulate her ideal vision of women's sovereignty and empowerment.

25.  Nancy Armstrong, *Desire and Domestic Fiction: A Political History of the Novel* (New York: Oxford University Press, 1987), 89, 99. For a fuller treatment of domestic ideology see above, introduction, 27–32.

26.  See above, introduction, 26.

27.  Moira Ferguson, ed. *First Feminists: British Women Writers, 1578–1799* (Bloomington: University of Indiana Press, 1985), 35.

28.  Mary Astell, *A Serious Proposal to the Ladies*, 4th ed. (1701; reprint, New York: Source Book Press, 1970), 14–20. Burney is also clearly working in a female literary tradition that valorized women's friendships and societies. The most prominent utopian vision of the period was Sarah Scott's *Millenium Hall* (1762).

29.  On which see above, introduction, 19–20.

30.  For typical readings, see Epstein, *Iron Pen*, 168; and Kristina Straub, *Divided Fictions: Fanny Burney and Feminine Strategy* (Lexington: University of Kentucky Press, 1987), 174.

31.  Albany, a madman who is always exhorting Cecilia to practice more charity, falls in love with a young woman who is seduced in his absence. When he discovers her infidelity, he "barbarously" beats her. In turn, she becomes a prostitute, and, in penance, she refuses to eat or change her clothes. Becoming "deaf, mute, [and] insensible," she eventually starves herself to death. Here madness is a response to violence and helplessness; Albany's lover has internalized his violent disapproval of her behavior (*C*, 705–6).

32.  During the scene of Mrs. Delvile's stroke, she warns the lovers about the threat of her husband's curses (*C*, 676).

33.  Epstein, *Iron Pen*, 168.

34.  Margaret Doody and Peter Sabor note that the *Daily Advertiser* listed many financial advertisements (*C*, 1002, n. 878). This, along with the fact that she is being held at a pawnbroker's, reveals how Cecilia, as she has been to Delvile, Harrel, and Briggs, is a commodity to the lower-class pawnbroker.

35.  Burney wrote to her surrogate father, Daddy Crisp, that if she were to restore

Cecilia's inheritance, she would betray the integrity of her project: "and I must frankly confess I shall think I have rather written a farce than a serious history, if the whole is to end, like the hack Italian operas, with a jolly chorus that makes all parties good and all parties happy!" (*DL*, 2:80). In response to Edmund Burke's complaint that a work of imagination should not have a mixed conclusion, she wondered, "[W]hen is life and nature completely happy or miserable? [*sic*]" (*DL*, 2:139).

## CHAPTER 3. MANNERLY VIOLENCE

1. *Diaries and Letters of Madame D'Arblay, 1770–1840*, ed. Austin Dobson (London: Macmillan, 1904), 2:380. This edition is hereafter cited in the text as *DL*, with volume and page numbers given parenthetically.

2. Margaret Anne Doody, *Frances Burney: The Life in the Works* (New Brunswick, N.J.: Rutgers University Press, 1988), 167–98. Doody does examine the ways in which Burney's hardships at court colored the tragic plays she wrote during her five-year tenure. However, she is most interested in exploring the alterations in Burney's psychological health and does not seize the opportunity to investigate the thematic connections between the court journals and *Camilla;* both texts, I would contend, are complex social histories. We can learn more from these journals, as Doody herself suggests, than just the intimate details of court life.

3. "I am *married,* my dearest Susan — I look upon it in that light — I was averse to forming the union, and I endeavoured to escape it; but my friends interfered — they prevailed – and the knot is tied. What then now remains but to make the best wife in my power? I am bound to it in duty. . . ." (*DL*, 2:382). Charles Burney, however, delighted in the comparison: "[T]hough I have had the good fortune to marry to my own contentment three of my daughters, I never gave one of them away with the pride or the pleasure I experienced in my gift of last Monday." *Memoirs of Dr. Burney, arranged from his own Manuscripts, from Personal Recollections. By his Daughter, Madame D'Arblay* (London: Edward Moxon, 1832), 3:96.

4. Doody, *Frances Burney,* 172.

5. Norbert Elias points out that sixteenth-century texts on manners particularly charted those forms of proper behavior that had developed in court circles. The new court aristocracy learned how to behave at court and these codes of conduct soon disseminated downward to the rest of society. See his *The Civilizing Process,* trans. Edmund Jephcot (New York: Urizen Books, 1978), 99–102.

6. Doody, *Frances Burney,* 168–69; Julia Epstein, "Writing the Unspeakable: Fanny Burney's Mastectomy and the Fictive Body," *Representations* 16 (1986): 133. See also Epstein's *The Iron Pen: Frances Burney and the Politics of Women's Writing* (Madison: University of Wisconsin Press, 1989), 29–33.

7. Burney's record of her mastectomy (1811) is another famous example of her interest in narrating pain and violence. In her scrupulous analysis of this letter, Epstein argues that Burney can take control of the pain and repossess the self that had been utterly vulnerable in surgery. Moreover, according to Epstein, writing about this experience in particular and writing fiction in general was a painful and violent act for Burney: "narration — writing the intimate and vulnerable self — represents an act of violence, a wrenching exposure that amounts to a self-inflicted incision, an aggressive attack on the writer's self." See *Iron Pen,* 81. See also idem, "Writing the Unspeakable."

8. Epstein, *Iron Pen,* 29.

9. Elias, *Civilizing Process,* 100–101.

10. Elias carefully investigates this relationship between manners and social status (ibid., 66).

11. See, for example, Karen Horney, *Feminine Psychology*, ed. Harold Kelman (New York: W. W. Norton, 1967), 226–29. Doody interprets Burney's illness as both a "revolutionary bid for freedom" and an obvious gesture of suicide (*Frances Burney*, 192–94).

12. Fanny Burney, *Camilla; or, A Picture of Youth*, ed. Edward A. Bloom and Lillian D. Bloom (London: Oxford University Press, 1972), 17. All future references are to this edition, abbreviated as *Ca*, and will appear parenthetically in the text.

13. *The Journals and Letters of Fanny Burney, 1791–1840*, ed. Joyce Hemlow (Oxford: Clarendon Press, 1978–84), 3:117.

14. Recent feminist film theorists have defined the peculiarly sadistic qualities of the male gaze; they show how pleasure lies in ascertaining guilt, asserting control, and subjecting the woman under the gaze to punishment. See, generally, Laura Mulvey, *Visual and Other Pleasures* (Bloomington: University of Indiana Press, 1989); and E. Ann Kaplan, *Women & Film: Both Sides of the Camera* (New York: Methuen, 1983).

15. Evelyn Fox Keller has noted that the proponents of the "new science" used sexual metaphors to describe the relation between the scientific mind and its object of study. Bacon, for example, viewed this object as female: "Let us establish a chaste and lawful marriage between Mind and Nature," and "I am come in very truth leading you to Nature with all her children to bind her to your service and make her your slave." As Keller argues, the aims of the new science were to conquer and master nature; she sees this early modern understanding of science as fitting neatly into a "patriarchal tradition." See "Gender and Science," *Psychoanalysis and Contemporary Thought* 1, no. 3 (1978): 413. On the role of the new spectatorial philosophy for this development in patriarchal rule see, above, 31–36.

16. It will be an ongoing assumption of this chapter that the phrase "patriarchal gaze" refers to this complex modern invention.

17. Joyce Hemlow, "Fanny Burney and the Courtesy Books," *PMLA* 65 (1950): 732. For a more recent discussion of the influence these conduct manuals had on the domestic novel, see Nancy Armstrong, *Desire and Domestic Fiction: A Political History of the Novel* (New York: Oxford University Press, 1987), chap. 2. Armstrong contends that courtship narratives in particular "seized the authority to say what was female" (4–5).

18. See *Married Women's Separate Property in England, 1660–1833* (Cambridge: Harvard University Press, 1990), 222. On new ideological developments that support the subordination of women on more affective grounds, see above, introduction, 22–23.

19. See Hemlow, "Courtesy Books," 732–61; Kristina Straub, *Divided Fictions: Fanny Burney and Feminine Strategy* (Lexington: University of Kentucky Press, 1987), chap. 4. Straub specifically focuses on the correlations between courtesy books and *Evelina*.

20. Hemlow, "Courtesy Books," 760.

21. Doody, for example, implies that such associations can rob *Camilla* of its philosophical power and reduce it to a simplistic ethical tract (*Frances Burney*, 206, 220). Epstein makes the same comments about *Evelina*. See *Iron Pen*, 95. I would counter, however, that conduct books raised serious social and cultural issues; to examine such an association may complicate rather than simplify our reading.

22. In a letter to Burney, her eldest sister Esther (Hetty) makes a suggestive reference to "Mrs. Arlbery (whom we are apt to call *d'Arblay*)." Quoted in Doody, *Frances Burney*, 250. Hetty wryly observes that Mrs. Arlbery shares the same natural wit and proclivity for trenchant satire as her author. At a young age, in fact, Burney secretly wished to subvert some of the more stifling commonplace rules of proper behavior. Her reactions to her outspoken

stepsister Maria Rishton underscore this desire. See *The Early Journals and Letters of Fanny Burney*, ed. Lars E. Troide (Oxford: Clarendon Press, 1988), 166. Burney meant to praise the first person who might "at least shew the way to a new & Open path."

23.   George A. Starr, "'Only a Boy': Notes on Sentimental Novels," *Genre* 10, no. 4 (1977): 524–25. Mitzi Myers observes that Starr is too quick to associate the female bildungsroman with a woman's "arrested development"; that is, according to Starr, she need never grow up. Myers argues that often these eighteenth-century heroines are never given the chance to develop moral insight because they are trapped in courtships that codify female powerlessness. See "The Dilemmas of Gender as Double-Voiced Narrative: Or, Maria Edgeworth Mothers the Bildungsroman," in *The Idea of the Novel in the Eighteenth Century*, ed. Robert W. Uphaus (East Lansing, Mich.: Colleagues Press, 1988), 68–69.

24.   For a different reading of this scene, see Claudia Johnson, *Equivocal Beings: Politics, Gender, and Sentimentality in the 1790s: Wollstonecraft, Radcliffe, Burney, Austen* (Chicago: University of Chicago Press, 1995), 150–51. Generally speaking, Johnson argues that *Camilla* participates in a complex dialogue involving the politics of sentimentality in the last decade of the eighteenth century. Because "sentimentality entailed . . . the 'masculinization' of formerly feminine gender traits," according to Johnson, it was valued in men rather than in women, and, as a consequence, women's feelings were considered "inferior, unconscious, unruly, or even criminal" (14).

25.   On the relationship between Protestant ideology and the social origins of the novel, see Michael McKeon, *The Origins of the English Novel, 1600–1740* (Baltimore: Johns Hopkins University Press, 1987), 189–205.

26.   On which see above, introduction, 29–30.

27.   Adam Smith, *The Theory of Moral Sentiments* (1759; reprint, New York: Garland Publishing, 1971), 38.

28.   Lawrence Stone has shown how in the "closed domesticated nuclear family," there was "increasing stress" placed upon personal privacy. Aristocratic and bourgeois domestic homes, for example, separated servants from the rest of the family, and children from adults; they contained separate rooms for the two sexes. See *The Family, Sex, and Marriage in England 1550–1800* (New York: Harper and Row, 1977), 253–57. For a slightly different discussion of these same issues in *Pamela*, see Armstrong, *Desire and Domestic Fiction*, 124, 278 n. 42.

29.   It is appropriate—and significant—that Marchmont should be Edgar's tutor in matters of courtship and marriage, since his first wife—"another Camilla"—had betrayed him with another man. His second wife, who was "gay" and dissipated, just barely escaped a "temptation" that would have "impeached his honour" (*Ca*, 643–44). Marchmont is clearly fearful of women's sexual allure; he sees himself as twice duped by powerfully shrewd and flirtatious women.

30.   Camilla has fallen into the common trap of "emulative spending." For a fuller discussion of this phenomenon, see above, introductio, 26–27. In this case, if Camilla wants to win back Edgar's moral approval, she must appear in public, the only place she is likely to meet him, and thus she is forced, in the end, to spend money she does not have for a fashionable ball gown. Quite simply, she is in an untenable situation. For the role of fashion in the rise of eighteenth-century consumerism, see Neil McKendrick, "The Commercialization of Fashion," in *The Birth of a Consumer Society: The Commercialization of Eighteenth-Century England*, ed. Neil McKendrick, John Brewer, and J. H. Plumb (Bloomington: University of Indiana Press, 1982), chap.2.

31.   On which see above, introduction, 25–26.

32.   On this relationship see McKeon, *Origins of the English Novel*, 198, 205–7. In his

discussion of progressive and conservative ideology, McKeon points out the symbolic significance of terms like "trust" and "credit." Capitalists recognized the importance of these words in a society based on exchange value; "credit," then, could allude to their own version of aristocratic honor.

33.  The phrase was coined by Harold Perkin; see above, introduction, 26.

34.  McKeon, *Origins of the English Novel*, 231.

35.  Jean-Christophe Agnew has offered a convincing reading of the similarities shared by Smith's seemingly disparate theories about the economy and about the dynamics of moral sympathy and spectatorship. See *Worlds Apart: The Market and the Theater in Anglo-American Thought, 1550–1750* (Cambridge: Cambridge University Press, 1986), 186. As John Brewer has taught us, the relationship between borrower and lender was a fairly intimate one, requiring the debtor to accept the uncomfortable fact that the creditor could and would pass moral judgments about his or her worth "over and beyond the immediate transaction." See "Commercialization and Politics," in *Birth of a Consumer Society*, 229. On this relationship, see above, introduction, 25. In this example from *Camilla*, moral and financial behavior become dangerously conflated.

36.  Doody, *Frances Burney*, 271.

37.  Epstein reads this scene as paradigmatic for all of Burney's novels. For here we see the heroine facing the blank page, an allegory for Burney's own anger and defiance, as writing signifies vulnerability, public exposure, and indelicacy. She further argues that Burney is working through her own ambivalence about writing, asserting authority with the patriarchal pen. See *Iron Pen*, chaps. 1 and 4.

38.  Joanne Cutting-Gray, *Woman as "Nobody" and the Novels of Fanny Burney* (Gainesville: University of Florida Press, 1992), 80. Hélène Cixous argues that a feminine mode of writing will "always surpass the discourse that registers the phallocentric system; it does and will take place in areas other than those subordinated to philosophico-theoretical domination." See "The Laugh of the Medusa," trans. Keith Cohen and Paula Cohen in *New French Feminisms*, ed. Elaine Marks and Isabelle de Courtivron (New York: Schocken Books, 1981), 253.

39.  At the conclusion of her copy of *Camilla*, Jane Austen remarked that "[s]ince this work went to the press, a circumstance of some assistance to the happiness of Camilla has taken place, namely that Dr. Marchmont has at last died." Quoted in Doody, *Frances Burney*, 272.

## CHAPTER 4. *EVELINA* REDUX

1.  *The Journals and Letters of Fanny Burney, 1791–1840*, ed. Joyce Hemlow (Oxford: Clarendon Press, 1972–1984), 6:716.

2.  Fanny Burney, *The Wanderer; Or, Female Difficulties*, ed. Margaret Anne Doody, Robert L. Mack, and Peter Sabor (Oxford: Oxford University Press, 1991), 11. All future references are to this edition, abbreviated as *W*, and will appear parenthetically in the text.

3.  See above, introduction, 30.

4.  Edmund Burke, *Reflections on the Revolution in France* (1790), in *Edmund Burke: Select Works*, ed. E. J. Payne (Oxford: Clarendon Press, 1877), 2:89.

5.  The influence of Wollstonecraft on *The Wanderer* is often acknowledged but has been left unexplored. See, for example, Claire Tomalin, *The Life and Death of Mary Wollstonecraft* (1974; reprint, New York: Penguin Books, 1992), 307–9. Wollstonecraft roundly criticized Burke's ideas; she particularly complained about his notion that "to be loved" was "women's

high end and great distinction." See *A Vindication of the Rights of Men*, 1790, in *The Works of Mary Wollstonecraft*, ed. Janet Todd and Marilyn Butler (London: William Pickering, 1989), 5:45.

6. For convenience' sake, I will refer to Burney's heroine as "Juliet" throughout the chapter.

7. Samuel Richardson, *Pamela; or, Virtue Rewarded* (1740; reprint, edited by T. C. Duncan Eaves and Ben D. Kimpel, Boston: Houghton Mifflin, 1971), 328. For a discussion of Lady Davers's resistance to Pamela's and B.'s marriage, see Nancy Armstrong, *Desire and Domestic Fiction: A Political History of the Novel* (New York: Oxford University Press, 1987), 130–31; and Michael McKeon, *The Origins of the English Novel 1600–1740* (Baltimore: Johns Hopkins University Press, 1987), 377–79.

8. See above, introduction, 140 n. 19.

9. Thomas R. Edwards, "Embarrassed by Jane Austen," *Raritan* 7 (1987/88): 66–67. See also Erving Goffman, *Behavior in Public Places: Notes on the Social Organization of Gatherings* (New York: Free Press, 1963), 196–97. In a social situation, "each person becomes a potential victim or aggressor in the potential occurrence of violent interpersonal actions, such as physical or sexual assault, blocking of the way, and so forth." I owe this reference to Ruth Bernard Yeazell, *Fictions of Modesty: Women and Courtship in the English Novel* (Chicago: University of Chicago Press, 1991), 142. Margaret Doody defines embarrassment as "an immediate manifestation of a flux of social power." See *Frances Burney: The Life in the Works* (New Brunswick, N.J.: Rutgers University Press, 1988), 59.

10. The image of the cruel, unfeeling plantation wife was a common one in the Abolitionist literature of the eighteenth century; she was often represented as politically powerless. See Moira Ferguson, *Subject to Others: British Women Writers and Colonial Slavery, 1670–1834* (New York: Routledge, 1992), 160–61.

11. The Somerset decision of 1772, handed down by Lord Mansfield, declared it illegal to force slaves to leave England. The Abolition Act itself did not pass until 1807. See ibid., 116. It was a popular misconception of the time that Mansfield had freed all of the slaves in England. Teresa Michals has argued that this misunderstanding is rooted in the fact that to the court, James Somerset was "neither an autonomous individual nor a piece of merchandise." See "'That Sole and Despotic Dominion': Slaves, Wives, and Game in Blackstone's *Commentaries*," *Eighteenth-Century Studies* 27, no. 2 (1993/94): 195.

12. It is worth noting that Mrs. Ireton's lapdog is described as "a tiny old" animal (*W*, 478), suggesting its mistress's decaying value in the aristocratic patriarchal culture she struggles to uphold. This satiric jab at her sexual impotence, linking her with her equally impotent brother–in–law Sir Jaspar (I will discuss him later), illustrates just how desperately deluded and powerless she is in her attempt to preserve her place in an attenuating aristocratic society. Like Sir Jaspar, however, she fights this inevitable loss of social and cultural hegemony by striking out at the weakest among her.

13. Michals has noted that the most steadfast champions of slavery were conservative landowners who saw the abolition of the slaves as one more step towards a less status-based, deferential society ("That Sole and Despotic Dominion," 205).

14. Orlando Patterson, *Freedom in the Making of Western Culture* (New York: Basic Books, 1991), 237.

15. In her recent work on Burney, Joanne Cutting-Gray makes a similar observation: "Juliet's namelessness makes her alienation culturally absolute." See *Woman as 'Nobody' and the Novels of Fanny Burney* (Tampa: University of Florida Press, 1992), 86.

16. Doody, *Frances Burney*, 40–41.

17. On this problem of the single woman, see above, introduction, 20.

18. Laura Brown has made this observation about the figure of woman in early-eighteenth-century English literature. See *Ends of Empire: Women and Ideology in Early Eighteenth-Century English Literature* (Ithaca: Cornell University Press, 1993), 20.

19. For the importance of this romance convention, see McKeon, *Origins of the English Novel*, 213.

20. Ferguson has noted that colonial slavery was a commonly used "referent" for British women writers to describe their social and cultural status (*Subject to Others*, 23). She further argues that the more conservative women writers displaced their own status anxiety onto slaves and treated them as objects of charity, while the more radical authors, like Wollstonecraft, saw the colonized as subjects who deserved their own self-determination (197).

21. Doody, *Frances Burney*, 350.

22. See Daniel Defoe, *Robinson Crusoe* (1719; reprint, edited by Michael Shinagel, New York: W. W. Norton, 1975). "How like a King I look'd. First of all, the whole Country was my own meer Property. . . ." (188).

23. Eva Figes notes that when Juliet first appears in the novel, "everything but her sex is in doubt: her age, class, nationality, and even race" are unknown. See *Sex and Subterfuge: Women Writers to 1850* (London: Macmillan, 1982), 53.

24. For a discussion of women and work see above, introduction, 20.

25. The *London Magazine* (1760) conceded how much the poor were needed to sustain the life of the propertied Englishman: "There is nothing more clear, than that we owe all to the labour of the lower class of people; it is this that supports all that deem themselves above work." This writer hopes to tweak the conscience of the well-to-do, stressing their debt to the working poor; charity sermons often made such references as well. Quoted in Paul Langford, *Public Life and the Propertied Englishman, 1689–1798* (Oxford: Clarendon Press, 1991), 458–59.

26. Rose-Marie Cutting has also posited that Mrs. Ireton's "sadism" is a consequence of upper-class ennui. See "A Wreath for Fanny Burney's Last Novel: *The Wanderer*'s Contribution to Women's Studies," *Illinois Quarterly* 37, no. 3 (1975), 56–57.

27. The phrase "ingeniously tormenting" echoes Jane Collier's text, *An Essay on the Art of Ingeniously Tormenting: With Proper Rules for the Exercise of that Pleasant Art* (London: A. Miller, 1753). Collier claims that "insulting taunts" are an effective method of controlling one's servants (49). On Collier's relationship to the novel, see Doody, *Frances Burney*, 357.

28. In a somewhat similar instance, Evelina decides that Mme. Duval, "who is the uncontrolled mistress of her time, fortune, and actions," allows Captain Mirvan to harass her because she "scarce knows how to employ herself." Fanny Burney, *Evelina; or, The History of a Young Lady's Entrance into the World* (New York: Norton, 1965), 61.

29. On the situation of the humble or paid companion, see above, introduction, 20. When she was at court, Burney felt that she was no more than a humble companion to her immediate superior, Mrs. Schwellenberg: "I saw myself expected by Mrs. Schwellenberg, not to be her colleague, but her dependent deputy! not to be her visitor at my own option, but her companion, her humble companion, at her own command!" *Diary and Letters of Madame D'Arblay, 1778–1840*, ed. Austin Dobson (London: Macmillan, 1904), 3:9. Doody has also remarked on this similarity (*Frances Burney*, 176), as has Betty Rizzo in *Companions Without Vows: Relationships Among Eighteenth-Century British Women* (Athens: University of Georgia Press, 1994), 99–104.

30. See Mary Wollstonecraft, *A Vindication of the Rights of Woman* (1792; reprint, edited by Carol H. Poston, New York: W. W. Norton, 1975), 143.

31. Ibid., 57.

32. As in *Cecilia*, Burney offers many scenes of social debate. Aristocratic pride in birth often comes under attack: "'Why then you are descended from somebody who was rich without either trouble or merit; for that's all that your gentleman is, as far as belongs to birth. The man amongst your grand-dads who first got the money, is the only one worth praising; and he, who was he? Why some one who baked sugar, or brewed beer. . . .'" (*W*, 258–59.

33. See above, introduction, 25–26.

34. At one point, Juliet is alone in public and needs someone to accompany her home; afraid of Sir Lyell's effrontery, she seeks aid from Mr. Tedman: "[R]ejoicing in any safe and honest protection, [she] entreated that Mr. Tedman would have the goodness to order one of his servants to see her home. . . . She then eagerly followed Mr. Tedman out of the room; while Sir Lyell merely vented his spleen . . . in a hearty laugh, at the manners, the dress, the age . . . of her chosen esquire" (*W*, 254–55).

35. Wollstonecraft, *Vindication of the Rights of Woman*, 147.

36. Ibid., 44.

37. See "Reform or Ruin: 'A Revolution in Female Manners,'" *Studies in Eighteenth-Century Culture* 11 (1982): 206.

38. Wollstonecraft, *Vindication of the Rights of Woman*, 150.

39. See Janet Todd, *Women's Friendship in Literature* (New York: Columbia University Press, 1980), 317–18.

40. Wollstonecraft, *Vindication of the Rights of Woman*, 144–45.

41. For a discussion of this historical phenomenon, see above, introduction.

42. Doody, *Frances Burney*, 342.

43. Doody has suggested that Elinor's obsessive and suicidal love for Harleigh owes something to Wollstonecraft's relationship with Gilbert Imlay and her subsequent suicide attempt. See ibid., 309, 333, 341–42. I would add as well that in this episode, Burney shows the same suspicion of passion and extreme sensibility as Wollstonecraft. See Wollstonecraft, *Vindication of the Rights of Woman*, 55–77.

44. See Julia Epstein, *The Iron Pen: Frances Burney and the Politics of Women's Writing* (Madison: University of Wisconsin Press, 1989), 188.

45. For a particularly illuminating and suggestive discussion of the similarities between Elinor's suicide attempt and Burney's mastectomy, see Doody, *Frances Burney*, 343–44. Burney had bled profusely, while crowded in by seven male doctors. Indeed, it does seem as if Burney is reworking this episode from her life; but this time the female patient has taken control of the knife and the surrounding spectators: "Elinor would not suffer the approach of the surgeon; would not hear of any operation, or examination; would not receive any assistance" (*W*, 360).

46. See Claudia Johnson, *Jane Austen: Women, Politics, and the Novel* (Chicago: University of Chicago Press, 1988), 19–21. Although Johnson notes that Elinor allows Burney to express some unorthodox ideas, I disagree with her observation that Elinor is "dismissed by 'sensible' characters." See, for example, Juliet's acknowledgment of Elinor's intelligence and liberal heart, above, 130.

47. Elinor's lament, of course, echoes Hotspur's final words in *1 Henry IV*, 5.4.84–86. Janet Todd argues that Elinor's inability to kill herself is a sign that women are not allowed to participate in male violence; both physical and verbal violence is masculine (*Women's Friendship*, 316). While I would agree that Elinor is not allowed to die heroically, I obviously take issue with Todd's curious claim that women are not implicated in the novel's wide range of violence.

158 Notes to Chapter 4

48. Elinor's suicide attempts do indeed attract attention; the scene reminds us of Harrel's suicide at Vauxhall. See Fanny Burney, *Cecilia; Or, Memoirs of an Heiress*, ed. Margaret Anne Doody and Peter Sabor (Oxford: Oxford University Press, 1988), 412–17. The men watch Elinor's agony more like "spectators of some public exhibition, than as actors in a scene of humanity" (*W,* 360).

49. J. W. Croker, *Quarterly Review* 11 (April 1814): 125–26. Croker is clearly upset with Burney's politics. In fact, he complains that it is Juliet who is most "violent" in her relationships with her female guardians (127). He even defends these women's desire to "exclude" Juliet from their company (127).

50. Kristina Straub also notes this theme, but she does so in an ahistorical way: "[F]rom Delvile through Harleigh, the doubts, uncertainties, and weaknesses of the male role . . . suggest a structural weakness within the system that relegates female happiness to male protection." See *Divided Fictions: Fanny Burney and Feminine Strategy* (Lexington: University of Kentucky Press, 1987), 210.

51. On women writers' use of the bourgeois ethic in debates about their rights, see above, introduction, 27. Miranda J. Burgess has curiously suggested that *The Wanderer's* conclusion is Burney's most "unequivocal," for it upholds traditional aristocratic values, decisively assails the modern inventions of a commercial society, and preserves the "ancient ideal of marriage." While Burgess sees Burney's fourth novel as an elegiac narrative that delineates a "fictive historical return" to a precommercial society, I argue that, unlike the Burney of *Evelina*, the author of *The Wanderer* posits not a nostalgic return to a past era, but an uneasy acceptance of some of the new innovations of modernity. See "Courting Ruin: The Economic Romances of Frances Burney," *Novel: A Forum on Fiction* 28, no. 2 (winter 1995): 143 n. 29, 147–48.

52. Janet Todd notes this characteristic of sensibility. See *Sensibility: An Introduction* (New York: Methuen, 1986), 13.

53. Compare Claudia Johnson, *Equivocal Beings: Politics, Gender, and Sentimentality in the 1790s: Wollstonecraft, Radcliffe, Burney, Austen* (Chicago: University of Chicago Press, 1995), 178, who argues that the "institutional power of patriarchy is spared direct criticism" because of the excessive cruelty of the novel's women. But, as I argued earlier, Burney largely attributes the women's brutality to the patriarchal structures of late-century society, which, I would suggest, is indeed a direct attack on patriarchal institutions.

54. Laetitia Hawkins, *Letters on the Female Mind, its Powers and Pursuits. Addressed to Miss H. M. Williams, with particular reference to her Letters from France in 2 vols.* (London: Hookham and Carpenter, 1793), 2:194.

# Bibliography

Agnew, Jean-Christophe. *Worlds Apart: The Market and the Theater in Anglo-American Thought, 1550–1750.* Cambridge: Cambridge University Press, 1986.

Allen, Walter. *The English Novel: A Short Critical History.* New York: E. P. Dutton, 1954.

Anderson, Earl R. "Footnotes More Pedestrian than Sublime: A Historical Background for the Footraces in *Evelina* and *Humphry Clinker.*" *Eighteenth-Century Studies* 14 (1980): 56–68.

Andrew, Donna T. "The Code of Honour and its Critics: The Opposition to Duelling in England, 1700–1850." *Social History* 5, no. 3 (1980): 409–34.

Armstrong, Nancy. *Desire and Domestic Fiction: A Political History of the Novel.* New York: Oxford University Press, 1987.

Astell, Mary. *A Serious Proposal to the Ladies.* 1701. 4th ed. Reprint, New York: Source Book Press, 1970.

———. *Some Reflections Upon Marriage.* London: John Nutt, 1790.

Blackstone, Sir William. *Commentaries on the Laws of England.* 19th ed. New York: W. E. Dean, 1841.

Brophy, Elizabeth Bergen. *Women's Lives and the Eighteenth-Century English Novel.* Tampa: University of South Florida Press, 1991.

Brown, Laura. *Ends of Empire: Women and Ideology in Early Eighteenth Century English Literature.* Ithaca: Cornell University Press, 1993.

Brown, Martha G. "Fanny Burney's 'Feminism': Gender or Genre?" In *Fetter'd or Free? British Women Novelists 1670–1815,* edited by Mary Anne Schofield and Cecilia Macheski, 29–39. Athens: Ohio State University Press, 1986.

Burgess, Miranda J. "Courting Ruin: The Economic Romances of Frances Burney." *Novel: A Forum on Fiction* 28, no. 2 (winter 1995): 131–53.

Burke, Edmund. *Reflections on the Revolution in France.* 1790 In *Edmund Burke: Select Works,* edited by E. J. Payne. Vol. 2. Oxford: Clarendon Press, 1877.

Burney, Fanny. *Camilla; or, A Picture of Youth.* Edited by Edward A. Bloom and Lillian D. Bloom. London: Oxford University Press, 1972.

———. *Cecilia, or Memoirs of an Heiress.* Edited by Margaret Anne Doody and Peter Sabor. Oxford: Oxford University Press, 1988.

159

————. *Evelina; or, The History of a Young Lady's Entrance into the World.* New York: W. W. Norton, 1965.

————. *Memoirs of Dr. Burney, Arranged from his own Manuscripts, from Personal Recollections. By his Daughter, Madame D'Arblay.* 3 vols. London: Edward Moxon, 1832.

————. *The Wanderer; Or, Female Difficulties.* Edited by Margaret Anne Doody, Robert L. Mack, and Peter Sabor. Oxford: Oxford University Press, 1991.

Campbell, D. Grant. "Fashionable Suicide: Conspicuous Consumption and the Collapse of Credit in Frances Burney's *Cecilia.*" *Studies in Eighteenth-Century Culture* 20 (1990): 131–45.

Campbell, Gina. "How to Read Like a Gentleman: Burney's Instructions to her Critics in *Evelina.*" *English Literary History* 57 (1990): 557–84.

Castle, Terry. *Masquerade and Civilization: The Carnivalesque in Eighteenth-Century English Culture and Fiction.* Stanford, Calif.: Stanford University Press, 1986.

Cixous, Hélène. "The Laugh of the Medusa." Translated by Keith Cohen and Paula Cohen. In *New French Feminisms,* edited by Elaine Marks and Isabelle de Courtivron, 245–64. New York: Schocken Books, 1981.

Clark, Anna. *Women's Silence, Men's Violence: Sexual Assault in England, 1770–1845.* New York: Pandora Press, 1987.

Clark, J. C. D. *English Society, 1688–1832: Ideology, Social Structure, and Political Practice during the Ancien Regime.* Cambridge: Cambridge University Press, 1985.

Collier, Jane. *An Essay on the Art of Ingeniously Tormenting: With Proper Rules for The Exercise of that Pleasant Art.* London: A. Miller, 1753.

Copeland, Edward. "Money in the Novels of Fanny Burney." *Studies in the Novel* 8 (1976): 24–37.

Croker, J. W. *Quarterly Review* 11 (April 1814): 123–30.

Cucchiari, Salvatore. "The Gender Revolution and the Transition from Bisexual Horde to Patrilocal Band: The Origins of Gender Hierarchy." In *Sexual Meanings: The Cultural Construction of Gender and Sexuality,* edited by Sherry B. Ortner and Harriet Whitehead, 31–79. Cambridge: Cambridge University Press, 1981.

Cutting, Rose-Marie. "A Wreath for Fanny Burney's Last Novel: *The Wanderer*'s Contribution to Women's Studies." *Illinois Quarterly* 37, no. 3 (1975): 45–64.

Cutting-Gray, Joanne. *Woman as "Nobody" and the Novels of Fanny Burney.* Gainesville: University of Florida Press, 1992.

Davidoff, Leonore, and Catherine Hall. *Family Fortunes: Men and Women of the English Middle Class, 1780–1850.* Chicago: University of Chicago Press, 1987.

Defoe, Daniel. *Robinson Crusoe.* 1719. Edited by Michael Shinagel. Reprint, New York: W. W. Norton, 1975.

Dobson, Austin, ed. *Diaries and Letters of Madame D'Arblay, 1770–1840.* 6 vols. London: Macmillan, 1904–5.

Doody, Margaret Anne. *Frances Burney: The Life in the Works.* New Brunswick, N.J.: Rutgers University Press, 1988.

Earle, Peter. "The Female Labour Market in London in the Late Seventeenth and Early Eighteenth Centuries." *Economic History Review,* 2d ser., 42, no. 3 (1989): 328–53.

Edwards, Thomas. "Embarrassed by Jane Austen." *Raritan* 7 (1987/88): 62–80.

Elias, Norbert. *The Civilizing Process.* Translated by Edmund Jephcot. New York: Urizen Books, 1978.

Epstein, Julia. *The Iron Pen: Frances Burney and the Politics of Women's Writing*. Madison: University of Wisconsin Press, 1989.

———. "Writing the Unspeakable: Fanny Burney's Mastectomy and the Fictive Body." *Representations* 16 (1986): 131–66.

Erickson, Amy Louise. *Women and Property in Early Modern England*. London: Routledge, 1993.

Ferguson, Moira, ed. *First Feminists: British Women Writers, 1578–1799*. Bloomington: Indiana University Press, 1985.

———. *Subject to Others: British Women Writers and Colonial Slavery, 1670–1834*. New York: Routledge, 1992.

Figes, Eva. *Sex and Subterfuge: Women Writers to 1850*. London: Macmillan, 1982.

Fizer, Irene. "The Name of the Daughter: Identity and Incest in *Evelina*." In *Refiguring the Father: New Feminist Readings of Patriarchy*, edited by Beth Kowaleski-Wallace and Patricia Yeager, 78–107. Carbondale: Southern Illinois University Press, 1989.

Fordyce, James. *Sermons to Young Women, in Two Volumes*. London: A. Millar and T. Cadell, 1766.

Goffman, Erving. *Behavior in Public Places: Notes on the Social Organization of Gatherings*. New York: Free Press, 1963.

Greenberg, Janelle. "The Legal Status of the English Woman in Early Eighteenth-Century Common Law and Equity." *Studies in Eighteenth-Century Culture* 4 (1975): 171–81.

Harth, Erica. "The Virtue of Love: Lord Hardwicke's Marriage Act." *Cultural Critique* 9 (1988): 123–54.

Hawkins, Laetitia. *Letters on the Female Mind, its Powers and Pursuits. Addressed to Miss H. M. Williams, with Particular Reference to her Letters from France*. Vol 2. London: Hookham and Carpenter, 1793.

Hayley, William. *A philosophical, historical, and moral essay on old maids. By a friend to the sisterhood*. 3 vols. London: T. Cadell, 1785.

Hemlow, Joyce. "Fanny Burney and the Courtesy Books." *PMLA* 65 (1950): 732–55.

———, ed. *The Journals and Letters of Fanny Burney, 1791–1840*. 12 vols. Oxford: Clarendon Press, 1972–84.

Hill, Bridget. *Women, Work, and Sexual Politics in Eighteenth-Century England*. Oxford: Basil Blackwell, 1989.

Horney, Karen. *Feminine Psychology*. Edited by Harold Kelman. New York: W. W. Norton, 1967.

Huang-Mei. *Transforming the Cinderella Dream: From Frances Burney to Charlotte Brontë*. New Brunswick, N.J.: Rutgers University Press, 1990.

Johnson, Claudia. *Equivocal Beings: Politics, Gender, and Sentimentality in the 1790s: Wollstonecraft, Radcliffe, Burney, Austen*. Chicago: University of Chicago Press, 1995.

———. *Jane Austen: Women, Politics, and the Novel*. Chicago: University of Chicago Press, 1988.

Kaplan, E. Ann. *Women and Film: Both Sides of the Camera*. New York: Methuen, 1983.

Keller, Evelyn Fox. "Gender and Science." *Psychoanalysis and Contemporary Thought* 1, no. 3 (1978): 409–33.

Kelly, Gary. "Jane Austen and the English Novel of the 1790s." In *Fetter'd or Free: British Women Novelists, 1670–1815*, edited by Mary Anne Schofield and Cecilia Macheski, 285–306. Athens: Ohio State University Press, 1986.

Kincaid, James R. "Anthony Trollope and the Unmannerly Novel." In *Reading and Writing Women's Lives: A Study of the Novel of Manners,* edited by Bege K. Bowers and Barbara Brothers, 87–104. Ann Arbor: U.M.I. Research Press, 1990.

Kramnick, Isaac. *Bolingbroke and His Circle: The Politics of Nostalgia in the Age of Walpole.* Cambridge: Harvard University Press, 1968.

Langford, Paul. *Public Life and the Propertied Englishman, 1689–1798.* Oxford: Clarendon Press, 1991.

Lasch, Christopher. "The Suppression of Clandestine Marriage in England: The Marriage Act of 1753." *Salmagundi* 26 (1974): 99–104.

Laslett, Peter. *The World We have Lost Further Explored.* 3d ed. New York: Charles Scribner's Sons, 1984.

Lévi-Strauss, Claude. *The Elementary Structures of Kinship.* Translated by James Harle Bell, John Richard von Sturner, and Rodney Needham. Boston: Beacon Press, 1969.

Lewis, Jayne. "Compositions of Ill Nature: Women's Place in a Satiric Tradition." *Critical Matrix* 2, no. 2 (1986): 31–69.

MacFarlane, Alan. Review of *The Family, Sex, and Marriage in England, 1500–1800,* by Lawrence Stone. *History and Theory* 18, no. 1 (1979): 103–26.

Marshall, David. *The Figure of Theater: Shaftesbury, Defoe, Adam Smith, and George Eliot.* New York: Columbia University Press, 1986.

McKendrick, Neil, John Brewer, and J. H. Plumb, eds. *The Birth of a Consumer Society: The Commercialization of Eighteenth-Century England.* Bloomington: Indiana University Press, 1985.

McKeon, Michael. "Historicizing Patriarchy: The Emergence of Gender Difference in England, 1660–1760." *Eighteenth-Century Studies* 28, no. 1 (1995): 295–322.

———. *The Origins of the English Novel, 1600–1740.* Baltimore: The Johns Hopkins University Press, 1987.

Michals, Teresa. "'That Sole and Despotic Dominion': Slaves, Wives, and Game in Blackstone's *Commentaries.*" *Eighteenth-Century Studies* 27, no. 2 (winter 1993/94): 195–216.

Mullan, John. *Sentiment and Sociability: The Language of Feeling in the Eighteenth-Century Novel.* Oxford: Clarendon Press, 1988.

Mulvey, Laura. *Visual and Other Pleasures: Theories of Representation and Difference.* Bloomington: Indiana University Press, 1989.

Myers, Mitzi. "The Dilemmas of Gender as Double-Voiced Narrative: Or, Maria Edgeworth Mothers the Bildungsroman." In *The Idea of the Novel in the Eighteenth Century,* edited by Robert W. Uphaus, 67–96. East Lansing, Mich.: Colleagues Press, 1988.

———. "Reform or Ruin: 'A Revolution in Female Manners.'" *Studies in Eighteenth-Century Culture* 11 (1982): 199–216.

Neale, R. S. *Class in English History, 1680–1850.* Totowa, N.J.: Barnes and Noble, 1981.

Newton, Judith Lowder. *Women, Power, and Subversion: Social Strategies in British Fiction 1770–1860.* Athens: University of Georgia Press, 1981.

Nussbuam, Felicity. *The Autobiographical Subject: Gender and Ideology in Eighteenth–Century England.* Baltimore: The Johns Hopkins University Press, 1989.

Okin, Susan Moller. "Patriarchy and Married Women's Property in England: Questions on Some Current Views." *Eighteenth–Century Studies* 17, no. 2 (1983/84): 121–38.

Olshin, Toby. "'To Whom I Most Belong': The Role of the Family in *Evelina*." *Eighteenth-Century Life* 6 (1980): 29–42.

Pateman, Carol. *The Sexual Contract*. Stanford, Calif.: Stanford University Press, 1988.

Patterson, Orlando. *Freedom in the Making of Western Culture*. New York: Basic Books, 1991.

Paulson, Ronald. *Satire and the Novel in Eighteenth-Century England*. New Haven: Yale University Press, 1967.

Perkin, Harold. *The Origins of Modern English Society, 1780–1880*. London: Routledge and Kegan Paul, 1969.

Plumb, J. H. *England in the Eighteenth Century*. New York: Penguin Books, 1950.

Pocock, J. G. A. *The Machiavellian Moment: Florentine Political Thought and the Atlantic Republican Tradition*. Princeton: Princeton University Press, 1975.

———. *Virtue, Commerce, and History: Essays on Political Thought and History, Chiefly in the Eighteenth Century*. Cambridge: Cambridge University Press, 1985.

Poovey, Mary. "Fathers and Daughters: The Trauma of Growing Up Female." *Women and Literature* 2 (1982): 39–58.

———. *The Proper Lady and the Woman Writer: Ideology as Style in the Works of Mary Wollstonecraft, Mary Shelley, and Jane Austen*. Chicago: University of Chicago Press, 1984.

Richardson, Samuel. *Pamela; or, Virtue Rewarded*. 1740. Edited by T. C. Duncan Eaves and Ben D. Kimpel. Reprint, Boston: Houghton Mifflin, 1971.

Richetti, John. "Recent Studies in the Restoration and Eighteenth Century." *Studies in English Literature* 30, no. 3 (summer 1990): 517–54.

Rizzo, Betty. *Companions Without Vows: Relationships among Eighteenth-Century British Women*. Athens: University of Georgia Press, 1994.

Rogers, Katherine. "Fanny Burney: The Private Self and the Public Self." *International Journal of Women's Studies* 7 (1984): 110–17.

Smith, Adam. *The Theory of Moral Sentiments*. 1759. Reprint, New York: Garland Publishing, 1971.

———. *The Theory of Moral Sentiments*. Edited by D. D. Raphael and A. L. Macfie. Oxford: Oxford University Press, 1976.

Spacks, Patricia Meyer. *Desire and Truth: Functions of Plot in Eighteenth-Century English Novels*. Chicago: University of Chicago Press, 1990.

———. "Dynamics of Fear: Fanny Burney." In *Imagining a Self: Autobiography and Novel in Eighteenth-Century England*, 158–92. Cambridge: Harvard University Press, 1976.

———. *The Female Imagination*. New York: Alfred A. Knopf, 1975.

Spring, Eileen. "The Family, Strict Settlement, and Historians." *The Canadian Journal of History* 18 (1983): 379–98.

———. "Law and the Theory of the Affective Family." *Albion* 16 (1984): 1–20.

Spring, Eileen, and David Spring. "The English Landed Elite, 1540–1879: A Review." *Albion* 17 (1985): 149–66.

———. "The English Landed Elite, 1540–1879: A Rejoinder." *Albion* 17 (1985): 393–96.

Starr, George A. "'Only a Boy': Notes on Sentimental Novels." *Genre* 10, no. 4 (1977): 501–27.

Staves, Susan. "*Evelina*, or Female Difficulties." *Modern Philology* 73 (1976): 368–81.

———. *Married Women's Separate Property in England, 1660–1833*. Cambridge: Harvard University Press, 1990.

————. "Pin Money." *Studies in Eighteenth-Century Culture* 14 (1985): 47–77.

Stone, Lawrence. *The Crisis of the Aristocracy, 1558–1641*. Oxford: Clarendon Press, 1965.

————. *The Family, Sex, and Marriage in England, 1550–1800*. New York: Harper and Row, 1977.

Stone, Lawrence, and Jeanne C. Fawtier Stone. *An Open Elite? England, 1540–1880*. Oxford: Clarendon Press, 1984.

Straub, Kristina. *Divided Fictions: Fanny Burney and Feminine Strategy*. Lexington: University of Kentucky Press, 1987.

Thompson, E. P. *Customs in Common*. New York: The New Press, 1991.

————. "Eighteenth-Century English Society: Class Struggle Without Class?" *Social History* 3, no. 2 (1978): 133–65.

Todd, Janet. *Sensibility: An Introduction*. New York: Methuen, 1986.

————. *Women's Friendship in Literature*. New York: Columbia University Press, 1980.

Tomalin, Claire. *The Life and Death of Mary Wollstonecraft*. 1974. Reprint, New York: Penguin Books, 1992.

Tompkins, J. M. S. *The Popular Novel in England, 1770–1800*. London: Constable & Co., 1932.

Troide, Lars E. *The Early Journals and Letters of Fanny Burney*. Oxford: Clarendon Press, 1988.

Trumbach, Randolph. *The Rise of the Egalitarian Family: Aristocratic Kinship and Domestic Relations in Eighteenth-Century England*. New York: Academic Press, 1978.

Tucker, Irene. "Writing Home: *Evelina*, the Epistolary Novel, and the Paradox of Property." *English Literary History* 60, no. 2 (summer 1993): 419–39.

Vopat, James P. "*Evelina:* Life as Art—Notes toward Becoming a Performer on the Stage of Life." *Essays in Literature* 2 (1975): 42–51.

Wayne, Don E. *Penshurst: The Semiotics of Place and the Poetics of History*. Madison: Wisconsin University Press, 1984.

Williams, Raymond. *The Country and the City*. New York: Oxford University Press, 1973.

Wollstonecraft, Mary. "Thoughts on the Education of Daughters." 1786/87. Reprinted in *A Wollstonecraft Anthology*, edited by Janet M. Todd. Bloomington: University of Indiana Press, 1977.

————. *A Vindication of the Rights of Men*. 1790. Reprinted in *The Works of Mary Wollstonecraft*, edited by Janet Todd and Marilyn Butler. Vol. 5. London: William Pickering, 1989.

————. *A Vindication of the Rights of Woman*. 1792. Edited by Carol H. Poston. Reprint, New York: W. W. Norton, 1975.

Wrightson, Keith. "The Social Order of Early Modern England: Three Approaches." In *The World We Have Gained: Histories of Population and Social Structure*, edited by Lloyd Bonfield, Richard M. Smith, and Keith Wrightson, 177–202. Oxford: Basil Blackwell, 1986.

Yeazell, Ruth Bernard. *Fictions of Modesty: Women and Courtship in the English Novel*. Chicago: University of Chicago Press, 1991.

# Index

Allen, Walter, 13
aristocracy, crisis of, 14, 19, 21, 24, 28, 41–
    42, 46, 55, 61–63, 134–37, 155n. 12
Armstrong, Nancy, 28, 79
Astell, Mary, 22, 80
Austen, Jane: and the novel of manners,
    30; reaction to *Camilla*, 134n. 39

Barbauld, Anna Letitia, 13
Blackstone, Sir William, 16
Burke, Edmund, 17, 19, 113–14
Burney, Frances: description of *Camilla*, 91;
    explanation of *Cecilia*'s conclusion, 83,
    150–51n. 35; mastectomy, 151n. 7,
    157n. 45; relationship with father, 55–
    57, 85–86; service at royal court, 85–
    90, 151n. 3. *See also specific works*

*Camilla*, 32, 33, 49, 114, 120, 123, 128,
    138; code of manners in, 94–102,
    111–12; financial distress of women in,
    103–7, 153n. 30; influenced by FB's
    service at court, 86, 88–89, 90, 94,
    108; the male gaze in, 94–102, 110;
    self-repression in, 107–10; women's
    friendships in, 94, 98–99
Campbell, Gina, 53–54
Castle, Terry, 67, 78
*Cecilia*, 15, 22, 33, 49, 50, 58, 86–87, 92,
    93, 96, 103, 123; aristocratic rule in,
    61–67; bourgeois guardians in, 67–73;
    Burney's response to ending, 150–51

n. 35; madness, 82–83; and patrilineal
    ideology, 61, 76, 80–81; social
    assimilation, 70–73; and suicide, 71–
    73; women's communities in, 73–81
Chapone, Sarah, 16
class, formation of, 24–25, 31. *See also*
    violence
companionate marriage: definition of, 22;
    and "free choice," 22–23
conduct books, 28, 79, 93–94
Cowper, Sarah, 27
credit: and consumerism, 26–27, 105;
    financial, 25–26, 71; as reputation, 71,
    104–5
Croker, John Wilson, 134

Davidoff, Leonore, 20
domestic ideology: and charity, 28, 78–80,
    119; self-regulation, 27–28, 29, 79,
    97–98; and women's empowerment,
    27–29
Doody, Margaret Anne, 13–14, 39, 46, 50,
    57, 66, 85–86, 87, 121, 123, 131, 132,
    133

Edwards, Thomas, 41, 47, 119
Elias, Norbert, 31, 88
Epstein, Julia, 14, 61, 83, 87, 88, 132,
    151n. 7
Erickson, Amy Louise, 19
*Evelina*, 13, 15, 17, 32, 33, 60, 71, 80, 83,
    91, 92, 93, 94, 96, 101, 109, 111, 113,

165